Good and Mad Women

MATTHEWS, Jill Julius. Good and mad women: the historical construction of femininity in twentieth-century Australia. Allen & Unwin, 1985 (c1984). 223p bibl index 84-71002. 27.50 ISBN 0-86861-657-5; 12.50 pa ISBN 0-86861-665-6. Australian CIP

In a wonderful exercise in feminist scholarship, Matthews draws on a wealth of economic, demographic, and historical information, and on sociological, psychological, and feminist theory. Moreover, she displays sensitive attention to the research process itself and writes very well. Her subject matter is the expectations surrounding Australian women, i.e., what good women are supposed to do. Matthews explores these expectations by looking at women who did not fulfill them—psychiatric patients. In Matthews's hands, the case notes of these ordinary women reveal extreme failures of what all women are trying to do—tread tightropes and escape from the contradiction-laden maze of ideal femininity. Matthew concludes with an optimistic overview chapter, an appendix concerned with admissions to the psychiatric institution whose documents she analyzed, a lengthy bibliography of references used in the text, and a subject index. Although concerned with Australia, the ideology of femininity uncovered in this book is nearly identical to that found in the US and thereby illuminates our own situation as well as informing us about Australia. Four-year college and university libraries.—*S. Reinharz, Brandeis University*

GOOD AND

The Historical Construction of Femininity

George Allen & Unwin
Sydney   London   Boston

MAD WOMEN

in Twentieth-Century Australia

JILL JULIUS MATTHEWS

First published in 1984
Second impression 1985
George Allen & Unwin Australia Pty Ltd
8 Napier Street, North Sydney, NSW 2060 Australia

George Allen & Unwin (Publishers) Ltd
Park Lane, Hemel Hempstead, Herts HP2 4TE England

Allen & Unwin Inc.
Fifty Cross Street, Winchester, Mass 01890 USA

National Library of Australia
Cataloguing-in-Publication entry:

Matthews, Jill Julius.
Good and mad women.

Bibliography.
Includes index.
ISBN 0 86861 657 5.
ISBN 0 86861 665 6 (pbk.).

1. Women — Australia — Social conditions — 20th
century. 2. Femininity (Psychology). 3. Sex Role. I. Title.
305.4′2′0994

Library of Congress Catalog Card Number: 8471002

Set in 10/11 pt Baskerville
by Eurasia Press (Offset) Pte Ltd

Printed in Hong Kong

Contents

v

Tables

Acknowledgements

*T*his book has been helped and nurtured by many people over many years. I wish primarily to thank the women of the Australian Women's Liberation Movement, without whom I would never have defined the problem, and because of whom there is the possibility of change.

I wish to acknowledge my gratitude to the South Australian Director of Mental Health Services, the Superintendent of Glenside Hospital, and the Glenside Hospital Research Committee, who granted me permission to use the Glenside Hospital casenotes. I have taken careful regard throughout the book to discharge the responsibility they placed upon me to preserve the privacy and confidentiality of the patients whose notes I had access to. I have never met any of the women whose casenotes I have used. I cannot be grateful for the suffering that brought them to hospital and turned their lives into cases. But I am indebted to them, and can only hope that my commentary on their experiences will be of value to other women.

During the writing of the book, I was assisted by the people and facilities of the University of Adelaide, the Research School of Social Sciences at the Australian National University, and the University of Wollongong. The typing of the manuscript was shared by Janice Aldridge, Anthea Bundock, Bev Gallina, Helen Macnab and Ann Webb.

Many people have given generously of their time and ideas in commenting on various arguments and drafts: Rosemary Pringle, Liz Fell, Anna Gibbs, Susan Sheridan, Fran Hausfeld, Anna Yeatman, Julia Ryan, Helen Mills, Dorothy Broom, Heather Radi, Pat Quiggin, Venetia Nelson, Hugh Stretton, Allan Martin, Stephen Foster, John Iremonger.

In particular, I am grateful to four friends who, throughout the process of working on the book, talked to me about me and my ideas and my writing: Jenny Pausacker, Eva Cox, Biff Ward and Pam Benton.

To all these people I am very grateful. None of them is, of course, responsible for the shortcomings of the book, but without their help it would not have finally surfaced.

Part I
Introduction

Good Women and Failure

*I*n 1945, Vera King was admitted to an Australian public mental hospital claiming, 'I am no one, there is no food to eat, it is no use doing anything. I don't know what my name is.' She was 45 years old, married with several daughters, and dominated by 'delusions of guilt and unworthiness'.

Her casenotes reveal that when first examined in hospital, she told of her childhood—a large happy family, wonderful parents, happy at school, good kind employers—'up to the age of about 15½ years, when her story ceased with an abrupt and rapid, "Anymore I don't remember"'. Her psychiatrist pressured her to remember. She became distressed, and pleaded to be let alone.

> When it was impressed on her that she could not remember because she did not want to recall unpleasant things and that therein lay the cause of her illness, and that by recalling them she would cure herself, she was incredulous and surprised and began to co-operate well, at first hesitantly and disjointedly, then more rapidly and coherently, interrupted by frequent thought-blocking followed by mild and moderate abreactions. The information thus elicited was...All 8 children were cruelly and harshly treated by the father, especially, and by the mother. Frequent thrashings of such severity as to occasion police intervention several times, and threats, abuse and depreciation were regular treatment. Vera feared him terribly and thought he might kill her, judging by his outbursts of threats and his expression of hate. He told her she was useless and that all 6 of his girls would not make one good woman. Her mother differed only in degree. School life from age 7 to 13: a period of fear and misery, dominated by a cruel schoolteacher feared and hated by all the children who used to thrash them with her riding whip. Working life: most of her employers were unkind to her, demanding a great deal and giving little reward, materially or otherwise. After the age of 15½ (where her thought blocking became apparent) her employers were particularly hard, and she was treated as a drudge, again

suffering threats, abuse and depreciation for all her work. 'I felt that I could never do anything right; they used to tell me I was useless and lazy', rather pathetically. 'I used to try so hard; but I was never any good', tearfully. (Did they frighten or harm you?) 'I thought they would hit me.' (Why? People are not allowed to do that.) 'I don't know. They used to look at me as though they would.' When aged 24 she went to work for a Mrs Grey. 'She was the best and kindest woman I have ever known; they were all good and kind to me', naming the members of the family...After 13 years there, she left to get married. Again thought-blocking became marked. Little information about her courtship and marriage was given, and she made frequent pleas, 'Leave me alone. It's not a bit of use, doctor, I can't remember. Why do I have to be plagued like this?' She became distressed when pressed, and betrayed much anxiety. It became apparent that Mr King's mother aroused intensely the old pattern of reaction founded by her parents and fostered by her schoolmistress and earlier employers. 'She said I was not fit to be her son's wife, and was so unpleasant that I would not go to their home even with my hubby.' When she died they were married...She told me of her marital happiness, and how good her 'hubby' was; but resistance and emotion reappeared, answers becoming very disjointed. No further information about Mrs King was obtained, but one significant point about her husband emerged unexpectedly, viz., that he said to her, 'All your daughters together will not make one good woman'. Vera then said to me, 'my father used to say that'. Her responses then became very disjointed and she became very upset and the examination was not pressed any further.

Vera was diagnosed as schizophrenic, a woman whose thought processes and behaviour were deeply distressing to herself and her family. A woman in extremity, an exception. But her story itself is recognisable. The relationships within which she lived, with parents, schoolteacher, employers, mother-in-law, husband and children, are meaningful to most white women in present-day Australia. The demand that she be a good woman, and the condemnation of her failure, are identifiable in our own lives. Her anxiety to be a good woman is an anxiety shared by us all. In other words, while the circumstances of Vera's life and the content of her thoughts are extreme, they are not alien. Vera was mad, we are not, but the difference beween us is one of degree, not of kind.

This book is about our identification with Vera's story. It is an investigation of what it is to be a good woman, and what it is to fail. It is about the most basic and taken-for-granted part of our lives as twentieth-century white Australian women: our woman-ness, our femininity.

Woman creates herself and is created by her specific circumstances. Her nature is not a fixed quality, but peculiar to her time and place. As

Simone de Beauvoir pointed out so succinctly,

> One is not born, but rather, becomes a woman...it is civilization as a whole that produces this creature, intermediate between male and eunuch, which is described as feminine. (1960:9)

My concern in this book is to understand the specific meaning and experience of becoming a woman in twentieth-century Australia, to analyse the civilisation that produces us, to uncover the peculiar circumstances in and from which we have made ourselves. To paraphrase Marx, 'Women make themselves and their own history, but they do not make them just as they please; they do not make them under circumstances chosen by themselves, but under circumstances directly encountered, given and transmitted from the past. The tradition of all dead generations weighs like a nightmare on the brain of the living.' (cf. Marx, 1968, 97)

Woman is a social being, created within and by a specific society. As societies differ, so too do women. It is easy to forget this and to see 'woman' as a timeless, changeless category. Woman in ancient Greece is seen to be the same as woman today; only their circumstances differ. From this view emerges an ahistorical sense of the meaning of being a woman, and of the simple continuity of our oppression. An anti-woman quotation from Xenophon sits comfortably beside one from St Augustine, and both chime in with those of Rousseau, Hegel and Norman Mailer. Woman, man and misogyny become constants, despite the world around them turning upside down.

I would argue instead that women and men and the nature of misogyny and oppression are all qualitatively different in different times and places. The sense of similarity, of easily drawn parallels, is illusory. Women themselves change. It is precisely the differences in circumstances that is crucial to the meaning and sense of becoming a woman. We must therefore understand the particularity of our own circumstances in order to understand ourselves.

The process of making ourselves, of becoming women, is a two-sided, ever changing process. We are constrained by the world around us, by relationships, institutions and ideas. But we are also part of the world and our behaviour changes it, by resistance, by acquiescence. The world presents us with a limited series of possibilities, and we choose from among them. Many things limit our choices, such as class, race, education, money, health, a time of war or peace. Most crucially, we are limited by being born female.

All the component parts of our world are geared to distinguish between female and male and to offer different possibilities and choices. Because she is identified at birth as being the female of the species, a girl child is treated differently and expected and encouraged to behave differently from a boy child. The behaviour that she develops does not flow automatically from her biological make-up, but from her society's treatment of her. Such a distinction, between biological make-up and behaviour, is commonly identified as one between sex and gender:

> 'Sex' is a word that refers to the biological differences between male and female: the visible difference in genitalia, the related difference in procreative function. 'Gender' however is a matter of culture: it refers to the social classification into 'masculine' and 'feminine'. (Oakley, 1972:16)

Unfortunately, this distinction is not so clear cut as it first appears. Human biology is not unchanging; the human body is not an ahistorical entity. Both have changed over time and, more importantly, the significance or meaning given to both is social and hence historically created. (Gatens, 1983) This argument will be pursued further in chapter 2. For the sake of clarity, however, and in order to keep to the fore the social meaning of being or becoming a woman, I use the term gender exclusively throughout this book.

The process of our becoming women is conducted in a world that distinguishes down to the most minute level between the genders. Each component part of the world has its own standard of femininity, of how a good woman should conduct herself. Each specific institution, relationship and belief system within society holds a vision of its ideal type of woman. Through this ideal, each social element's interest in maintaining a gendered world is furthered. Woman is clearly distinguished from man or more usually, from man presented as the universal. Thus, the ideal of a woman worker is clearly different from the ideal of worker, who is male; within the family, the ideal of mother is quite distinct from either father or parent. Each vision of the good woman is composed of a relationship—a mother in relation to her children, a worker in relation to her employer, a student in relation to her teacher—and each relation is qualified by a set of abstract ideals—self-sacrifice, diligence, submission, nurturance. Such ideals are, of course, gender-specific. Diligence in a woman is different from diligence in a man, purity in a man is a very different quality from purity in a woman. (Hence the feminist list of alternative descriptions for the same behaviour. He is assertive, she is pushy; he is informative, she is gossipy.)

There is no specific behaviour which in itself will fulfil the ideals of femininity. The ideals are static, representing a state of being. But a woman is always in a process of becoming, of making herself. She cannot, for example, achieve 'purity' once and for all. She must always be striving to become and to remain pure. She can only try to live up to the counsels of perfection throughout the various and changing circumstances of her life. As Greer Litton Fox argues in her article, 'Nice

Girl', femininity, or what she calls 'lady' and I term 'good woman', is a state that can never be achieved:

> A woman (or man) must earn the label of 'feminine' (or 'masculine') through traditional sex-appropriate behavior, and one must act feminine (or masculine) continually in order to retain the label. Rarely is there carry-over of the label from one arena of action to another, and there is little allowance for even one transgression of sex-appropriate norms if one is to retain one's claim to femininity (or masculinity). In sum, the lady is always in a state of becoming: one acts like a lady, one attempts to be a lady, but one never is a lady. In effect, then, throughout her lifetime a woman's behavior will reflect continued efforts to attain what is essentially an unattainable status. There is no respite from the demands for ladylike behavior—neither young age nor old age bring relief from such normative control of behavior. (Fox, 1977:809–10)

Any ideal of femininity is thus, by definition, unattainable. But the attempt to become a good woman, the pursuit of femininity, is further thwarted by the multiplicity of ideals, as noted before. These ideals coexist but are not necessarily compatible. As well, each woman carries her own ideal of femininity, derived from her social world. In most instances, this personal standard will be internally inconsistent, as well as at odds with the standards of some parts of her society. Some of the implications of such inconsistency can be seen in the story of Vera King.

Vera attempted throughout her life to be a good woman as was demanded by various people important to her, but she was confronted by a series of incongruous meanings which she could not reconcile. In the end, she succeeded only in creating a negative image. She herself was 'not a good woman'. This negative image drained her existence. 'I am no one...I don't know what my name is.' From Vera's casenotes, we can identify at least five sets of agents who invoked the 'good woman' image: her parents (whose definition was challenged on occasion by the police), her schoolteacher, employers, prospective mother-in-law (whose definition was challenged by her fiancé), and finally by her husband. As well, her psychiatrist was drawn implicitly into the debate. The meaning or content given to the image in each case was different. Only the formula itself remained constant. This formula acted as a reprimand. It was used to warn Vera that she was not doing what someone else thought she ought to be doing. More importantly, she was not being the sort of woman they wanted her to be.

In other words, femininity is an empty shell. It purports to be the truth, the essence, the absolute meaning of being a woman. But, instead, it is a concept waiting to be given meaning by whoever conjures it into use. Such meaning is always political because it is always prescriptive (Millett, 1971, 23). The sort of woman she ought to be is laid down by each individual and institution which has power and authority over her. The prescriptions are many and bewildering. Every woman's body and life, everything she does, thus become the objects of struggle for control by competing forces, each force proclaiming itself the upholder of the true ideal of femininity.

The process of becoming a woman is the process of the pursuit of femininity, the attempt to live up to the various standards of her society, the struggle to behave like and to be a good woman according to her own and her society's standards. Because femininity is an idealised and illusory quality, and because it is composed of inconsistent and contradictory parts, its pursuit is doomed to failure. She cannot please all of the people all of the time. To be a woman is thus necessarily to carry a sense of failure.

It is this failure which is instantly recognisable as what women have in common. It is the part of Vera King's story which has immediate meaning. This failure is inherent in the pursuit of femininity, a failure all women share whether mad or not. This book presents an analysis of the nature of this failure, showing how it has been constructed, indicating the impossibility of the task we have been set and accepted. It is a history of the traditions of Australian society which have influenced the meaning of our femininity. It is a history of the contradictions and constraints that the world imposes upon those born female as we become women. It is a history of the lives of individual women who have been confronted by the maze of gender imperatives, the demand that they be 'good women'. Its purpose is to uncover the processes of becoming a woman in twentieth-century Australia so that, by understanding our historical construction as women we may expand our opportunities and choose less inhibiting and destructive possibilities.

We cannot abolish gendering, the division of the world into masculine and feminine. Even feminists have standards of femininity. The point is not to renounce femininity but to restructure and widen its meaning. The purpose of this book is to show the historical construction of the inevitable sense of failure that comes from living within the constraints of a particularly repressive social definition of femininity. From that understanding, we may seek to be more autonomous creators of our own woman-ness.

The first step in unravelling this history of the process of becoming a woman in a specific society, the pursuit of femininity in twentieth-century Australia, is a theoretical one. The next chapter looks at the question, what is a woman and what is her history? It elaborates upon some of the points raised so far. In particular, it argues that there is no meaning of woman that is simply given for all time, an essential femininity. Every aspect of our lives is historical and changing: our bodies, our consciousness of our selves, our treatment by society, the sense of our commonality as women.

2

Feminist Theory and Historical Methodology

Feminist theory

'In comparison with men, we as women suffer inferiority and exploitation in many ways.' Something like this has been said at each upsurge of feminist thought and activity in the western world since the sixteenth century. The first task for feminists has been to name those ways. The more we have looked, the more we have seen. The naming and listing of injustice eventually leads to our seeing it as a complex web of systematic oppression: all social institutions, beliefs and relationships, each in its particular ways, discriminate against women. Worse, the system turns us against ourselves: all women, each in our own particular ways, accept most of such discrimination as normal. We are therefore doubly trapped.

For feminists, the next step is necessarily confused. 'Who do we blame for this state of affairs?' Externally, various targets can be identified and attacked, ranging from the particularly unjust discriminations of education or employment or law, to more abstract opponents such as capitalism, patriarchy, or all men. Internally, this attack can be undermined by self-doubt, or turned on ourselves. We wonder in anger: 'why didn't they (our mothers and sisters) tell us about this before and do something to change it?' We become embittered by frustration: 'why don't they (other women) recognise their own suffering and join us in the struggle for change?' We despair and blame ourselves: 'why do they, how do we all collude in our own oppression?' We have seen the enemy and he is not only out there but among us and within us.

From this twofold apprehension of our oppression and our collusion arise the questions: 'who are we? how did we get to be like this? and how can we free ourselves?' The stock answers given by defenders of the status quo across four centuries have been, when reduced to their most basic: 'women simply are; they and their state are simply given, having neither history nor need for explanation nor possibility of change.' In response, feminists over four centuries have tried to redefine the nature or essence of woman in such ways as to justify her claim to release from bondage: 'she is equal to man; she is equal but different; she is superior.' Between the conservatives and the feminists then develops an argument of 'it is/it isn't' at various levels of sophistication, couched in the languages and paradigms of science and faith of the time.

In general, then, arguments about women's place in the scheme of things, and feminist attempts to improve that place, have been couched in terms of woman's nature, that is, her femininity. The peculiar quality of femininity has been hotly debated, but both conservatives and many feminists have accepted that some such quality or essence does exist and has existed from the beginning. They all hold that this essence has and always will distinguish women from men, no matter what their shared circumstances.

The existence of such an essence is, of course, a possibility. However, there is no evidence at all as to its character beyond faith and belief. The circumstances of women's and men's lives have never been shared. As far as we know, every human society has distinguished between women and men, and their lives and possible choices have been shaped through that distinction. There is no way beyond mere assertion to tell apart the essential from the social in this situation. Further, we who observe are ourselves distinguished into women and men by our own society. Both the observed and the observers are gendered beings, and are incapable of knowing our essence—if we have one. What we are capable of knowing, however, is the social character of gender. We can uncover the changing constitution of the distinction between women and men, the changing circumstances of our lives and how they affect who we are, how women in the past differ from or are the same as women in the present. That is, we can discover the social meanings of femininity.

In European societies and their extensions during the past several centuries, there seem to have been four levels to the question, what is a woman? Each level of meaning is historical, that is, it changes over time, over both the individual's life cycle and the society's history. These four levels of woman are the biological, the psychological, the systemic, and the social. Or, to put it another way, there are four histories: of she, the female body; of me, the woman; of it, the gender system; and of us, the women. When discussing women—our subjectivity, our history, our oppression—there is a strong tendency to fuse several of these levels, which leads to horrible confusions of meaning. We would do better to separate them. Such separation, of course, can never be complete because each level deeply affects the others. Thus, in the following analysis, there is necessarily some overlap and recapitulation. The point is that it is the same integrated being, woman, whom I am circling around, looking at from the four perspectives.

Firstly, the history of she, the female body. Biological woman is the female of the species. All we know for sure is that what distinguishes her from the male of the species is her potentiality for child bearing and feeding, a potentiality that she need not use and will still remain female. All the rest of what is termed human biology, and is often considered both innate and immutable, is indeterminate. Most of the so-called sex-differences between women and men in body size, shape and effectiveness, in thinking patterns and ability, and in endocrinal functioning, are affected by social practices to an unknown extent. [Brennan, 1982] The biological polarity of female and male is by no means clear-cut. Variations in anatomy, hormones and chromosomes need to be considered along a continuum, or as two overlapping normal curves. In the middle fall a range of bodies that are not clearly either female or male: hermaphrodites, transsexuals. To either side are bodies that are recognisably female or male, but lack certain crucial aspects of femaleness or maleness, or carry significant characteristics of the 'opposite' sex: eunuchs, impotent men, infertile women, hirsute women and breasted men. The exclusive and exhaustive biological segregation into female and male that is part of commonsense is more a demand of our culture than a neutral description of reality. (Yudkin, 1979, 98)

For example, in an individual life, a woman who consistently eats a high-protein diet, engages in rough-and-tumble play and weight lifting, takes steroids, and is sympathetically trained in geometry, will look and act and think more like a man than most men. Again, the story of the changing physique of the Japanese people since the second world war is well-known. Through dramatic changes of diet and lifestyle, they have grown taller, more muscular, more angular. Certainly, there is still a substantial and visible difference between the physiques of Japanese women and men in general. But a Japanese woman of today is also physically different from her sister of 100 years ago and, indeed, her body shares certain similarities with the men of that time.

Thus, cause and effect of biology and social behaviour are appearing, as more research is done, to be increasingly entangled. Eventually, it may be possible to write a social history of human bodies, their abilities, potentialities and modifications. But clearly, there is no essential meaning of the nature of woman to be found at this level.

So to the second level of history: me, the woman. Psychological woman is the identity and sense of being woman. It is an awareness that is usually so fundamental as to be taken for granted. It is also a very ambiguous awareness, incorporating unknown and shifting proportions of biology and social behaviour. Such occurrences as menstruation, pregnancy and menopause, as having a breast removed or getting wrinkles—these are biological, physical events with considerable social implications and significance. Having a boyfriend, being softly spoken and emotionally mercurial, sitting to urinate and being poor at maths—these are all social events that are often taken as normal biology, facts of physical life. All such occurrences are part of our self-awareness, our identity as women.

The distinction between female and male is made into a rigid polarisation by western culture. This creates problems for anyone, woman or man, who does not consistently and unambiguously feel themselves to be womanly or manly. The culture insists that gender identity be clear and certain. A woman in our society is supposed to feel herself in no way manly or masculine. Ambiguity or non-conformity leads to psychological tension in the woman herself and in those who cannot work her out. (This tension fuels vast industries in the capitalist west. For example, real women have only head and pubic hair, thereby producing an intense need for depilatory agents, with surgical and psychiatric backup.)

Every known society distinguishes between women and men, but the particular forms of this distinction vary. Women feel themselves to be women in different ways in different societies. As well, the degree of difference between women and men, and the degree of tension created by ambiguity vary. These variations produce different kinds of identity in people, none of which are essential or unchanging. Here, the emerging history of homosexuality is important. It is beginning to reveal that forms of sexuality differ between societies, that attitudes towards those forms vary, and that exclusive heterosexuality is not an essential part of becoming and feeling oneself either a woman or a man (Padgug, 1979; Rich, 1980; Weeks, 1981). Reproduction is a biological imperative for the human species. Desire and ability to reproduce, however, are not essential to an individual's gender identity as woman. There are no fixed and constant desires or behaviour, sexual or otherwise, that constitute the sense of being a woman. We are therefore now able to hypothesise a history of gender identity, a history of the changing meanings and consequences of feeling oneself to be a woman.

From quite another direction over the past decade, there has been considerable feminist interest and research into this same psychological level of being a woman. Beginning with Freud's work on sexuality and its development by various others, such writers as Juliet Mitchell (1974), Dorothy Dinnerstein (1976), and Nancy Chodorow (1978) have sought to understand how individuals come to identify themselves as and learn to act like women. They have analysed, in somewhat different ways, how consciousness and the unconscious become gendered. In Mitchell's terms, what is under question is 'how femininity is lived in the mind' (Mitchell, 1974:7).

These feminist analysts recognise the combination of biological potentialities, social forces and material conditions that together establish the content of femininity in any particular society. But generally, they have been concerned with a more abstract notion of femininity, one that is appropriate to most of western history. They have not yet applied their analyses to any specific period. In fact, however, their analyses seem to fit best the processes of becoming a woman in industrial society, that is, of the last several centuries. Nonetheless, despite this unacknowledged specificity, their work is vitally important. They deny any essential femininity, any true nature of woman. Rather, they seek to understand why people go on consenting to unjust and distressing relations between the genders. Their purpose is that, with this understanding, we might undermine that consent and change the relations.

The histories of these two levels of becoming a woman—the biological and the psychological—are yet in their infancy. The scale of time over which changes have occurred is not clear, nor are the causes of those changes. Some reference will be made to these levels in the rest of this book, but they are not my central focus. Rather, I will be concentrating upon changes over a shorter period of time at levels that are more immediately recognisable as social.

This brings us to the third level of women's history: the systemic. Despite the extreme relativity of all the meanings of woman (and equivalently, man), all individuals and all societies tend to treat what they have created as women and men as essential, and as necessary to their sense of rightness and order. Indeed, they build up the specific and relevant differences and relationships between women and men into an order in its own right. This ordering according to gender is one of the main ideological and material grids within which social meaning is created, an ordering which encompasses the entire society, sub- or super-imposed on all other orderings. This gender order is a systematic process of power relations that, for the individual, begins at birth and turns barely differentiated babies into either women or men of the approved types, thereafter keeping them to the mark as the definitions change. It is a systematic process of power relations that, for the society, establishes a basic division of labour, an initial social differentiation that permeates and underpins all other distinctions. As systematic ways of creating social women and men, and of ordering the patterns of relations among and between them, it is not logically necessary that such gender orders should be hierarchical, inequitable or oppressive. Unfortunately, as far as we yet know, all of them are and have been, and the inequality is consistently balanced. The masculine has always been taken as superior to and hence as having the right to dominate the feminine.

This does not mean, of course, that all men have benefited equally from the oppression of women, nor that every individual man is superior to every individual woman. There are other orderings of society that cut across the gender order and deflect and modify it. Only within a specific group of men and women who are otherwise equal is it possible to see gender domination clearly. For example, among every class of slave owners that we know of, the women are inferior to the men; similarly among the class of slaves. But in cross-class relations, the pattern becomes confused. The female slave owner clearly oppresses the male slave as a slave, but she is also vulnerable as a woman to the complex desires of the slave as a man. His desire for revenge, his desire to be like the superior male slave owner, can both be most readily fantasised if not expressed through his sexual domination of women of the superior class (Fanon, 1968). Class, caste, and race are all gendered. The power relations of each of these other orderings are always affected by gender and suffused with sexuality. The resulting tangle of relations is infinitely complicated, and only in the last two decades has it become the subject of serious investigation.

Thus, when I use the term 'gender order', I am aware that I have merely named an abstraction. I have simplified the unruliness of social relations in order to be able to talk about one element in isolation, knowing that such isolation never occurs in reality. A similar mode of simplification operates in recent feminist discussions of 'patriarchy'. Patriarchy has been variously defined, but probably the most useful are Juliet Mitchell's 'the law of the father' (1974:xvi) or Michèle Barrett's 'an over-arching category of male dominance' (1980:11). Since both gender order and patriarchy may seem to mean the same thing, I wish to clarify briefly what I see as the distinction. As I have mentioned above, every known society distinguishes between women and men. 'Gender order' expresses this fact, but does not specify the nature of the distinction. Thus, a gender order could be matriarchal or patriarchal or egalitarian. By analogy, we can talk of an economic order as being the ordering of people's relationships to the means of production and consumption which exist in every society. Such an ordering has no essential nature, but may be variously feudal or capitalist or communist. To distinguish between general form and specific content in this way seems to me to be a useful step away from extreme generalisation of assumptions. Certainly, the form, or ordering of gender relations has always existed; this is a valid assumption. That the gender order has always been patriarchal, however, cannot be assumed but must be proven for each specific society. This content must always be arrived at from evidence, and always qualified by the phrase 'as far as we yet know'.

The specific nature or content of any gender order is constantly in process, being formed and changed. It is fashioned by the actions of individuals who are themselves formed in that interaction. It is created in the struggles and power strategies and contradictions and unintended consequences of a multitude of social groups and individuals and interests. Some of these strategies are deliberately designed to exercise direction over some or all women or over some or all men. Some are determined to resist such control. Some come to affect women or men only as indirect spin-offs or side effects. The femininity and masculinity that are forged of these countervailing forces are never constant but always changing and, more often than not, internally inconsistent if not contradictory.

Clearly, any particular gender order affects both women and men, as individuals and groups, as well as the relations between them. The problem of the meaning of woman is paralleled by the problem of the meaning of man. I do not know whether these problems are equivalent. Throughout this book there are places where apparent analogies could be drawn between the genders: men suffer from the constraints of masculinity in an inflexible gender order. I do not draw these analogies because they require separate and detailed investigation. Assumptions cannot be made about the specific content of gender. My concern here is with women and femininity. I am thus deliberately looking at only one aspect of the gender order.

For women, the gender order of any particular•society creates an ideology of femininity, which establishes both the imperative and the meaning of being a good or true woman. This ideology is a patterned set of ideas and beliefs about women that influences both the behaviour and the treatment of all women in the society. That part which propels the imperative to be a good woman works at the psychological level, discussed above. It is concerned with the development of gender identity. It involves strategies to instil in each woman the desire and need to be feminine. Such desire and need become part of the woman's sense of herself, and direct the path of her becoming. The other part of the ideology of femininity establishes the meaning or content of being a good woman. Such meaning is constructed by a series of strategies which establish a complex hierarchy of ideal attributes. This hierarchy can perhaps best be conceived as a checklist of specific forms of appearance, behaviour, thought, speech and activity. These forms establish a basic inventory of femininity. Their detailed meanings depend on such things as class, age, race, locality, group status, historical context. Each woman can then be judged according to her performance against the appropriate checklist. Each woman is constantly subjected to scrutiny, by others and by herself. What is at issue is not whether she is a woman (except in the rare cases of transsexuality or hermaphrodism); rather, it is a question of what sort of a woman.

Femininity at this systemic level does not consist of one thing, but of many. It contains a sufficient range of variations on the basic womanly inventory to encompass all women in any particular society. Neither the specific inventory, nor its variations, are always and ever the same, but vary between societies and over time. In any particular society, there are a multitude of ideals of good women, suitable for each recognised social grouping. Within each group's ideal is a pinnacle from which the variety of less good positions slide, eventually falling into the anti-ideal of the bad woman. But these social groupings, and their appropriate ideals, are themselves ordered as a hierarchy. Some good women are better than others.

For example, in western societies since the nineteenth century, even such a social grouping as prostitutes has its hierarchy of shifting feminine ideals. At the top is the good prostitute, who is forced into the life through circumstances beyond her control and who thereafter displays her heart of gold. Other prostitutes fall away from this ideal in specific ways (e.g., stealing from their clients, growing old, being unrepentant). Eventually they come to be seen as unredeemably vicious and barely deserving, according to the ideology of the gender order, the name of woman. Obviously, however, throughout the same period, the group of prostitutes and their ideal come somewhere near the bottom of the more inclusive social hierarchy of the good woman. Near the top, in Australia, is the woman who is Australian-born of British stock, heterosexual and monogamous, happily married with several lovely children, comfortably off, living in her own home, perhaps working in a service occupation (but not while the children are young), careful of her appearance, clean and tidy, abstemious but hospitable, moderately religious (Protestant). The details of this ideal of the good woman will be more extensively discussed in Parts II and III.

As well as strategies to create, instil and proclaim such ideals, the gender order has further strategies to cajole and compel women to pursue them. Such strategies provide backup to the various ideological prescriptions about appropriate, feminine behaviour through material incentives and deterrents and, ultimately, through threats and the actuality of violence. At this systemic level, then, the meaning of woman is the history of the ideals of femininity, and of the ways they have been imposed.

Finally, we come to the social level of the meaning of woman, the history of we the women. This is the level which is constructed by and encompasses all the others. Women as social beings are biological entities and self-aware identities who live within the strategies of prescription and punishment of the gender order. The meaning of the nature of woman, of femininity, at this level is therefore highly ambiguous, vacillating between self-perception and others' recognition, between actuality and expectation, between behaviour and prescription. Whereas the history of the body and the history of feminine identity are played out over extremely long periods, the history of women as a social category involves much shorter and more precise periodisation.

Such a history would focus firstly on the diversity of woman. Women were not and are not any particular sub-group, caste, race or minority, but comprise approximately half of virtually every major social grouping, are approximately half of humankind in general, half of all societies and each of their categories. By their identification as members of all these specific categories, women are radically differentiated from each other. The only universally distinguishing feature of women is the social attribution to them of the status as other than men. Thus, there can be no unified history of women, only a multitude of histories of women as members of specific social groupings, groupings to which men also, usually, belong.

Secondly, this history would focus on the different experiences of women and men in any of these social groupings. At the very least, there must be two histories, the women's and the men's. We cannot assume that the experiences of women will be the same as men's in the same group. Nor can the concepts derived from such men's historical experiences be simply transposed in the attempt to understand those of women. For example, trade unionism in contemporary Australia does not necessarily mean the same thing to working-class women as it does to men of that class. Nor does it mean the same thing to women of the capitalist class. Notions of solidarity, of industrial matters, of work relations will mean different things to the three groups. In other words, women are both different among themselves, and different from men, and such diversity must be accommodated in any women's history. (Similarly, men's history must be acknowledged as such, and not falsify the past by claiming to be universal.)

Beyond acknowledgement of diversity among the groups of women, there is the need to acknowledge the diversity of each individual woman. There are neither heroines nor villains who are exclusively that. Each woman in any society is not simply a member of one definite social category, but is a unique and female focus of a multitude of coexisting and competing social groups and relationships. She might be white, legitimate, well educated, a football player, lesbian, divorced, mother of five, a typist, suburban, a member of a local council, a Buddhist. Each of these relational attributes, whether ascribed or achieved, is suffused with a particular set of ideals of femininity. This woman will have a sense of herself as a woman, and some unconscious desire to be a good woman. It is unlikely that this desire will be so imperative or so clear as that postulated by psychoanalysts, since, in practice, gender inscription is rarely complete or fully successful. Nonetheless, even if this desire were fully functioning, it would necessarily miscarry. Her pursuit of any, let alone a unified, ideal of femininity in this maelstrom of changing and contradicting ideals must inevitably lead to failure at some point or another. She will inevitably transgress some norms of femininity no matter how diligently she tries to conform to a true pattern. Indeed, such transgression is structured into the very pursuit itself, since the individual desires an internally consistent femininity, whereas the ideal is socially structured as inconsistent.

The three other levels of being a woman come together at this fourth level as the experiences and behaviour of women in a particular time and place. This is most centrally the arena of feminist history. The history of we the women can look very like traditional history. But it is not, because it is by and for and about ourselves. Here 'women' are not simply objects of study: the feminist historian recognises herself as part of the history she writes.

Feminist history is not impartial; it is deeply partisan and politically committed history. It takes the experiences of women as central, and denies the validity of those histories that do not—except in so far as those others self-consciously accept that they are equally partisan, masculine histories; not universal, not objective, not neutral. There is no unified history. Women's and men's bodies and subjectivities and experiences of the world are differently constructed over time. Women and men share the same world, but act upon it and are acted upon by it differently. Women's and men's histories are crucially different.

But history is appropriated by the powerful, and so women's experiences have been made subordinate and relative to men's. Men's histories have been presented as universally human. The frameworks, concepts and priorities of these 'universal' histories reflect male interests, concerns and experiences. These interests are, of course, internally diverse, but they are all different from female interests, which are similarly diverse. 'Universal' histories, of society, politics, culture, economics, are nothing more than the histories of those with the power to define themselves as insiders. The powerless are defined as outsiders, and have created for them special, 'sectional' relations to the universal. Hence all the book titles, 'Women and...' At least these are accurate. But where are all the titles, 'Men and...'? They turn into 'The History of...'

One task of feminist history is to break down these masculine universals. It is a difficult, political task. The social world has been created in the image of the powerful—men. Its reality has been presented as perceived through male eyes. Our very language is deeply structured by masculine symbolism. The words we use fit men's experiences and deny the different experiences of women. Feminist history tries to split apart the unities and the universals and reveal their gendered differences. The historical meanings of war, of work, of leisure, of politics, of migration, are vastly different for women and men. There is no single, 'human' experience of them.

A related task is to create the patterns of an autonomous women's history. 'Universal' male histories have established certain patterns of time and events. 'Women and...' histories have established the different significances for women and men of these same events. The next step is to locate the independent patterns of women's historical experiences. For example: exploration, colonisation, convicts, more exploration, sheep and gold, representative government, land legislation, class politics, federation, may be the standard pattern for understanding the 'universal' (ruling class male) history of nineteenth-century Australia. It does not provide a particularly useful pattern for understanding women's experience.

Feminist history is not simply women's history. Feminist historians are not simply women historians. Every historian is either female or male, and knows the world as a gendered being. To make sense of the past, the historical record, each historian must select, interpret, create patterns and invent meanings. These processes all involve the historian's subjectivity, which is gendered. That subjectivity has also, however, been disciplined by historical training. Within western societies, the discipline of history has been, until recently, thoroughly imbued with a masculine view of the world. The histories that the profession has created have, despite their other differences, reflected masculine interests. In so far as these interests have been presented as universal human interests, in that guise they have been adopted by some women historians. Further, histories of women have been written within this masculine discipline, by both women and men. Such histories have studied women as a group of outsiders. Their experiences have been interpreted and judged according to the norms of male experience.

Feminist history takes the complexity of women's experience of and in the world as the norm. The feminist historian looks first at women, not in relation to men, but as autonomous shapers and creators of meaning, makers of our own history within the bounds of our physical, psychological and social circumstances.

Historical methodology

That is one way of putting it: a theory of feminist history rather than a feminist history itself. But it is a theory that emerged in the process of trying to write such a history. An outline of that process might best serve both to show some of the inevitable discrepancies between theory and practice, and to introduce in more detail the rest of this book: a feminist history of femininity in twentieth-century Australia.

My initial project was a mixture of social history and women's history. I was interested in the history of the everyday lives of the women among whom I lived in South Australia. I wanted to know what life had been like, what it had meant, what were the constraints and freedoms, what was the experience of ordinary women during the twentieth century. With this general interest, I spent some time picking up and modifying and discarding information, concepts and theories about everyday life and women.

I then decided that I needed to ground the abstraction of 'ordinary Australian women' and, coming from that grand British tradition of empiricism, I went forth to find some empirical data. These were the early days of both anti-psychiatry and of Women's Liberation, so I decided to investigate the casenotes kept about women admitted to the local state psychiatric hospital: Glenside Hospital. There were two rationalisations I made for this choice. Firstly, such records seemed to me to provide a rich, untapped source of information about people who left no other records. In general, most people leave no personal account of their lives. A few write biographies, more write letters—few of which survive—some write diaries, some are interviewed by oral historians. For the rest, they remain anonymous except in the mass. Only the repetitious, cyclic, common aspects of their lives are recorded by the state: birth, baptism, marriage, taxes paid, death—bureaucratic detail which gives meaning to the actions of the bureaucracy but little to the subject.

To this anonymity, however, there is an exception. When an apparently ordinary person transgresses some law or tenet of behaviour, when she or he steps across the boundary of legitimate ordinariness into some form of deviancy, then the state requires an explanation. The nature of the transgression, its explanation and what is done by authority are recorded, and the transgressor becomes a 'case'. All institutions that deal with cases build up records of people's lives containing different types of detail according to each institution's concern with a specific type of deviancy.

The two major institutional systems dealing with deviance in twentieth-century Australia are the judiciary–police and the medical profession—with the institution of social work spanning the two. The legal system is mainly concerned with those individuals who are held to have intentionally transgressed against a specific and socially sanctioned norm, who are therefore individually responsible for their behaviour, and hence must be punished. Accordingly, the minimal case records of this system are concerned with the immediate deviant behaviour, the nature of the punishment, and the effects of inflicting that punishment. The medical system, in contrast, concerns itself with those individuals who are held to have unintentionally deviated from more general norms, who are not responsible for their behaviour, which is caused instead by social, familial, biological or physical factors, and hence can be treated or cured. The more extensive medical records are thus concerned with the immediate deviant behaviour, not in itself, but as a specific manifestation or symptom of a wider illness or physical or mental disability whose nature must be discovered historically, accurately defined or diagnosed, then appropriately treated. Within the psychiatric profession, casenotes are expected to contain extensive biographies of the patients, recorded in the hope that the doctor will find in the patient's family and personal history the source of her or his madness.

The other reason for choosing psychiatric casenotes as my empirical data had to do with alternative interpretations of the meaning of madness:

1   Madness is the antithesis of sanity, hence mad women's lives are the antithesis or negation of the lives of ordinary women. Therefore, I had merely to reverse the experiences that were these women's madness, and I would know the experiences of normality and ordinariness.
2   Mad women were defined as mad because they deviated from social norms. If I traced the pattern and content of each woman's behaviour as her sanity began to be questioned, I would be able to determine the content of that which she was deviating from, namely, normality and ordinariness.
3   Madness is a label applied to those who deviate from certain social norms. In so far as a person is not labelled, she is not mad. Therefore, mad women were ordinary up to the point of being labelled. Consequently, I could simply deal with each woman's history up to that moment of her being labelled mad, consider it ordinary, and ignore the rest.

With these justifications for using the data, I set forth to collect them. It took quite a time, as did the process of understanding enough about Glenside Hospital as the institution that had generated the notes, and the system of knowledge by which their meanings as casenotes was established. By the end, I had begun to feel distinctly that this data was far too intractable. All the reasons I had formulated for using them were either wrong or inadequate. As an untapped source of biography, the casenotes were too embedded in the purposes for which they were collected. They were fragmentary, cryptic, the minimum information required by the doctors for the purposes of their day-to-day treatments which were required to be legally accounted for. As for my three versions of the meaning of madness, and their consequences for the meaning of normality, neither the cases themselves nor my researches into psychiatric and deviance theories could provide a simple and clear-cut correlation: madness is an undefined state or experience (Scheff, 1966). There are no objectively definable criteria for its existence; there are no objectively established social norms whose transgression leads to the label of mad being applied. Any and all behaviour can be called mad, depending upon the social context, the values held by and the relationship of power between the judge and the judged. Even in the case of the medical profession, which alone can legitimately and conclusively diagnose or define a person as mad, each doctor's judgment is subjective, inevitably biased according to her or his age, sex, class position, etc.; and in so far as the judgment is made of behaviour alone, it is inevitably a moral judgment about what ought to be.

At this point in my research, as well as losing my justification for using the data, I had also lost sight of my original project which, since it had never been precisely defined, was not surprising. The closest I could get back to it was something to do with the meaning of being a woman in twentieth-century Australia. I was floundering without a conceptual framework to cling to, bogged down in apparently useless data. All I could do was the magician's trick of pulling arbitrary sociological and historiographical concepts out of a hat, and attempt to work the casenote data into some sort of shape. But the concepts didn't work. I tried production, reproduction, ideology, everyday oppression, power, society, class, public and private...Then I realised I was back with the old problem. These were concepts derived from male experience of society and history. All the theorists I was reading to help me to define the terms refused to deal with women's experience. They either ignored it, and by implication subsumed it within a universal that was male, or they tacked it on the end in a subsidiary or 'special case' category. Thus the concepts, and the frameworks, were there, but I couldn't translate them into either female or, indeed, accurately universal (that is, equally female and male) terms. This line of approach, indeed, led me to think that women didn't exist, or at best, were invisible; which didn't tally with my self, my politics, or my data. This incongruity led me to an extraordinarily simple discovery: the root of the problem lay in the fact that the very concept of 'women' was not defined, but was a taken-for-granted category.

To define the concept, however, was a much more difficult proposition than determining the need. To repeat a statement made above, women were not and are not a particular sub-group, but comprise approximately half of all social groupings. By their identification as members of specific groups, women are radically distinct from each other. The only universally distinguishing feature of all women is their gender. In so far as gender is a social category, it is relational. Thus the only situation in which women can be considered as a homogeneous group is in relation to men.

Having got that far with my definitional problems, I jumped to the conclusion that, in order to analyse accurately the everyday life of Australian women, I would have to relate their experiences to those of the men of the same time and place, which would mean compounding the problems of my intractable data and taking a comparable sample of the casenotes of men admitted to Glenside Hospital. But how could such a sample be made comparable? In terms of the relation of women and men as such, I would have to adjust or stabilise all other social attributes in order to make sure that I was dealing with gender alone. Class, race, age, diagnosis, would all have to be made equivalent. There were just too many variables. Moreover, such a comparison with this sort of data would lead inevitably into a fragmentary, atomised, individual-by-individual tabulation, leaving gender as that which was left over after everything else had been taken away. And how would I recognise this remnant?

Once again, gender distinction had been made peripheral and minimal by my method of analysis. But 'everybody knows' that gender is a basic and most fundamental difference between people. There is a coherent and very rigid ordering of society on the criterion of gender which is reproduced generation after generation without the need for individual conscious intervention. (An individual may say and believe that classes do not exist in present society, but they cannot say that there is no distinction made between women and men.) It is this gender order that establishes the definition or the meaning of 'women' and 'men' in any particular society by sanctioning the patterns of relations between women and men as gender groups, and between individual women and men as members of those specific groups. I thus came to see that the everyday lives of ordinary women that I had been interested in was really a concern with the nature and operation of this gender order: how it was maintained and how it changed; how 'women' were made and how they lived, within this order, both as individuals and as members of their gender group.

It seemed to me that one way to understand that gender order, and to investigate the lives of women within it, was to postulate that the gender order of any particular society at any particular time was premised on a specific ideal of the relations between women and men, and that the component parts of that order attempted to shape everybody's lives towards that ideal. In other words, the function of the gender order was to transform people into ideal good women and men; and in so far as people regarded themselves as 'women' and 'men' (that is, having the gender identity of women and men), they were operating within the framework of that order and were in some sense, in many senses, measuring themselves and others against their understanding of the ideal standard, of true or good women and men.

What I saw now as my project was to pursue the meaning of trying to be a good woman in Australian society during the twentieth century: to establish the components of the society that shaped the gender order, the ways in which they enforced the order, the ways in which women lived within that order; to establish the precise content of the ideal of the good woman and the consequences of trying to achieve it. Obviously, this was an enormous undertaking since the gender order was the most fundamental, most pervasive, and most taken-for-granted structure of the society. Every condition of an individual's life was affected by it, and I could not hope to encompass all aspects. Selection was necessary, and must be of significant, substantial elements. With no other theoretical criteria to go on, I decided to accept those of the institution whose workings I knew best by now—psychiatry.

Psychiatry is an institution very strongly implicated in the maintenance of the gender order in so far as it is concerned with 'curing' deviation and restoring normality. This normality is gender-specific: not normal individuals but normal women (and men) is the hoped-for goal, and normal women, by definition, pursue the ideal of becoming good women. At Glenside Hospital, the method employed for this restoration of normality involved, initially, understanding the personal and social history of each patient in order to discover what had gone wrong when. The plan for recording such case histories was as follows:

> Begin with the onset, duration and progress of the patient's illness,
> including their complaint—*verbatim*. The next part will normally be
> an account of any previous psychogenic disorder. Then follows the
> history of the patient's life with comments on the presence or
> otherwise of familial or hereditary diseases, alcoholism or epilepsy,
> with notes on the home atmosphere and influence. A profile of near
> relatives is useful. The personal history should include notes on early
> development; neurotic traits in childhood; play life and sociability;
> school and work records; premarital and marital sex history.

What this plan sought to elicit was information that could be translated into medical terms. Psychiatry saw madness predominantly as an illness caused by genetic, constitutional, or accidental factors. It did recognise as well, however, that some forms of madness were due to social maladjustment, and sought information about the patient's past and present environments. This was the information of interest to me as it established and named those areas of social life in which adjustment was essential if psychiatrists were to consider one normal. From the plan outline I extracted three social areas that psychiatry judged important to normality: family life, sexual life and work. There was a fourth category that was also recorded in all patients' records and was taken to influence strongly the patient's social background: 'native place' or nationality.

From my initial forays into the Glenside Hospital record room, I had extracted the casenotes of 60 women, admitted between 1945 and 1970, who were diagnosed as suffering from functional mental disorders, that is, whose madness had no known organic cause but was defined solely in terms of the peculiarities of their behaviour. (The process of selecting the cases, and the details of those used, are contained in the Appendix.) I was granted permission to use the casenotes by the South Australian

Director of Mental Heath Services and the Superintendent of Glenside Hospital. The sample was selected by random process, and the cases used were coded. The women were given invented names which bore no resemblance to their real ones. For those women who were not Australian-born, their names were invented so as to retain a semblance of ethnic authenticity. I decided to use surnames as well as first names in order to reduce confusion between the cases, and to attempt to invest them with more individual identities. The names of all the women whose casenotes I use throughout this book are totally fictitious, having no relationship whatsoever to real individuals or real families who may bear those names. Details from the notes which might be used to identify any actual woman have been altered, except on rare occasions when they are intrinsically important to my analysis.

The casenotes varied considerably from year to year and from patient to patient in the quantity and nature of information they contained. At the minimum, they contained only basic administrative details: name, age, marital status, whether sober, address, birthplace, dates of admission and discharge, details from medical certificates requesting admission. Beyond that, they contained some sort of psychiatric history, record of diagnoses made and treatments given and, occasionally, reports by ward nurses, psychologists, social workers, mental-health visitors, occupational therapists and outpatient clinic staff.

Such casenotes are not autobiographical material. The person whose life has been thus captured has no say in its recording. Even verbatim reporting of her own words is not under her control. Usually such words have been elicited by specific questions containing explicit or unspoken assumptions and expectations which guide her answers. Nor are casenotes strictly biographical. They do not seek to understand a person's life in any terms other than those which further the interests of the institution compiling the notes. Such recorded lives have no autonomy, but are slotted into prearranged patterns. I came to call the notes 'captured biographies'.

By the time I had decided to embark afresh on my pursuit of the history of the good woman through analysis of the gender order, I had at hand 60 such captured biographies. These I proceeded to sort out and categorise in terms of the information they contained about family, sexuality and work. It was a tedious and horrific task. The psychiatric record laid out in stark detail the extremes of unhappiness and hopelessness of these women's lives, because that was where the psychiatrists sought to find the clues to their present condition. Eventually, I was able to see that the horror was partly produced by the method of recording. I learnt how to recount the traumas of my own and my friends' lives in such a way as to leave out everything else, and so create the semblance of a psychiatric record, and wonder why we weren't in hospital too. In other words, the types of extreme, traumatic events recorded in the casenotes occur in most women's lives, but most women do not undergo so many of them and are not so seriously affected. For most women, such events are counterpoised with many other, happier events, and are not linked together to form an interpretive framework of their lives as was done by the psychiatrists for their patients. The lives of mad women are certainly not ordinary, but there is no one who can say how much out of the ordinary they are.

So I began to come to terms with the cases, as biographies. But each case, each life, was unique. How to pattern these lives to give a general meaning to being a woman in twentieth-century Australia became the next problem. And again, the solution was a matter of trial and error. I found myself rewriting the traditional history of Australian society, constantly trying to reconceptualise the frameworks and categories so as to bring out their relevance for women. In the process, the uniqueness of the cases became incongruous. The broad sweep of historical change that affected all women I found difficult to relate to the lives of particular women. It was a long and still unfinished process, balancing out the general and the unique, breaking down a universal history into its masculine specificity, beginning to reread specifically female meaning into the past.

In the book as now presented, the captured biographies play a less significant part than they did in its making. But the process of struggling to make sense of them as social documents has been crucial to my understanding of feminist history. As well, the continuing uneasy tension that they introduce, the play of social forces and the lives of individuals, is a vital corrective. In what would otherwise be a straightforward history that makes coherent patterns of social experience, they are a constant reminder of the anomalies, the gaps, the untidiness of real social life. History is only made coherent after the event by omission of what does not quite fit.

In the end, this book has come to be about the history of women making themselves in twentieth-century Australia, under circumstances not chosen by themselves, but directly encountered, given and transmitted from the past (cf. Marx, 1968:97). It looks at the recorded experiences of certain women, and seeks to understand what was the content of the femininity they sought and were propelled to achieve. It looks at certain elements of the Australian gender order, at various institutions and relationships which directly affected women's lives by defining for them an approved and necessary femininity. It is about the ordered circumstances that existed, the pressures that were applied, the choices that were presented to women, and about their experiences within those circumstances.

Chapter 3, 'The pattern of probabilities', is a demographic and statistical overview of changes in Australian women's lives. It sets out the patterns of life and death, of childbearing, of marriage and divorce over the twentieth century. These patterns were the result of a multitude of individual choices made in uniquely personal circumstances which, by accumulation, became social phenomena. I do not present here any arguments as to why circumstances changed, nor why large numbers of women made the choices they did. Such arguments come later. Chapter 3 is an abstract description of what changed in the sociophysical expectations of life for the generations of Australian women. It includes a discussion of migration, because Australia has always been an immigrant country, and many Australian women have been foreign-born. Their expectations had to accommodate a sea change.

Part II is an examination of some of the social forces that structured the gender order. It shows them at work in creating the ideal of femininity. These social forces were manifold; they overlapped and intertwined and contradicted each other; they changed direction. I have grouped them into three categories. The economy was the arena of daily subsistence through production and consumption. Women's lives were fundamentally affected by two interrelated economic processes: the elaboration of a gender division of labour, and the expansion of a technologically organised capitalist marketplace into all areas of daily work. The second arena, of ideology, was one of competing ideals and purposes. Over the century, two ideologies held sway, at different times, over the meaning of femininity. The first, from the 1890s to the 1930s, was an ideology of population. The second, from the 1950s, was one of permissive consumerism. Both ideologies, in their heydays, were so deeply believed as true representations of how the world worked that they became taken-for-granted bases of commonsense. They were the background systems of understanding upon which were played out all the other, more specific, theories and practices. The third significant force of the gender order was its system of organisation. Over the century, the 'hidden hand' of classical economics was replaced by a more visible one. Similarly, ideology no longer appeared to drop from the sky, but could be seen in the process of its formation. Or so 'it seemed, as a new group of experts emerged who claimed to organise it all. These new professionals were scientific managers of people and social processes. They rationalised the processes of the economy, organising its expansion into mass production and mass consumption. They regulated the private lives of individuals and families, adjusting them to appropriate standards of behaviour. In all their operations they clarified and standardised gender differences in the name of efficiency. As a by-product, they made explicit not only the ideal of the good woman, but revealed the processes of its construction.

Part III is about women's attempts to live the impossibility of this ideal. This section introduces the captured biographies of the women of

Glenside Hospital. Three of the most significant dimensions of their lives as women were their sexuality, work and mothering. Each of these dimensions was changed and ordered by the processes discussed in Part II. The gender order prescribed by rules and regulations and expectations a path of true femininity for each woman to follow throughout life. But the gender order was itself ever changing and inconsistent. The path was a maze. Each woman inevitably failed in her pursuit of the ideal.

My purpose in writing this book has been to understand the lives of Australian women in order that we might change our condition of subordination. There are two main directions in which feminists have sought such understanding. In the direction of origins, we seek first causes. These tend to be found in such differences between women and men as: childbearing rendering women in need of masculine protection; or women's inferior strength; or the male demand for certified paternity; or in the rise of private property; or in kinship obligations being secured by the exchange of women. The other direction is less concerned with first causes, and more interested in continuation, with the means by which gender oppression is maintained and enforced today, or in some other specific period. This is the approach I take: looking at the peculiar interrelationships of the strategies that fashioned and maintained the Australian gender order and the meanings of femininity in this century. My basic question is not how did this happen, but rather, what does this mean for women and the ideal of the good woman.

As for the problem that I have discussed throughout this introduction—that of the masculine bias of our language and its organisation of reality—I have dealt with this in two ways. Firstly, wherever I have been able to see through them, I have broken down apparently universal categories into their masculine specificity, and brought to the surface submerged female experience, for example, in my discussions of the economy and work. Similarly, I have attempted to retranslate masculine interpretations of female experience, as in the discussions of lesbianism, prostitution and motherhood. Secondly, I have not held the categories of analysis to their conventional places with their rigidly defined boundaries, but have let them wander. This has involved circling around the same spot for a while, repeating the same point in juxtaposition with a number of different points, allowing categories to overflow and overlap in order to encompass a more integrated understanding of women's experience. For example, the fact that Australian women throughout the century have received less pay for the same or similar work done by men is not merely an economic fact, restricted in meaning to women's working lives. It has not been merely a discriminatory effect of the workings of the capitalist market in search of enhanced profits. It has as well been supported by the ideological stances of trade unions, the legal arbitration system, churches, parliament, and community groups. Unequal pay has been deeply embedded in the gender order, and has had significant bearing on many aspects of the lives of women beyond their work: compelling them into heterosexuality, making marriage a necessity, affecting the patterns of their mothering and their experiences as migrants.

I would make one final point about a history that seeks to understand in order to change. Between the two lies unpredictability and indeterminancy. The meaning of being a woman cannot, ultimately, be deduced from however much data. That meaning is a lived, and hence perverse reality, and the accuracy of any understanding must be tested by all of us who live it. Similarly, the accuracy of any understanding about how to free ourselves from gender oppression must be tested by us in the streets.

3

Patterns of Probability

*O*ver the past century, the process of becoming a woman has been affected by and been part of dramatic changes in Australian society. The meaning of femininity in the 1980s is very different from its meaning in the 1890s. Before examining these transformations of meaning, in Parts II and III, I want in this chapter to establish the nature of the sociophysical changes that occurred in the life expectations of white Australian women. The life expectations and experiences of Aboriginal women were and are significantly different from those of non-Aboriginal women, whether Australian-born or immigrant. Regrettably, here and throughout the book, I can make only occasional mention of these differences. As well, regional distinctiveness has been flattened out. The 'Australia' I write about is an averaged nation, its patterns closer to those of the more populous southern and eastern mainland states than to the frontiers and isolation of the north and west.

The patterns of each individual's life are created by personal decisions made in unique circumstances: whom to marry and when, what work to do, what beliefs to adhere to, which pair of shoes to buy. But the circumstances are generally shared by many others, and the decisions also have to be made by everybody else. The accumulation of all the individuals' circumstances and decisions, averaged'out so as to blur each individual's uniqueness, allows us to create the patterns of the social order. The value of such patterns is that they establish the boundaries of probability. Everything is possible; only some events are probable in any particular society.

A woman born in, for example, 1949, might have dreamt of living to a hundred, marrying seven times and having ten children, being an astrophysicist and an Olympic hurdler. All this was possible. The probability, however, can be calculated from all the sociophysical circumstances into which she was born and through which she passed. In general, it can be expected that she would have done what others like her did, made similar decisions to her peers, been dissuaded from the unusual. She would have fitted into the life patterns of her time and place. Change any of the particular circumstances of her life—born of wealthy rather than poor parents, encouraged to stay at school rather than taking a job at fifteen, not marrying because her first boyfriend didn't like her jumping fences—and the patterns into which she was likely to fit would change slightly. New probabilities would enter her life.

Many circumstances and decisions of individual life are highly idiosyncratic. Many others are widely shared. What, then, were the major shared circumstances and decisions of Australian women over the past century? What were the probable life expectations and experiences of women in the 1890s? How different were they for women in the 1980s? Throughout the century, the patterns of probability for women in Australia were bounded by changes in three major sociophysical patterns: those of life and death and the balance of the genders, of reproduction, and of migration.

Life and death and the balance of the genders

At the beginning of the period, in 1891, the total Australian non-Aboriginal population numbered just over three million. (Recent estimates put the Aboriginal population at about 111 000 in 1891 (Smith, 1980:210). Ninety years later, the population (including 155 000 Aborigines, who were counted in census returns for the first time in 1966) had multiplied to over fourteen and a half million. In contrast with the earlier immigrant–settler period, by 1891, 84 per cent of the non-Aboriginal population was Australian-born, mainly of British ancestry. The rest was predominantly British-born. By 1976, the Australian-born proportion was still high, at 80 per cent, but the ethnic or cultural Britishness of the population had altered considerably as a result of continuing streams of European migrants after the second world war.

Australia in 1891 was very much a man's world, at least statistically. The first century of settlement had been marked by a superfluity of men. The colony was founded by almost 800 men, over 200 women, and 36 children, gender unspecified (O'Brien, 1950:154; Shaw, 1974:6; Gandevia, 1978:13). Half a century later, the gender ratio was 226 males for every 100 females. Even in 1891, there was an excess of fifteen men per 100 women. From the first world war, however, a more even balance was achieved and maintained. Across the whole period, of course, there were considerable fluctuations year by year and region to region, and considerable differences between age groups. Australian culture valued heterosexuality highly, and the imbalance in numbers between women and men meant that the few women were in high demand. The culture also valued monogamy, which meant that many men would be denied the sexual and housekeeping services of women. In consequence, both heterosexuality and monogamy were adhered to less in practice than in belief (Hirst, 1983:200; Smith, 1975; Clark, 1977:117–8). Further, a division among women was intensified. The respectable reserved their services for one man; the disreputable chose or were forced to make themselves available to several or to many (Summers, 1975:267–89; Perrott, 1983:99–103; Grimshaw & Willett, 1981).

As the years of settlement passed, the population as a whole became more urban, the female population especially so. As early as 1890, approximately two-thirds of Australians lived in areas classified by the census as urban. In particular, the population was concentrated on the coast in the six state capital cities which held 35 per cent of the total in 1900, 51 per cent in 1947, and 64 per cent in 1979. This reality of Australian settlement was rarely acknowledged in the masculine images of national identity. An ideology of Australia as a bush paradise rose and subsided periodically over the century (White, 1981), as did arguments for the need to populate the vast hinterland lest it be coveted by the 'teeming hordes' of Asia. Governments, philanthropic bodies, the Christian churches, nationalist intellectuals and imperial apologists, all tried at various times to encourage soldier settlement, boy farming, rural villages, a stalwart yeomanry (Shields, 1982; Campion, 1982:105–6; Christo, 1974; Forsyth, 1954). Various schemes were begun. Most failed, and the suffering of women during such failures was great (Lake, 1981). Even on farming ventures that succeeded, women's lot was not easy. The same body of literature that eulogised the bush for its stimulation of mateship among men accepted the loneliness and terror of the mate's wife. Though some women thrived in the country, by and large modern Australian femininity took an urban guise.

Although there were substantial regional differences and national fluctuations, over the century individual life expectancy at birth rose: from 55 to 77 years for women, and from 51 to 70 years for men. Aboriginal life expectancy at birth in the early 1970s was about 52 years for both women and men (Hetzel, 1974:25–7; National Population Inquiry, 1975:515–20). Much of this expanding lease of life for the white population was provided, statistically, by the sharp decline in infant mortality rates over the first several decades of this century. (The circumstances of this decline, and its effects on femininity, are discussed in chapters 5 and 6.) The rate of death of infants under one year had peaked in the 1870s and 1880s. In South Australia in 1875, of every 1000 children born live, 180 died before reaching their first birthday. In New South Wales and Victoria in 1889, respectively 125 and 153 infants died (CBCS, 1939:167). (Until well into the 1900s, all such mortality rates must be treated with extreme caution, since registration and compilation were extremely haphazard. Once again, it is only the general trend over time that is of specific interest here.) From the turn of the century, the rate of infant mortality declined substantially. After 1904, it never again rose above 100 deaths per 1000, and by the mid-1930s only about 40 infants out of every 1000 died in their first year. This substantial improvement in infant health was brought about through environmental control rather than medical advances. Not until the late 1930s did the first of the antibiotics become available. By the 1930s, total infant deaths within the first year of life had stabilised at about 8 per cent of all deaths in Australia. By 1978 they had fallen to about 2.5 per cent of total deaths, with over three-quarters occurring within the first four weeks of life. Of every 1000 infants born in 1978, only about twelve died within their first year (CBCS, 1939:167; Thame, 1974:200–2;·Mendelsohn, 1979:232; ABS, 1981:227). Aboriginal children did not share in this enhancement of life chances. Even in 1971, Aboriginal infants continued to die at the appalling rate of 120 in every 1000 (National Population Inquiry, 1975:518).

The same antibiotics effecting the second stage of decline in infant mortality were instrumental in the initial decline in maternal mortality from the 1940s. Before that date, Australia's record was worse than many European countries, with well over five mothers dying out of every 1000 giving birth. During the 1920s, death in childbirth was the second major cause of death, after tuberculosis, among married women in early and middle adulthood. In that same decade, it was estimated that up to 80 more women out of 1000 childbearers suffered from puerperal infections, and that half of all mothers suffered from 'some weakening of bodily function following childbirth' (Thame, 1974:160–4). Following the widespread availability of antibiotics in the 1940s, the maternal death rate began falling, from four in 1000 live births in 1940 to 1.1 by 1950, dropping right away to 0.06 in 1975 (Mendelsohn, 1979:168). For at least half of the century, then, and probably longer in popular memory, the good woman's fundamental task of childbearing was attended by the probability of pain and suffering, and the possibility of death, for either mother or child or both. This is discussed further in chapter 9.

Apart from such general considerations about the condition of life and death of the population, there were two specific phenomena of great significance in the making of Australian femininity: the demographic transition, and migration.

The demographic transition

At the beginning of Australia's demographic transition in the 1860s–

1880s, married women bore and reared large families. At its completion, in the 1960s, their families contained only two or three children. This phenomenon of fertility decline was shared by most western countries over slightly different time spans (Ruzicka & Caldwell, 1977; Richards, 1978:13–20). For the individual Australian woman, the demographic transition was experienced as a set of changes that marked her off from both the generations of women before and the generations after: changed attitudes to her body, changed expectations of her life patterns, changed relationships with all the people in her intimate life—parents, siblings, friends, husband, children.

According to the available Australian statistics, the birth rate began to drop steeply in the early 1860s (CBCS, 1939:163). At that time, the annual crude birth rate stood at 43 live births per 1000 total population. (The crude birthrate is not a particularly sensitive measure, since it ignores gender ratio and age distribution. Moreover, before the 1900s and the introduction of compulsory, and eventually reliable, registration of births, the crude birthrate was quite inaccurate. Nonetheless, it is useful to indicate broad trends over time.) The birthrate fell, with slight fluctuations, from the 1860s to the mid-1930s when the lowest rate of 16.4 was recorded. From 1935 to 1947, the rate rose again, stabilising at about 23 births per 1000 until 1961. Thereafter, until 1976, there was another sudden downturn, falling once again to the 1930s level of 16.4 Since then, the annual rates have been unstable, producing as yet no clear pattern (Ruzicka & Caldwell, 1977:71–86; Caldwell, 1980).

In the last two decades of the nineteenth century, this decline in fertility was apparently brought about through changing marriage patterns (McDonald, 1974:103–13). These same decades also saw the peak in infant mortality rates, and a very high rate of death of mothers in childbirth, which continued until the early 1940s. These death rates probably affected the choices people made about childbearing (Quiggin, in progress; Thame, 1974:160–98). The major alteration in marriage patterns was for both women and men to delay the wedding. By marrying at older ages, the number of fertile years women spent within marriage was reduced and, therefore, the possible number of children they could bear was less. Further, as the disproportionate ratio of men to women declined, the proportion of women who never married rose. By 1891, in urban areas where the gender ratios were more evenly balanced, about 8 or 9 per cent of women never married, taking them out of the statistical fertility market (McDonald, 1974:103–13).

From the 1890s marital fertility came gradually to be controlled less by restricting the years in marriage, and more by deliberate contraception. By means of abstinence, rhythm, withdrawal, mechanical and chemical contraceptives and abortion, married couples, or women by themselves worked to control the number of their children (Ruzicka

& Caldwell, 1977:320–35; Allen, 1982). As knowledge of and access to these various methods increased, despite the illegality or official restriction of some, so too did the sense of the possibility of effective control of childbearing within marriage grow. (The implications of this situation will be dealt with in more detail in chapter 7.) Couples saw postponement of marriage as less necessary, and gradually the pattern reversed. Marriage became progressively more universal and was entered upon at earlier ages. 1921 marked the end of the old, delayed marriage pattern. In that year, almost 17 per cent of women and 20 per cent of men over 49 years had never married. Average age at first marriage stood at about 24–25 years for women, and about 26 years for men (McDonald, 1974:133, 140). Thereafter, the ages at which women and men married for the first time declined slowly. By the 1970s, women tended to marry at about 21, and men at about 23. During the decade of the 1970s, the decline was arrested, and there was, for women, a slight rise in age, and for men a stabilisation (Krupinski, 1978:9). As well, by the 1970s, close to 95 per cent of both women and men could expect ultimately to marry.

Before the demographic transition began in the 1860s–1880s, married women on average ended up with families of about seven children. High rates of miscarriage and infant mortality meant that most married women would have been pregnant more often than this. About 60 per cent of all families contained more than six children, but all other sizes of families, from childless to more than ten, were common. Further, the average size of families varied considerably according to certain characteristics of the parents: religion, national or ethnic origin, education, regional location, occupation (Ruzicka & Caldwell, 1977:131–50; National Population Inquiry, 1975:49–57). From the 1870s the average completed family size dropped steadily until by 1954 it contained the proverbial 2.43 children. There was a slight increase in the following decades, but no new clear pattern has yet emerged.

As well as family size thus declining, families became more uniform. The spread across the range of possibilities from none to more than ten children diminished. Increasingly, everybody had two to three children, regardless of religion, birthplace, occupation, etc., though wives who had jobs in the commanding workforce generally had smaller families than those who did not (National Population Inquiry, 1975:83–9, 357–61). These two or three children were born in a shorter period of time than ever before. That is, childbearing became a highly concentrated activity. In terms of family lifecycle, by the 1970s, most children (over three-quarters) were born within a ten-year period—the first decade of marriage when the mother was between 20 and 30 years old—rather than being extended across the mother's fertile life.

This overall reduction in family size and length of time devoted to childbearing was accomplished by the deliberate choices of married couples. Birth control by various means was well established in Australia before the contraceptive revolution associated with the marketing of the anovulant pill in 1961. The pill did not fundamentally change the prevailing fertility patterns, but did increase the efficiency of avoiding unwanted pregnancies and of the timing and spacing of pregnancies. The pill was, however, crucial to women's sense of control of their fertility and hence of their lives and futures. Its apparent certainty meant that effective choice was for the first time possible.

There were several other relevant aspects to the demographic change that Australian society underwent in the century to the 1980s. From the statistics, more women could expect to spend more of their extended lives in the married state, with fewer children to bear and rear. A woman born after 1960, with a life expectancy well into her late seventies, could expect to marry in her early twenties, have her two or three children before the age of 30 and, overall, spend almost three-quarters of her whole life with one man. Counteracting this trend, however, was the increasing rate of divorce. At the beginning of the century, only 4 per cent of marriages ended in divorce, while by the 1960s this proportion had risen to about 12 per cent (Day, 1970:294). This increase occurred with little encouragement from the law, under which divorce was a long, expensive and harrowing experience until 1975 (Finlay, 1978:113–8). By comparison, the other two forms of marriage dissolution, permanent separation and death, retained remarkably steady rates over the century. The status of permanently separated was first recorded in the census of 1954, and from then until the 1971, the rate remained constant. The rate jumped in the 1976 census, probably because permanent separation for one year had become the sole legal ground for divorce. In 1975, the Family Law Act established 'no fault' divorce on the sole basis of 'irretrievable breakdown of marriage'. The first year of the Act's operation, 1976, saw the divorce rate reach an exceptional peak. Many couples who had been estranged or separated for some time took advantage of the new leniency of the law to formalise the end of their marriages. Thereafter, the rate of divorce fell substantially, and by 1980 had apparently settled back into a more regular, slow increase.

This trend to increasing divorce was itself counteracted by another: an increasing tendency to remarriage. Whereas in the five years before 1970, only 6 per cent of brides had been previously divorced, by 1980 almost 19 per cent had. In this latter year, almost 30 per cent of all marriages involved one or both partners who had been previously divorced (ABS, 1980b:4). Thus, the married state was still, and increasingly, the usual status of women throughout adult life, but not necessarily with the same husband. The significance of marriage and its alternatives is discussed in chapter 7.

There was only one major demographic dimension that appears to run against this trend of marriage as the increasingly expected experience of adult women: that of births outside marriage. From 1921–30, almost 24 per cent of all confinements of women between fifteen and nineteen years, and almost 7 per cent of those between twenty and twenty-four years, produced illegitimate children. By 1978, these rates had increased respectively to 48 per cent and 12 per cent. (ABS, 1978:11; 1980a:31). Moreover, until the 1970s, over 40 per cent of brides under twenty years were pregnant on their wedding day. Thereafter, the pregnancies kept happening, but fewer of the women married before giving birth. Only 23 per cent of births to women under twenty in 1978 occurred within eight months of marriage (ABS, 1978:11). In other words, marriage was decreasingly a prelude to maternity for young women. Nonetheless, it became the epilogue, with most single mothers eventually marrying, though not necessarily the father of the first child.

The causes of the demographic transition, and of each of its component patterns, are still the subject of much discussion (McDonald, 1974; Ruzicka & Caldwell, 1977; Quiggin, in progress). The particular priorities and processes of the changes are unclear. They were subject to influence by, and in their turn influenced, all the other social processes to be discussed later—economic, ideological, political. As a setting for the construction of modern Australian femininity, however, it is the very fact of the changes that is of most importance. Throughout the century from the 1880s, heterosexual relations and childbearing remained the core experiences of the good woman. But the permitted latitude of behaviour, and the content of the ideal of femininity changed, as did the patterns of the average life experiences of the generations of women.

Migration

The experience of trying to be a good woman was an especially complex one for many of the millions of women living in Australia during the century from the 1880s. These were the women who were born outside and migrated to Australia at some point in their lives. They brought with them the standards of femininity of their various homelands, some similar to, some greatly at odds with Australian standards. They were kept to some of their native standards by their kin and compatriots, for whom a particular patterning of gender relations was vital to their sense of well-being and order. At the same time, the people and customs and laws of their new Australian homeland compelled change, at different rates for different individuals within the migrant communities. For many women, the path between the two sets of standards was a tortuous one. Moreover, the difficulty of reconciling the two versions of femininity was not necessarily only experienced by those women who themselves migrated. Often the discrepancy was maintained within the families and communities of migrants to bedevil the lives of later generations of Australian-born daughters.

Non-Aboriginal Australia has always been a migrant society. Everybody's family has come from somewhere else within the last two hundred years. Between 1860 and 1919, over one million migrants arrived and stayed in Australia, mostly from the United Kingdom, providing about 24 per cent of total population growth. Nearly half had been financially assisted by one or other of the Australian governments. They came in two waves, on either side of the depressed 1890s (Crowley, 1954). Another 2 million arrived in the years between the wars, many of whom left again because of the depression. Over 500 000 people arrived in Australia in the decade of the 1930s, but the excess of arrivals over departures was only 30 000 (Department of Immigration, 1973:9). In the twenty years following world war two, over 2 million people migrated to and stayed in Australia, constituting an average of almost 40 per cent annual population growth. For the first time, this last wave included substantial numbers of non-British-born migrants.

Before world war two, immigrants were preponderantly single and young. In general, government-assisted schemes tried for a balanced gender ratio, but unassisted migrants were overwhelmingly male (Crowley, 1954:76). In the postwar period, government policy favoured families, but economic factors favoured young single men once more. This led to striking, but usually short-term, gender imbalance among certain national groups, with consequent intensified demand by men for the services of women within and close to such groups. But, again, overall gender ratios tended to stabilise near parity (Immigration Advisory Council, 1969).

Until 1920, immigration policy was in the hands of each colonial or state government. In that year, a State–Commonwealth agreement was negotiated which empowered the Commonwealth government to take over the responsibility for recruitment and transportation of all assisted migrants to Australia, while each state retained the responsibility for advising the Commonwealth about the numbers and types of migrants it was prepared to receive. Throughout the whole period of non-convict immigration, Australian governments maintained a strong dual, and somewhat contradictory, interest in the process: in the rapid build-up of a labour supply, and in the development or re-creation of an idealised British civilisation (Hamilton, 1982:15–22; Crowley, 1954).

There was always present a certain element of xenophobia and insularity, succinctly expressed in 1905 by the New South Wales parliamentarian, and later premier, William Holman, who insisted that, 'the best of all immigrants is the Australian baby' (Crowley, 1973, I:84). Forty years later, this insularity was recognised by the Commonwealth

Minister for Immigration, Arthur Calwell, as a potential stumbling block to the success of the mass immigration programme:

> The Australian people must help newcomers to become assimilated. We have been too prone in the past to ostracize those of alien birth and then to blame them for segregating themselves and forming foreign communities. It is we, not they, who are generally responsible for this condition of affairs. (Calwell, 1945:1218)

But there were also always strong countervailing ideological interests in favour of migration. Strongly expressed in the years between the wars was the imperial interest, whose objective was 'the redistribution of the white population of the Empire in a manner most conducive to the development, strength and stability of the whole' (Wood, 1928:108–9). From before the turn of the century, and throughout the next 80 years to the present, other groups of pro-white, anti-Asian immigration lobbyists maintained their vociferous presence, seeking to fill the continent's 'vast, empty spaces' with white settlers in order to pre-empt the 'land-hungry teeming races in the East'. The geographic orientation of this lobby tended to be skewed by a belief that Britain was home. Some of the background to this population debate is given in chapter 5.

Whatever the specific economic or ideological arguments of the time, Australian governments generally regarded their bailiwicks, and the country as a whole, as having enormous potential that could and must be made productive and prosperous. This potential could only be achieved by a large population, which in turn could only come about through immigration to supplement natural increase. To make Australia great, migrants were needed. The question was, who should the migrants be?

The basic standard employed by both state and Commonwealth governments as to who should be received was the very vague concept of 'desirability'. On the negative side, this concept became enshrined as the 'White Australia Policy': the attempt to exclude all Asian, black, and coloured immigrants. A dictation test was used—the ability to write out not less than 50 words dictated in any prescribed language—to establish the standard of desirability as meaning 'white'. But 'whiteness' itself was not absolute. Rather, it involved a sliding scale premised on racial theories about the superiority of British and northern European peoples and their cultures over all others. In this context, 'white' meant something more than simple skin pigmentation. It meant close approximation to the Australian ideal in terms of lifestyle, language, culture, work ethic, values. From this position, the positive aspect of the standard of desirability involved the importation of migrants who would not disturb and would indeed advance the peaceful and prosperous economic development of Australia. In addition, desirable migrants were those who would work at jobs in which there was a shortage of Australian labour, who would not compete with native-born workers for scarce jobs, and who would not upset the delicate balance between Australian workers and employers by accepting lower wages than the native-born received.

By and large, the standards of desirability and of the Australian ideal were masculine. Women were almost invisible. Domestic servants were the only class of female migrants ever explicitly discussed before the 1920s. In general, immigration policy makers tended to subsume female migrants within a universal (that is, masculine) rhetoric, or else to ignore them in favour of specifically male concerns. From the 1920s there was some slight recognition of the existence of a 'woman problem': some families were believed to be returning to England because of the failure of the wife to 'acclimatise'. Such concern, however, was sporadic and very much in the background. Women were simply assumed to be adjunctive to male migration. They came as members of families headed by men. Or they followed, once their menfolk had established a measure of security and prosperity. This latter was especially the case with non-assisted southern European chain migration. The women arrived in Australia as mothers, brides, wives, daughters, cousins of male migrants. Their movement was subordinate, not independent.

In the 1960s, the Department of Immigration began, suddenly and belatedly, to worry about female migration. The problem, as politicians and bureaucrats saw it, was one of the possibly deleterious effects of an imbalance of the genders. Peripherally, it also concerned the difficulties of female migrants' assimilation into the Australian community. On the balance of the genders, the Immigration Advisory Council reported to the Minister in 1969 that, indeed, an imbalance did exist, but was not so great as was generally believed and was being rapidly minimised by government measures; its persistence had a beneficial effect upon the economy by increasing the available mobile male labour force, but it did not drive migrant men to insanity nor to commit violent sexual crime; the Australian economy was working well because migrant women, both married and single, had a substantially higher rate of participation in the paid workforce than Australian-born women; the family was being staunchly defended, with most migrant groups maintaining the same or a higher percentage of married people than the Australian population. With a little more emphasis on employment, accommodation, and information for single women, the already highly satisfactory situation could be rendered excellent (Immigration Advisory Council, 1969). In other words, the emphasis was on the needs of the state and of men, with women useful only as factory and marriage fodder.

The other aspect of the migrant woman problem, assimilation, was not resolved any more equitably. To a limited extent, researchers came to recognise that the feminine condition itself was not good for female migrants. There was a conflict between women's adjunctive, dependent, familial status, and the demand for their assimilation into the community. Surveying studies of migrant mental health, the medical administrator, Jerzy Krupinski, reported in 1967 that

> In females, the late onset of mental illness could be precipitated by the onset of menopause, and predominantly by the termination of the mother's former role within the family, i.e. when the offspring have become adult, independent, assimilated into the community and leave her behind. (Krupinski, 1967:272).

There was nothing specific to migrant women in this analysis. The 'empty-nest syndrome' was becoming a commonplace explanation of all middle-aged women's unhappinesses and illnesses in the 1960s and 1970s (Bart, 1971). However, being a migrant could exacerbate the situation. Krupinski went on:

> Further, a high proportion of female non-British migrant patients did not speak English even after several years of residence in this country. Their husbands learn English at work and their children become assimilated at the school. The mother remains the only non-assimilated person in the family and becomes isolated in her own family, while her role as mother and wife begins to diminish with the progressive assimilation of her family into the community. (Krupinski, 1967:272)

The implication of this explanation was that, by staying in their expected place, the home, and by performing their expected tasks, as wives and mothers, that is, by attempting to conform to a basic ideal of the good woman, female migrants as women were inadvertently contravening the ideal of assimilation set for them as migrants.

Women at home were considered crucial to the stability of their families, and hence of family members' wider social relations. In 1970, the Minister for Immigration eulogised: 'as wives and mothers, they are the rock to which their families are anchored. They are, in a very real sense, the new pioneers of the 20th century' (Lynch, 1970:5). But, by staying in the home, women would have little opportunity to assimilate (a term rarely if ever defined in the literature), while their husbands and children would have enforced contact with the Australian community through their presence in the paid workforce and the school. It was all very well to argue, as did one psychiatrist, that '[t]hough all opportunities for assimilation should be given no pressure should be used. It is essentially the children and grandchildren of the migrants who should be the ones to commence assimilation and complete it' (Schaechter, 1962:461). But the enforced assimilation of the husband and children tended to create embarrassment in them about the unassimilated mother at home. Consequently, they left her behind, isolated in a family that needed her to stay put as an 'anchor' while they drew away into the wider community. The problem was known, and was considered to be insoluble. Individual alleviation was merely to be hoped for. In 1967, the Department of Immigration issued a pamphlet, directed specifically at intending British female migrants, which loosely defined the problems and the hope:

> Your greatest problem will probably be homesickness. While your husband is busy with his new job, and your children are settling in at school they won't have time to be homesick. You may have more time on your hands in which to be lonely. But these pangs will pass, and as time goes on will lessen. (Department of Immigration 1967)

The problem was a social one, created by the inevitable loss of emotionally supportive relationships through a migration process in which women were largely adjunctive to men, combined with the social expectation of good women being wives and mothers at home (Richardson, 1974:55; Minc, 1972:86). The solution needed to be a social one, but was left instead as an individual concern. It is, of course, obvious that most migrant women did find individual solutions short of madness, and that they prospered and flourished in their new country. The point is, however, that almost all migrant women came up against and had to fight through this contradiction between home and assimilation which was inherent in Australian immigration policy. Each confronted a series of conflicting demands: to stay at home but to become part of the community; to provide enough emotional support for family members to be able to make the transition to their new support groups in the new social environment but not, herself, to seek beyond the home; to maintain the old culture for the sake of the emotional continuity of the family but to engage with the new culture in order to ameliorate its disruptive effects on the family; to stay the same ('anchor') but to change ('assimilate').

Changed patterns

What then were the major changes in the patterns of probability within which non-Aboriginal Australian women pursued the goal of femininity across the century? On average, by the 1980s, Australian women lived longer in a more suburban environment. They were more likely to marry and bear fewer children, the production of whom would be more under their own control as to number and timing, and was less likely to be accompanied by illness and death. They were more likely to change husbands, and to engage in heterosexual activity outside marriage. Australian women in the 1980s were less likely to be of British stock, and this would bring them into conflict with the standards embodied in the dominant Australo-British culture. To foreshadow some of the discussion of the next section, married Australian women in the 1980s were likely to have jobs in the commanding economy as well as in and around the home; to be active consumers in a permissive society; and to be reliant upon and hedged around by the ministrations of professional social managers.

Part II

Constructing the Ideal of Femininity

So far, I have discussed a theory of femininity, and sketched the broad statistical outlines of white women's lives in twentieth-century Australia. In the following section, I am looking at three dimensions of society that were significant in establishing the specific content of femininity. I sketch out the patterns of change and continuity in the economic and ideological spheres as they affected the choices and possibilities open to women. These patterns were forged within the power relations of individuals, groups and institutions which increasingly came under the direction of a new group of experts: professional managers of the gender order.

4

Economy

*I*n the economic dimension of social life, the most significant process shaping the meaning of Australian femininity was the gender division of labour. This gender division was the primary, most essential organising principle of Australian economic life, not a mere appendage or simple convenience. It was integral to every aspect of the economy, and was perpetuated throughout all other changes by a variety of mechanisms. In terms of the labour market, women and men have been and are segregated, working in different occupations, different places, different times. In terms of tools and technologies, of the material forces and processes of the production of living, women and men had, and still have, different access, different training, different skills. In terms of their expectations, circumstances and experiences of work, and hence, of their consciousness of the economic and social orders, women and men inhabit different worlds.

Certainly, these worlds intersect and affect each other, and certainly some women live working lives closely aligned to the masculine model (though far fewer men live close to the feminine model). Moreover, over the last century, the position of the gender boundary, or the line of demarcation between the feminine and the masculine economies, has altered dramatically. The opportunities and restrictions within and between the economies have changed. The economic expectations and behaviours of women and men have been transformed. But the fact of difference between the economic lives of women and men has remained constant, and oppressively so. Women as a group are now, and were in the past, more restricted, more exploited, less able to achieve economic independence, and generally treated as inferior, compared with men (Ryan & Conlon, 1975; Owen & Shaw, 1979: Hargreaves, 1982; Deacon, 1982a).

Within this gender division of labour, as well as the main division between women and men, a secondary division exists among women, between the young and single, and the married. In many ways, the working lives of young single women are closer to the patterns and processes of men's working lives than to those of married women with families. But the single woman is nonetheless treated as a distinct—and inferior—category of worker in the masculine economy because of the expectation that she would marry. Since the early decades of the nineteenth century, single women have been allowed and expected to work only until marriage. For a respectable woman to work for wages after marriage was deemed a sign of terrible failure on her husband's part, indicating the disintegration of the family ideal. This ideological demarcation affected all women's work. A young, single woman was not, and is not, considered equal or similar to a young single man because of the presumed difference in their futures. The gender ideology proclaimed for her, but not for him, a change of status and direction of work upon marriage. Whether or not she actually ever married, whether or not she remained in the home after marriage, this presumption inhibited her from working in certain fields, from acquiring certain skills, and hence denied or lowered her prospects for a career. The expectation of this status change coloured the working experiences and opportunities of all women.

In this chapter, I wish to establish the broad economic trends within which Australian femininity was constructed. What the standard texts have proclaimed as the historical trends in the economy have been, in general, those that derive primarily from the masculine economic world (Forster, 1970; Butlin, 1972; Sinclair, 1976). The significance of the gender division of labour—the existence of a dual, symbiotic economic order in Australia—has been largely ignored. By and large, the masculine economy has been taken as the only one—the 'invisible women' approach. Alternatively, but more rarely, the feminine economy has been observed and tacked on as a minor appendix to the supposedly universalistic analysis of the masculine economy—the 'add women and stir' approach. Both of these approaches end up with models or pictures of the economy, and with prescriptions as to how to fix it, that are invariably wrong. Trends in the feminine economy have occasionally been treated as significant in their own right, but the interrelation of the feminine with the masculine, their mutual repercussions, influences and stimuli, the very meanings of their coexistence and of the gendered nature of the economic order, have only just begun to receive attention (Game & Pringle, 1983).

Such inveterate denial of the gender division has distorted the very language of economic analysis, hampering attempts to develop more accurate understandings. Words have acquired meanings that apply only to the masculine economic world, but are used as if they were gender-free universals. Notions of labour, of skill, productivity, workplace, unit, time, career, working conditions, unemployment, wages: all have a different meaning depending upon whether they assume a cockeyed view of the masculine economy as comprising the whole economy, or whether they accommodate the fully gendered nature of that whole. Examples of such distortion are abundant, but a few will indicate its significance for the meaning of femininity. The notion of work does not commonly accommodate unpaid housework, childcare, shopping; that of the social relations of production does not encompass sexual harrassment; that of career does not take account of the rearing of children; that of the family wage ignores the existence of women supporting dependents. What follows, then, is a provisional description of the main changes in the economic order over the past hundred years, in so far as such changes were significant in the making of modern Australian femininity. The most overarching of these changes, in the shadow and because of which many others occurred, was an extension of the capitalist marketplace. Increasingly, all goods and services produced within the society became commodities to be bought and sold. This affected the nature of both production and consumption, enmeshing them irretrievably in the cash nexus.

Production: the commanding economy

In relation to the sphere of production, the expansion of the market has been treated by most economists and historians as a mere shift from small to larger scale, from a simple to a more sophisticated capitalism, a quantitative rather than qualitative change. Such writers have established that, around the turn of the century, the Australian economy was already established in the pattern that would simply expand and diversify throughout the twentieth century. They have concentrated, in making this assessment, upon the commanding heights of the economy—those sectors that have contributed most to the gross national product, that have generated the most profit and the most surplus for export.

The main export-earning industries in the 1880s and 1890s were pastoral, agricultural and mining. The growing of wool and wheat, the mining of coal, copper and gold, and later of lead, iron and zinc, were highly capitalised and open to technological innovation. These primary industries were served by banking and financial enterprises with strong imperial connections with Britain. In the early years of the century, these financial institutions began tentatively to support as well the growing manufacturing sector that had emerged in the 1870s as a small factory system to process local goods for a small domestic market. Other sectors that were less export-oriented but nonetheless vital to the development of the economy were building and communication. The cities grew at prodigious rates in the years before and after the 1890s depression, and railways and roads spread out from them to service the primary industries of the hinterland. The foremost economic historian of this period, N.G. Butlin, expressed his perception of the state of the Australian economy in 1890 thus: 'the foundations of an enduring western society had been established and the social and productive assets of a coherent, efficient economy and of a wealthy society installed' (Butlin, 1972:3–4).

The major sectors of the economy were all in place by 1900, the basic lines of Australian capitalist development set. Throughout the twentieth century, pastoral, agricultural and mining sectors remained pre-eminent in export trade. Even in the 1970s and 1980s, various governments consistently hailed yet another mineral resources boom to lift the whole economy out of its recession. The secondary sector, manufacturing industry, grew slowly in the first third of the century, with its major expansion beginning in the late 1930s and into the second world war. There was an industrial boom in the postwar years, especially concentrated in the metal industries, in whitegoods, and in electronics. All these sectors were the spotlit focus for both economic analysis and planning from the 1890s to the late 1960s. Throughout the entire period, all these undertakings and industries required, and received, massive state support, including provision of physical infrastructure (railways, roads, ports, housing, water, power), provision and training of labour (assisted immigration, strike breaking and punishing, schools), provision of research, financial and marketing apparatuses, and direct financial bailing out (preferential tariffs and taxation, large-scale grants and loans). These areas of the economy became, over the century, increasingly capital-intensive, technologically developed, and foreign-owned. The Australian economy, as analysed by the masculine economists, is now an entrenched monopoly capitalism, linked through foreign and multinational corporations to a world capitalist economy.

These commanding heights have always been very much masculine territory, not the least in terms of their personnel. Such masculinity has traditionally lent itself to statistical analysis. So, for the sake of brevity and conformity, I shall discuss changes in the commanding economy through four tables. It is important to point out, however, that they are inaccurate and useful only to indicate broad trends of change. The inaccuracy is intrinsic to the use of census data historically. Firstly, the census categories themselves have changed over the century with the changing structure and understanding of the economy. The definition of the workforce itself is variable with, for example, part-time workers and assistants being somewhat arbitrarily included or excluded. Only the censuses from 1966 are strictly comparable. Secondly, the compilation of the censuses has been premised on masculine experience, and much of the work of women has been dealt with arbitrarily. Such terms as 'usual occupation' and 'looking for work' have been extremely ambiguous for many women (Keating, 1967; Palmer, 1967; Deacon, 1982a). The following tables, therefore, provide only a rough guide to patterns of work in the commanding economy.

Table 1 indicates the fairly even spread of male workers throughout the major occupational sectors of the economy from 1891 till the second world war. Thereafter, the primary sector declined substantially as an area of male employment, becoming much more capital- than labour-intensive. After the second world war, an industrial boom brought employment in secondary industry to an increasing number of men. In this same period, however, it was the tertiary or service sector that expanded most rapidly. By 1981, the tertiary sector employed 45 per cent of all men in the labour force. This shift in male employment over the century is a manifestation of the major economic development recognised by masculine economists: from a rather primitive capitalist economy heavily dependent upon export of natural resources, to a monopoly or corporate capitalism, still heavily dependent upon the same primary exports, but also relying upon a massive service or tertiary sector to facilitate relations among and between giant corporations, the state, and the mass of consumer/workers. (Other economists described the shift as one from a pre-industrial to a post-industrial economy; still others wondered where the industrial stage went—and when.)

Table 2 indicates growth of this service sector across the century, employing 35.6 per cent of the total labour force in 1891, rising to 57.1 per cent by 1981. Further, it points to the feminisation of major areas of the sector in the postwar decades. By 1981, the clerical, sales and professional occupations alone employed almost 40 per cent of the total workforce and, significantly, 60 per cent of the female workforce. Moreover, as shown in Table 3, from the 1920s onwards, women in these tertiary occupations worked in disproportionately female environments. That is, their numbers in these jobs greatly exceeded the ratio of women to men in the workforce as a whole. By 1981, 37 out of every 100 workers were women, but they were concentrated in only a few, mainly service, occupations. For example, almost 70 out of every 100 clerical workers were women. Clerk, salesperson, typist, stenographer, nurse and teacher were women's jobs par excellence.

In terms of masculine universalistic interpretation, a 'working women's revolution' began in the late 1950s. The dramatically increasing percentage of women in the total workforce is shown in Table 4: it remains fairly constant at about 20 per cent from the 1890s to the 1950s, then almost doubles over the next three decades.

Even more striking was the rise in the participation rates of married women, also shown in Table 4. From being a tiny minority of the female workforce in the half century before the war, by the late 1960s

Table 1 Percentage distribution of workforce by occupational sector. Australia 1891–1981

	1891 M	1891 W	1891 T	1911 M	1911 W	1911 T	1933 M	1933 W	1933 T	1954 M	1954 W	1954 T	1966 M	1966 W	1966 T	1981 M	1981 W	1981 T
Primary	35.1	12.8	30.7	36.6	4.1	30.2	30.1	3.4	24.3	18.4	4.0	15.1	12.6	5.0	10.3	8.5	4.4	7.0
Secondary	32.8	22.3	30.7	28.9	28.4	28.8	34.5	23.6	32.1	42.1	28.1	39.0	43.7	15.9	35.5	39.5	9.1	28.1
Tertiary	31.2	60.4	37.0	34.5	67.5	41.0	35.4	73.0	43.6	39.5	67.9	45.9	42.9	76.0	52.6	46.0	77.7	57.8
Other/ inadequately defined	0.9	4.5	1.6	—	—	—	—	—	—	—	—	—	0.8	3.1	1.6	6.0	8.8	7.1
	100	100	100	100	100	100	100	100	100	100	100	100	100	100	100	100	100	100

Source: Censuses 1911, 1954, 1966, 1981.

Table 2 Employment in the tertiary sector 1891–1981. Percentage of workforce employed at census

Occupation	1891		1921			1966		1981	
	Female	Total	Female	Total		Female	Total	Female	Total
Commercial	6.6	12.3	17.2	15.3					
Clerical						30.0	14.7	31.9	17.1
Sales						12.5	7.7	11.5	8.5
Sub-total	6.6	12.3	17.2	15.3		42.5	22.4	43.4	25.6
Professional	10.2	6.2	17.2	8.7					
Professional, technical and related						13.2	9.3	17.0	13.6
Administrative, executive and managerial						2.6	6.3	1.9	5.3
Sub-total	10.2	6.2	17.2	8.7		15.8	15.6	18.9	18.9
Domestic	42.5	10.3	34.5	9.1		15.3	7.4	13.7	8.4
Service, sport and recreation									
Transport and communications	1.0	6.8	1.6	9.0		2.4	6.1	1.7	4.8
Total	60.3	35.6	70.5	42.1		76.0	51.5	77.7	57.1

Source: Censuses 1911, 1921, 1966, 1981.

Table 3 **Women as a percentage of the total workforce in tertiary occupations 1891–1981**

Occupation	1891	1921	1966	1981
Commercial	10.6	22.4		
Clerical			60.0	69.5
Sales			47.7	50.1
Sub-Total	10.6	22.4	55.8	63.0
Professional	32.3	39.7		
Professional, technical and related			42.0	46.4
Administrative, executive and managerial			12.0	13.0
Sub-total	32.3	39.7	29.9	37.1
Domestic	71.9	76.2		
Service, sport and Recreation			61.0	51.0
Transport and communication	3.0	3.5	11.6	6.5
Total tertiary workforce	32.2	33.5	43.1	49.8

Source: Censuses 1911, 1921, 1966, 1981.

Table 4 **Women in the commanding workforce 1891–1981**

Census Year	Female workforce as % of total workforce	Married female workforce as % of total female workforce	Female workforce as % of total female population—all ages
1891	19.7	—	18.2
1901	20.5	—	19.7
1911	19.6	11.1	18.4
1921	19.7	9.2	17.4
1933	21.8	11.0	19.2
1947	22.4	19.7	19.0
1954	22.8	30.8	19.0
1961	25.1	38.5	20.4
1966	29.5	47.8	25.0
1971	31.7	56.8	26.7
1976	36.0	64.0	32.2
1981	37.6	61.3	34.5

Source: Martin & Richmond, 1968; OECD, 1974; Dept. of Labour & National Service, 1967; Censuses 1911, 1954, 1966, 1971, 1976, 1981.

they had become a majority, and by 1981 comprised over 60 per cent. These married women increasingly worked part-time rather than full-time. Between 1966 and 1980, the number of married female part-time workers increased by 137.5 per cent. At the latter date, 45.1 per cent of all employed married women were working part-time (Women's Bureau, 1981:20–21). Further, married women progressively worked while their children were still under the age of 12. In 1969, 29 per cent of such familied women were in the labour force; by 1980, 42.5 per cent of them were (Office of the Status of Women, 1983:15).

Among the masculine economists, much argument still persists about the explanation of these phenomena, with causes traced to the postwar 'marriage revolution' depleting the work pool of single women, to the 'consumer revolution' requiring a bigger family income, to the 'technological revolution' opening up more suitably feminine jobs. All these explanations ignore women's historical and life-cycle working experience. They are premised on the assumptions of masculine experience and the processes of the masculine economy. To a large degree, the postwar 'working women's revolution' was a trick of perspective, not a radical change in women's experiences.

The trick lay in the definition of work, its nature and its place. By and large, masculine economists have classified as work only that which is clearly performed within the masculine capitalist market-place—the commanding heights; that which is directly organised by the traditional processes of that marketplace—as in large corporate or state enterprises; and that which is defended by the traditional institutions of the male working class—the trade unions. But the commanding heights have never comprised the whole economy, the processes of large enterprises have never monopolised the ways of making a livelihood, and the trade unions have both inadvertently and deliberately excluded many workers from their protection.

Production: the local economy

Throughout the nineteenth and twentieth centuries in Australia, there has existed a sector of small-scale production parallel with the large-scale, commanding economy. Such local or domestic enterprises produced for sale goods and services for domestic and local consumption: food and drink, clothing and footwear, building materials and services, blacksmithing, household and personal services. The work and production of this local capitalist sector was largely unperceived by orthodox economists, whose tools of analysis were too blunt and bent from being applied only to their own and their brothers' experiences in the commanding economy. Neither census enumeration, taxation data, closed-ended surveys, productivity data, inspection, arbitration, nor any other methods of assessment and control of the commanding economy could or would pick up the quiet details of small scale, under-the-counter, informal, home-based or family production. (As the depression of the late 1970s and 1980s deepened, some economists did begin to discover what they called an informal or cash economy in which men engaged in the shadow of the commanding economy (Gershuny & Pahl, 1979–80). Men on means-tested pensions and benefits supplemented their pittances by work for cash which was not declared to taxation or social-security departments. As with all imperialist discoveries, the natives have always known about it, but the economists have only just begun to quantify and systematise this 'new' phenomenon, trying to coerce it into their theoretical procrustean beds.) For most of its history in Australia, however, the local capitalist economy has been either ignored or treated as an anachronism or anomaly in discussions of the development of Australian capitalism. Nonetheless, some unquantified trends can be discerned, and within these trends some of the more important processes constructing the relation of modern Australian femininity to work become visible.

In general, the main trend in the local economy was in the same direction as that in the commanding masculine economy: the extension of the marketplace.

In small farming, production moved from the sphere of semi-subsistence to full integration with the market. In the 1890s, small farms worked by whole families were still common. The husband and older sons might engage in seasonal waged work: fencing, shearing, droving, dam building. The wife and younger and female children, and menfolk when available, produced as much as possible for daily living and to sell for cash: keeping a few chickens, cows and pigs, growing vegetables and fruit, preserving, making bread and clothes. Over the next few decades there was a shift towards concentration on a specialised and restricted range of cash crops and flocks to the detriment of production for household use. Small family farms continued to produce many basic goods for household consumption, but increasingly became dependent upon money to buy a wider range of goods in the public market.

With small-scale manufacturing and service work, the shift was similar, in that a greater dependence on the marketplace emerged. Or, rather, the reach of the marketplace extended and gradually overwhelmed the domestic sector. Most particularly, over the century, the locus or site of production moved away from the home. Many goods for household consumption and local barter, especially food and clothing, were made at home during the 1890s, from substances either grown there or in the neighbourhood. Such production slowly lessened, and household goods were made outside the home and bought for cash. Similarly, services once performed within and around the household were circumscribed and downgraded, and 'superior' replacements or improvements were offered for sale in the marketplace.

The importance of this local economy for women throughout the whole period was that its work could be accommodated to the rhythms and patterns and demands of family and house work. This latter work remained primary to the definition of femininity for a married women, especially with children. But money was equally primary for the necessities of life as the marketplace expanded. As the commanding economy spread to encompass local production, especially in the period after the second world war, the only way for familied women to retain their income-earning work was to find a new way of doing both.

For some women, this was impossible or undesirable, and they refrained from paid work. In 1963, American journalist Betty Friedan identified the 'problem that has no name' as a potential and debilitating fate of such women. It was later known as suburban neurosis. For others, a balance was achieved at enormous personal cost as they struggled to perform both sets of work. The sociologists Alva Myrdal and Viola Klein discussed this problem as 'women's two roles' in 1957, and it thereafter became standard terminology in discussions of women's work. For increasing numbers of yet other women, the solution was found in paid work that permitted the same balance with family work as did the old local economy. Such women were economically exploited by their employers, despised by trade unions, and ignored by the protective, controlling arm of the state. But they did retain some control over the balance between their dual priorities of family and money. (It is significant to note here that no one, not even most of the women caught in this dilemma, considered transforming the priority of family and house work. The prevailing standards of the gender order on this matter were considerably more intransigent than those of the economic order.)

In the postwar period, the place within the commanding economy that was most amenable to this third solution of part-time work for familied women was the newly colonised local economy. It did not have a tradition of, nor had yet had time to impose masculine conditions and processes of work. Not until the collapse of the economic boom in the 1970s did employers in major areas of the traditional commanding economy—such as clerical, sales, professional and service work—begin to consider part-time work as a profitable rationalisation.

Effectively, then, familied women have worked in the same income-earning occupations within a local economy, according to the same rhythms and patterns, for over a century. Before the second world war, they were barely visible to economic analysts because they were not immediately linked to the commanding economy. By the 1960s, that economy had spread its direct control over the local economy. Suddenly, these women became visible, as workers, and the masculine analysts proclaimed a 'working women's revolution'. Women had produced jams and breads and shirts invisibly at home in the 1890s; it is women who produce jams and breads and shirts more visibly in factories and workshops (and, as outworkers, at home) in the 1980s. It was women who cared for children, did the family account books, washed and nursed out of sight in the home in the 1890s; it is women who care for children in family day-care centres, work as part-time clerks and accountants in small businesses, work in laundromats and nurse in hospitals and nursing homes in the 1980s.

The downgrading of women's work

Women's experience of work in the local economy will be examined more fully below in chapter 8. Here, I wish to pursue a second aspect of the masculine monopoly of economic interpretation: the downgrading of women's work compared with men's. This downgrading was vital to the construction of the feminine ideal, at least until the 1970s. The good married woman did not work. This ideological precept meant that what a married woman did around the home was ignored, or considered to be natural maternal activity. What she could do before marriage was limited and poorly paid, making marriage itself the preferred alternative. Should she choose or be forced to work for wages after marriage, she was subjected as well to public denigration or pity, insecurity of tenure and a double workload.

At the 1891 census, only 18 per cent of all females were considered to be gainfully employed, as compared with 64 per cent of all males. The remaining percentage of males comprised children under sixteen, students, pensioners and inmates of institutions. A roughly similar percentage of females fell within these categories. The remaining wide discrepancy derived from the category, 'wives without gainful occupation'. Into this category, hundreds of thousands of women were pushed from sight and the value of their work denied.

This conceptualisation of women's work as non-work has been recently studied by sociologist Desley Deacon (1982a), who has uncovered its invention in the political intrigues of late-nineteenth-century statisticians. Before the 1891 census, the issue of what constituted work, employment or occupation had been determined according to various definitions of what was productive. In the case of women, these variations had meant that married women's work was 'in no two successive censuses classed alike' in either Britain or Australia (Jones, 1983:27). Generally, however, the range of women's work had been acknowledged as valuable and part of the productive activity of the nation, whether in the commanding or local economy, in the household, in charitable and artistic pursuits, as assistants to fathers and husbands, or in their own right. That is, types of work were distinguished, but their qualities or social value were not (Deacon, 1982a: 17–20). Only in 1891 did all the Australian colonies accept a new definition which divided the population into breadwinners and dependents. The new principle involved in this distinction, the basic criterion for having an occupation, became the receipt of income or wages for work (Deacon, 1982a:55–6; Jones, 1983:31). That is, the notion of productivity was replaced by one of remuneration. In the absence of a clear statement otherwise, women working in the sphere of the household, including helping in family concerns without pay, were classified as dependents. Such women were definitively labelled as non-workers for all purposes of economic discussion. Women's legitimate activities, under this new ideological dispensation, were restricted to the home, producing children, training them, maintaining the health and well-being of all family members.

Working on European material, the historians Louise Tilly and Joan Scott (1978:197–200) have discussed a real decline in married women's employment between 1870 and 1914 that was probably comparable to the situation in Australia (Sinclair, 1982). They claim that there was a contraction in those sectors of the economy that previously had employed married women, especially the casual work of childminding and servicing boarders. A rise in the real wages of men meant that a double income was less necessary. Improving health in the population led to fewer husbands dying or becoming invalided and thereby requiring fewer wives and widows to become breadwinners. Smaller families meant fewer mouths to feed, and the prolonged residence of adult children in the household increased both the family budget and the mother's house work. All these factors operated in Australia during the long boom from the 1860s to 1890 and continued into the early twentieth century. Because of them, numbers of women would have chosen to leave the waged workforce upon marriage, and not to return to it thereafter. Some married women jumped; others were pushed.

The conceptual alienation of women from the world of work was solidly entrenched in economic practice over the first two decades of the twentieth century. The state, through its arbitration and conciliation system, male workers, through their trade unions, and employers, through their employment practices, colluded to deny women (and most other categories of workers who were not Anglo males) equal access to and reward from work, now firmly defined in narrow masculine, white supremacist terms. The central process of this collusion was the sanctification of the 'family' or 'living' or 'basic' wage.

The family wage

Edna Ryan and Anne Conlon, in their book *Gentle Invaders* trace in detail the history of this concept from the late nineteenth century. Here, I will only sketch that development, beginning in 1907 with the first legal pronouncement of the specific Australian formula. In that year, Mr Justice Higgins of the Commonwealth Arbitration Court, in a judgment known as the Harvester Case (1907), introduced the concept of the basic wage as the basis for wage determination. The concept was premised on the priority of male workers as breadwinners and on a gender-segregated economy. Higgins wished to establish a 'fair and reasonable remuneration' for unskilled workers. The standard he set as appropriate was that of 'the normal needs of the average employee regarded as a human being in a civilised community' (Ryan & Conlon, 1975:90). When it came to assessing needs, Higgins made a fundamental distinction between women and men. Men he presumed were breadwinners, and their needs included those of their families. Women he presumed had only themselves to support, and should therefore receive a proportionally lower rate of pay. Whether or not particular men were bachelors, or whether particular women were responsible for the support of dependents, were irrelevant considerations in Higgins' general ruling.

All women working in the commanding economy were presumed to be single and awaiting marriage. They engaged in such work merely to fill in time and to buy themselves finery. In 1911, Higgins made his position clear:

> If the girls will have their finery at the sacrifice of other things more necessary, that is their business; but probably it is not fair to force the employers to pay for all that a girl may fancy as being necessary human requirements. (Ryan & Conlon, 1975:96)

Paid work was an interlude before permanent domestic work when women would be 'kept' by their husbands for whom public work was a life-long activity. The NSW Board of Trade declared in 1921 that

> A boy knows from birth he will be a breadwinner; that is his lot in life. A girl learns that in all probability she will marry. Her work will only be an episode in her life... The great majority live with their parents, and these should receive a wage which will relieve their parents of the whole expense of their upkeep but not necessarily one which will give their parents a profit. (Ryan & Conlon, 1975:83)

The Arbitration Court did recognise that some women would have to work after marriage, and that some would even have the care of dependents. But such women were considered exceptional. Their wages could not be increased because 'the minimum concept cannot be based on exceptional cases' (Ryan & Conlon, 1975:95). This strict determination of wages on the basis of gender, however, opened up a rather unfortunate possibility. If women were cheaper workers, then employers, in the interests of greater profit, might begin to employ more women, to the exclusion of men, who would be driven into unemployment and their families into poverty. This situation had to be guarded against. Higgins determined, therefore, that the wage should follow the job, not the person, and that each job must be assessed as being more suited to either women or men. If a job was usually done by men—for example, blacksmithing—it was to be classified as men's work and paid at a high rate; if usually done by women—for example, millinery—it became women's work to be paid at a lesser rate. If the job was usually done equally by both women and men—for example, fruitpicking—then the male rate applied. Any woman working in a job classified as male must be paid a man's wage (Mildura Fruitpickers' Case, 1912:72).

It was assumed by the Court that employers, faced with the prospect of having to pay the same wage to any employee, whether male or female, would automatically prefer a male worker. It was further assumed that a male worker would not wish to work in a woman's job because of the lesser rate of pay. Thus, each sex would be protected from the competition of the other. The concept of the differential living wage and the gender-segregated economy were strongly supported over the next 50 years by both employers and male trade unionists. The former gained half-price labour for all jobs they could define as female; the latter gained protection from competition and maintenance of a refuge in the family.

As well as denying women wage justice, the Arbitration Court also set restrictive conditions upon women's work. The various state parliaments reinforced this trend by passing legislation aimed specifically at working women. Such 'protective' legislation considered all women as potential or actual mothers, nothing more. Its primary concern was the size and well-being of the states' future population. (This issue will be discussed in chapter 5). From the 1870s, but more significantly from the 1890s into the early twentieth century, a series of Acts was passed by the states which regulated and restricted the employment of women (and of boys under sixteen or eighteen) in the name of the protection of those weaker sections of the community who were not as capable as adult male workers of protecting themselves. Women were considered weaker because of their childbearing potential and the Acts, paradoxically, protected that weakness itself, rather than the women whose potential it was. Gynaecological ailments, problems associated with parturition, and moral depravity were all claimed by medical and moral experts to be possible consequences of women's factory and shop work. Accordingly, the Acts restricted women in the hours they could work, the overtime they could perform, the machinery they could use, the substances they could work with, and the weights they could lift (Ryan & Conlon, 1975:32–49; Owen & Shaw, 1979:46–7, 57; Spearritt,

1975:38–41; Markey, 1980).

These legal restrictions applied only in the commanding economy, where their effect was to reduce women's competitiveness with men. The home, as the site of local work and outwork, was not covered by the legislation. In the home as a domestic workplace, there was never any question that a woman was able to lift more than 35 pounds of wet washing, tired infants, groceries, or bedridden relatives. There were no eyebrows raised about her being on call 24 hours a day for her babies' needs, and the law saw no contravention in her overtime house work after the day's paid work was complete.

As well as protective legislation, women's paid work was restricted by overt and covert practices by employers and male unionists. Women were denied access to apprenticeships, and in many jobs were forced to resign upon marriage. Ostensibly, in all these cases of legal and customary discrimination, the purpose was to protect women from their own frailty. In effect, the protection was of male privilege and monopoly in the commanding economy, and of male absenteeism in the domestic workforce. Paradoxically, however, the restriction of paid work for married women operated as a disciplinary process for their husbands, who were thereby compelled, as sole breadwinners, to be steady, compliant, reliable and docile. Hence the lesser industrial militancy of married men. What women got was lower wages and severely limited opportunity, the need to marry and compulsory economic dependence. Protective legislation reinforced the segregation of the labour force, the gender demarcation of occupations, and the inferior position of women in both commanding and domestic workplaces.

Many of these 'protective' restrictions were abolished in the 1960s and 1970s, and Anti-Discrimination Acts of limited scope have lessened some of the informal discriminatory practices of employers (Ronalds, 1979). But the consciousness lingers on, and women are still considered, in many quarters, as handicapped or deficient workers when compared with men.

The Arbitration Court only set wages and conditions for federally registered trades. At the state level, local boards and courts operated autonomously, but, in this instance at least, followed the lead of the federal court (Mendelsohn, 1979:146–8). From the second decade of the twentieth century, women's basic wage in most fields covered by either federal or state awards was set around 54 per cent of the male basic wage. (There was, strictly speaking, no legally defined female basic wage until 1950. Rather, it was a legal fiction or generally agreed formula among the groups of men engaged in wage fixing (Ryan & Conlon, 1975:104).) In certain other areas of employment, work was not covered by any awards, and wages were open to direct bargaining. Given the gender segregation of occupations, and the gender bias of economic power, such occupations were disproportionately female, and direct bargaining generally resulted in less than even the female basic wage being paid.

The effect of the legal legitimation of the family-wage concept was almost wholly negative. It sanctioned discrimination against women in terms of rates of pay, and of areas and conditions of work. It reinforced other forms of institutional and customary discrimination. As a positive move towards even a masculine notion of economic justice, it was a total failure. The actual amount of the family wage was never high enough to meet the real needs of a family, defined as a man, a wife, and three dependent children. A Royal Commission on the Basic Wage reported in 1920 that the Harvester equivalent based on the cost of living would then have been about £5.16.0; the actual Commonwealth basic wage stood at the time at £4.2.0 (Basic Wage Commission, 1920–21). Moreover, demographically, the large proportion of male workers did not support such a family. Ryan and Conlon recount that, in 1919, a New South Wales parliamentarian pointed out that 'a typical hundred active adult males had sixty five wives and one hundred children, or two thirds of a wife and an average of one child each' (Ryan & Conlon, 1975:108). It paid to be a bachelor.

Not until 1967 did the Arbitration Commission abandon the concept of the basic, family wage. By then, however, the notions of the male breadwinner and the superiority of male work had been thoroughly entrenched in economic consciousness for well over half a century. During that time, Australian women had become concentrated and segregated into seven or eight comparatively low-paying, low-promotion occupations in the commanding economy, not alone by nature or by choice, but because they were herded into them by the collusion of the courts, the employers and the unions, brought together in the arbitration system. For over 60 years, that system employed unsubstantiated gender theories of women's domestic nature and low productivity, and men's natural role as family breadwinners, in order to justify the limiting of women's opportunities and to keep women in their 'proper' place. Nonetheless, gradually, women did begin to push outwards the boundaries of that proper place.

Resistance and equal pay

In response to, and despite the strength of this economic misogyny, there had always been an opposition. Equal-pay campaigns were organised in the 1930s, during the war years, and through into the late 1960s and 1970s. The second world war brought out strongly the contradictions of the system of gender discrimination, and, for a short time, some women experienced near equality with men as workers. Those women who replaced the men who were drawn into the military machine received up to 90 per cent of the male rate of pay—and improved conditions—but strictly for the duration of hostilities. Meanwhile, those women who stayed in or entered 'female' occupations continued to receive only about 54 per cent of the male basic rate, eventually rising to 75 per cent in 1945 (Larmour, 1975; Ryan & Rowse, 1975; Hasluck, 1970:268). Apologists for the state had no delusions about the conscious turning on of economic gender equality, and made sure that it could be turned off again. As the wartime Australian News and Information Bureau (1942) explained:

> The national economy, for the last two generations, has been directed towards the establishment within the Australian home of an increasingly high standard of living.
> The direct result of this policy has been to consolidate the family unit, thereby withdrawing from employment the vast majority of women at marriage.
> The industrial economy has deliberately discouraged the entry of women into occupations where heavy manual labour, fatigue and monotony have been predominant features.
> Therefore, in seeking, under the driving necessity of war, to recruit woman power to its utmost industrial capacity, Australia has had to change overnight a psychology that has been fostered for generations.

Officialdom proclaimed the changes in the gender order brought about by the war to be temporary, an emergency aberration. Nonetheless, the war provided a crucial breach in the legitimacy of the ideology of the family wage. Women's experience in the war had shown that the gender division of labour and the gender differential in wage rates were premised solely upon an assumption that a stable and desirable society could exist only if women were mothers and men were breadwinners, and that this assumption was not necessarily correct. It had shown that assumptions about the relationship between femininity and paid work were not necessarily correct: that women's productivity was not automatically lower than men's; that men's jobs were not automatically more arduous or more skilled than women's jobs, and that women were as capable as men of doing most work; that it was not their feminine nature which restricted women to work in only six or seven major occupations, but rather the result of explicit denial of opportunity to work elsewhere. It had shown that assumptions about the relationship between marriage, motherhood and paid work were not necessarily correct: that women did not necessarily desire to leave the public workforce on marriage; that married women's public-workforce participation did not necessarily entail the destruction of the family.

In the postwar world, the rapid expansion of the marketplace, and its turning of virtually everything into a saleable commodity, created a new context and meaning for women's work and, hence, for femininity.

Women's production of goods and services at home, for private or local consumption, was appropriated by the marketplace. Some work was almost completely transferred to mass-production factories, which employed large numbers of women. As mentioned earlier, it became much cheaper to buy bread, preserved fruit, tinned and frozen food, clothes and furnishings, than to make their equivalents at home. Other work was transformed on the spot. Childminding, cleaning, laundry work, neighbourhood barter of produce, music teaching, sewing: women continued to do such work, but gradually the market organised them, and they became paid, or commission-earning, employees of capitalist companies (Matthews, 1982). Personal services, once performed in and organised from the home, expanded into work performed and organised by state-employed professionals, usually women: childcare, care of the aged, education and health services. Women's work came to be more visible within and assessable by the criteria of the marketplace. As a consequence of such visibility and women's continued struggles for equality, slowly and piecemeal some acceptance of the right to equal pay was achieved. Concrete application of the right has of course been dilatory and subject to the most tortuously devised loopholes. By the December quarter of 1983, the average total full-time weekly earnings of women workers in the commanding economy stood at only 66 per cent of male workers' earnings.

It may have been eroded in arbitration practice, but the notion of the male as breadwinner is still alive and well in economic practice—revealingly displayed in the continuous attacks on married women working in times of high unemployment (Alford, 1981). The gender division of labour has changed its shape, with women working in jobs previously defined as male (for example, bank tellers), and with a few men working in jobs previously defined as female (though most such men end up in newly created masculine jobs at the top of the female hierarchy, as in, for example, nursing and librarianship). But the division itself remains. Women's work is neither equal to nor interchangeable with men's (Power, 1975; Jones, 1979).

Consumption: the domestic-service economy

The world of work and production has changed dramatically over the past century, affected by the encroachment of the marketplace as we have seen. The second major change in the Australian economy, likewise affected, has been within the world of work and consumption. (Much of the discussion in the rest of this chapter is further elaborated in chapter 8.) Economists have hardly discussed this change at all, because most of its manifestations have occurred in and around the household, within the sphere defined as feminine, and hence, not economic.

Throughout the period, the work of consumption within the household revolved around the daily maintenance of household members:
the preparation of appropriate food, shelter and clothing for health and
well-being or, at the least, for daily physical survival. The nature of
such consumption obviously depended upon a variety of circumstances: the human composition of the household (the numbers, ages,
sex, health and relations of its members), its physical setting (size and
nature of house and whether urban, suburban or rural), its productive
activity (family enterprise or paid work), its cultural traditions (British,
Aboriginal, immigrant or ethnic), and so on. The processes of such
consumption, however, were less idiosyncratic, and were patterned
across the century as a shift from what can be called a domestic-service
economy to one of mass commodity consumption.

Domestic servants had been employed in non-convict, moderately
comfortable, Australian households from the beginning of British con-
quest. By the second half of the nineteenth century a widespread and
fully developed domestic-service household economy was flourishing.
The heyday of this economy occurred in the long boom of the 1870s and
1880s, as the whole society moved into a period of settled comfort
beyond the rigours and subsistence struggles of early colonisation
(Kingston, 1975:45–50; Davison, 1979:201–5, 226–7). There remained,
of course, households which did not share in this prosperity. The very
nature of the long boom generated pockets of poverty in both country
and cities (Fisher, 1981:161). From the 1890s, a long and slow decline
of the domestic-service economy set in. It began around the same time
as the expansion of the marketplace, the diversification of both local
and commanding economies in terms of manufacturing and commer-
cial services, and the beginning of the demographic transition.

Clearly, in the 1890s, not every household employed servants. Indeed, at the time of the New South Wales 1901 census, only about 10
per cent of all households did so (Kingston, 1975:47–9). But such a
figure does not take account of changes within the family life cycle, nor
of unpaid domestic service by female relatives. At certain stages in the
life of a family with a steady though not necessarily high income,
particularly when there were numerous small children around, a general servant could well become both a possibility and a perceived necessity. Little has been written on domestic service in Australia, and we do
not have a class analysis of those who employed servants. Moreover, for
the same reasons of masculine bias as discussed above, we do not know
how many women were actually working as servants. Unknown numbers of unmarried daughters, cousins and sisters acted as unpaid
servants in the households of their families. Unknown numbers of
women performed casual household services for others and avoided the
nets of enumeration.

Nonetheless, vast numbers of women were also officially recorded as private domestic servants (excluding those who worked in boarding houses and hotels). At the 1891 census (the first one in which women's work was systematically downgraded), there were over 96 000 women so classified, comprising 36 per cent of the recorded female workforce. The proportion of all women recognised as working in the paid workforce remained fairly constant over the next five decades (Martin & Richmond, 1968:2). (Perhaps more accurately, W.A. Sinclair (1982) has pointed to a slight downward trend in participation rates from 1871 to the first world war, which reversed to a slight rising trend during the war and after it.) However, within this fairly stable working situation over the first half of the century, the proportion of women recorded as private domestic servants declined greatly, with the most dramatic drops occurring in the years just before the first world war, from 1911 to 1915, and during the second world war (Keating, 1967:336). Very roughly comparable census figures are shown in Table 5.

The importance of the rise and fall of domestic service in the general transformation of the Australian economy and in the construction of modern Australian femininity is suggested, by analogy, in Theresa McBride's book dealing with domestic service in England and France, *The Domestic Revolution*. McBride argues that the economy of domestic service was a key element in the development of the modern family. It was the means by which families adapted themselves to the processes of industrialisation and urbanisation. While the commanding economy was being transformed by the factory system, the domestic or familial economy was being transformed by the system of domestic service. Through it, both middle-class and working-class women developed new social relations and skills appropriate to a world dominated by the marketplace.

On the one hand, the employment of servants initiated the middle-class woman into the role of employer/manager and initiated her into certain professional skills. On the other hand, for the servants themselves, service had a significant impact on the distribution of the labour supply and was an important channel for urban migration. Almost paradoxically, domestic service served as a means of the modernisation of rural labour and particularly of women. (McBride, 1976:117)

Domestic service in its nineteenth-century form was a transitional household economy.

McBride further points out (1976:17) that the ironic end of this transition to modern urban society was the decline of domestic service. What emerged instead was the modern housewife. That is, 'housewife' as the dominant definition of woman in the home was constructed at the boundary between the two classes of mistresses and servants,

Table 5   Women employed in private domestic service in Australia 1891–1954

Census Year	1891	1901	1911	1921	1933	1947	1954
Number	96 000	110 500	114 000	92 000	129 000	31 000	31 000
Proportion of total female waged workforce	37.7	33.4	29.2	20.0	21.5	4.4	3.6

Source: Censuses 1911, 1921, 1933, 1947, 1954.

gaining its strength as the old domestic economy declined.

Under the old domestic-service economy, there were three types of women who worked in the 'comfortable' home. One was the mistress, who employed a number of servants. At the 1901 New South Wales census, almost 70 per cent of all servants were employed in the 19 per cent of houses containing seven or more rooms. Over 52 per cent of such households employed two or more servants (Kingston, 1975:48). The work of the mistress in such households was primarily that of administration:

> The mistress acted in an administrative and executive capacity, hiring and firing the staff and overseeing the fairly large-scale catering and accommodation operations which a normal household required. Her responsibilities could be seen in part as personnel work assuming a kind of maternal care for her servants which extended to their health and morals, and in part as general management on a scale which is no longer seen except in institutions, small hotels and catering businesses. (Kingston, 1975:15)

Such women were not defined as housewives. Their position was determined rather by the ways in which they maintained social order within and outside their husbands' class. Within the class, they established and maintained the standards of respectable private and social life. They patrolled the social points of entry to the class, keeping out those whose ambition was greater than their credentials, and assuring those within that all was well. The rituals of visiting and calling, of entertainments and eating, of courtship and marriage, the maintenance of standards of domestic life—all of the rules of etiquette were their primary and complex responsibility (cf. Davidoff, 1973). Outside the class, they had the option of undertaking public philanthropic or civilising work, voluntary of course. (This was the period of intensive population campaigning, which will be discussed in the next chapter.) For such upper- and middle-class women, the home was the place in which they performed their work of creating order and maintaining civilisation as a feeling and set of personal relations. Essential to the development of such middle-class respectability was the employment of servants to perform the physical household labour.

In less well-off homes, the mistress herself was a house-worker, as well as a supervisor. These women were the first to be called housewives. Into this category fell the vast majority of servant employers. Again, at the 1901 New South Wales census, of the 10 per cent of households employing servants, 80 per cent employed only one (Kingston, 1975:48). The work in these households was basic, heavy and time-consuming. In this era before the expansion of the commodity market, such work was all by hand, using mainly unprocessed goods and tools. Beverley Kingston in her book *My wife, my daughter and poor*

Mary Ann details the arduousness of cleaning, washing and cooking when neither gas, electricity, nor internal plumbing, let alone hot-water services, fuel-less stoves, washing machines, refrigerators, vacuum cleaners or any processed food, existed. House work in such circumstances was highly labour-intensive, and even households of the artisan class (that is, with fairly steady though perhaps low wages coming in) deemed a general 'slavey' a necessity, not a luxury. Alternatively, unmarried female family members were dragooned into unpaid service.

The third category of house-worker was the servant herself. Servants were workers, not housewives, and indeed, throughout the nineteenth century, most servants were expected to be, and were, unmarried. They were daughters of the working class. Poverty drove them to work, and the gender-segmented and underdeveloped industrial economy provided personal service as their only significant opportunity for employment until the end of the nineteenth century. It was expected by the employing class that these young women would eventually marry and establish new working-class homes, taking with them, so the ideal went, many of the methods and values of middle-class housekeeping, and hence 'improving working class home life'. (See chapter 8.) As a South Australian parliamentarian declared in 1928: 'Nothing helps a girl to take her place in life as a married woman better than training in a good home' (Matthews, 1978, 206).

Domestic service was, in general, a temporary occupation for young working-class women between school and marriage, and high turnover rates were expected of them. Census figures are thus a very poor guide to the numbers who experienced at least a term in service. (Against roughly comparable census figures, McBride estimates that at least 'a quarter of all French and English women probably served as domestics for a period of time in the nineteenth century' (McBride, 1976, 119).) It was this widespread experience of service among single women, the widespread employment of a servant by married women at certain stages of the family cycle, and the widespread expectation that a servant was necessary for civilised domestic life, that establishes the existence of a domestic-service economy throughout most of the nineteenth century in Australia.

However, from the last decade of that century, as the economy became more diversified and more market-oriented, proportionally fewer young working-class women worked as domestic servants. Domestic employers generally gave up on the possibility of persuading native-born women into service, although some of the pressure on the state for education in domestic arts was based upon such a hope (Matthews, 1983). As well, girls who were state wards were compelled into service (Barbalet, 1983), and considerable effort was put into importing servants under the guise of state-assisted or privately sponsored immigration. Unfortunately, as Kingston puts it, 'the trouble was that the best servants also made the best wives, being girls who were well trained, neat, methodical and resourceful' (Kingston, 1975:30). Thus the demand for servants remained consistently higher than their supply throughout the second half of the nineteenth century and into the twentieth. But although the usual market mechanisms operated to try to rectify this by offering higher wages and better conditions, the 'Servant Problem' became insoluble when the supply of cheap and willing immigrants ran out.

There are no easy explanations for the demise of the domestic-service economy, but generally it seems to have been caught in the pincers of a refusal of supply and a lessening of demand, and just faded away. Around the turn of the twentieth century, both working-class and middle-class families were substantially altering. On the working-class, supply side, from the 1870s onwards, family incomes earned by the males of the household were rising, and hence daughters' wages were less necessary (Sinclair, 1982:290). For those households where daughters' incomes remained essential, or where the daughters sought some personal independence, other more congenial work in offices and shops, or even in factories, was becoming available. Domestic service was increasingly seen by both young working-class women and their families as demeaning rather than respectable and protective. As well, the numbers of young girls available for service, or any other work, were being undercut by the state. Compulsory schooling and labour legislation prevented from working those 11- and 12-year-olds who had been previously favoured as cheap household assistants, junior slaveys.

In general, after leaving school, young working-class women were increasingly moving from the work of production and service in the household to that of the marketplace. As a consequence, not only were they helping to produce and sell more and more commodities, but they were at the same time turning themselves into consumers and buying more and more commodities. The marketplace, with its less paternal relations as compared to those of households, with its opportunities for individual autonomy, an independent wage and things to buy with it, came to predominate in the working lives of working-class women. Over the years, the marketplace came as well to predominate in the married lives of working-class women, so creating the modern working-class housewife.

On the middle-class, or demand, side, other factors were at work, pushing towards the demise of the domestic-service economy. While working-class family incomes were generally rising, those of the large servant employers were relatively falling, being especially affected by the extensive depression of the 1890s (Sinclair, 1982:287; Davison, 1979:190–228). As well, families were becoming smaller and growing in intimacy and exclusiveness. The nature of domestic work was changing, and there was less willingness to accept outside intermediaries like servants coming between parents and children (cf. McBride, 1976:67). The various ideological changes, to be dealt with in the next chapter, especially the movements for public health and infant welfare, induced rising standards and expectations of nutrition and hygiene, of family health and childcare. Middle-class mothers came to believe that such standards could rarely be obtained from paid working-class servants. The complaints of a Servant Problem throughout the whole period were twofold. There was believed to be an absolute lack of women offering service and, at least as importantly, it was the lack of suitable women that was most vexatious.

These ideological changes were accompanied by physical ones which eased the burdens of time and weight in the work of many households. Indoor plumbing, improved sewage disposal, and electrification, all reduced the pure physical work of the home. No longer, for example, was a physically exhausting 16-hour Monday required to do the family washing. Smaller families brought about changes in domestic architecture which, along with the introduction of basic household appliances, altered the nature of housework, if not its quantity. With an automatic washing machine and drier the laundry work of the house-wife of the 1980s is certainly simpler and lighter and no longer requires help. However, standards of cleanliness and the amount of family clothing have both risen over the century, and the amount of time spent washing throughout the week is at least as long as her great grand-mother's Blue Monday (cf. Vanek, 1979:502; Oakley, 1974:92–112). (There is further discussion of this point in chapter 8.) From the second decade of the twentieth century, technology that was already in use in the industrial sphere came slowly to be adapted to domestic use, and, after the second world war, became cheaper and more widely available. After the Servant Problem was discarded as insoluble, technology came to the rescue, but by then, everything was different.

Consumption: the housewife's economy

In the years between the wars, the housewife as she is known today emerged into her own. Mistresses and servants persisted in an alterna-tive but dying economy until the second world war, and thereafter only in small and isolated enclaves. The two women in the home—mistress and servant—merged into one, and that one occupied a place within families that had not existed before.

The marketplace reached into both the working-class and middle-class home, altering the nature of women's work. Modern housewives in relation to their work are, to a large degree, of the one class. In general, they no longer produce goods for consumption from primary materials. Rather, their work (excluding childcare) involves the purchase of commodities—goods and services—and their transformation into things for the family to consume to maintain its daily life. The quantity, quality and variety of what is bought of course depend upon the household income. Economic class is certainly reflected in family lifestyle: laundromat or privately owned washing machine; ownership of freezer, dishwasher, blender, electric garbage disposal; the quality of floor coverings and cleaning machinery, etc. As well, households with greater income can purchase domestic services rather than servants in the marketplace: cleaning, ironing, childminding.

The modern home is an integral part of the marketplace, as clearly economic as a multinational. The home is itself a market, and the housewife is its coordinator, mediating some sort of a balance between the needs and fantasies of individual family members, the intrusive profit seeking of the corporations, and household income. The feminine ideal of this woman in the home is as the reproducer and daily maintainer of happy workers and dedicated customers.

5

Ideology

*T*he second major sector of social life within which femininity was fashioned was that of ideology: systems of ideas and beliefs and their expression in practice. Here, the shift of greatest significance for women was that from a central concern with the population to a preoccupation with permissive consumerism. Population ideology held that a large, healthy and 'racially pure' population was central to moral and economic progress. Permissive consumerism opposed moral and legal restrictions on personal behaviour and claimed that self-fulfilment could be bought in the marketplace. Each of these ideologies in its heyday was more than a simple set of conscious beliefs, held by a specific group of people. Rather, each formed the substratum of all social beliefs, a taken-for-granted aspect of commonsense, the foundation of the practices of all social institutions. All sides in any debate or disagreement accepted in some sense and operated within the framework each ideology established. In other words, each ideology became attached to the meaning of life and the pursuit of happiness.

Population ideology

Population ideology emerged in its specifically modern form in the eighteenth century in western Europe; that is, its birth coincided with that of British colonisation of Australia. By the late nineteenth century, this ideology was infused into all modes of Australian thought. It manifested itself in the 'White Australia' immigration policy; in defence and foreign trade; in state intervention in matters of education, welfare, industrial relations and rural prosperity; in economic debate over free trade and protection, religious debate over purity and decadence, scientific debate over evolution and degeneracy, political debate over socialism and liberalism; and in the secret knowledges of the expanding professions—law, medicine, town planning, psychology, social welfare, economics.

From the 1870s till the 1950s, the size, composition and health of each nation's population was an obsession in the western world, including Australia. There is as yet no clear understanding of this obsession in its comparative, international aspect. Despite a considerable degree of apparent commonality between at least English-speaking countries, especially Australasia, Britain and North America, the social, political and economic contexts of the obsession were different in each country, and its manifestations were various (Gordon, 1977; Searle, 1971).

In general, population ideology was concerned with the supervision and regulation of procreation, migration, mortality, the level of health, and life expectancy (Foucault, 1979:139). Thus, what appear at first sight to be purely biological processes were considered to be of great social and political significance for national efficiency. Each birth, each death, each illness or infirmity became a political event, to be counted and measured and placed in a pattern, to be encouraged or discouraged, to be ordered. The central focus of this population ideology was women's bodies; its principal mode of control was women's work within their families; its central icon was the Ideal Mother. Counter to the politics of this ideology were the individual and collective struggles of women to control their own lives and bodies, the struggle for a freedom of their own defining.

Within Australia, three specific concerns developed during the period: to increase the size of the population; to improve the standard of living of the population; and to oppose whatever stood in the way of these reforms. Among those actively involved in population politics, the three concerns were rarely separated out in practice, but which concern took priority depended upon the specific aims of each group and its favoured tactics. As well, there were four overlapping and shifting dimensions of factional involvement: the religious—between Protestant and Catholic; the sociobiological—between eugenist and environmentalist; the class-political—between Labor and non-Labor; and the gender-political—between pro- and anti-feminist or suffragist. The interests of each of these factional groupings were formed from various mixtures of the concerns of population ideology. They fought for and against dress reform, factory legislation, domestic-arts education, censorship, temperance, contraception, mixed bathing, immigration, bush nursing, public dances, and much more (Bollen, 1972; Hicks, 1978; O'Farrell, 1977; Bacchi, 1980a; Bacchi, 1980b; Rickard, 1976; Connell & Irving, 1980; Hyslop, 1982). Within any such reform group, the composition of membership, the positions taken and the concerns fought for cannot be explained by simple criteria of gender or class or race or religion. A wide variety of views of moral enlightenment worked hand in hand with, or against, a variety of beliefs about economic development and social and national advancement.

What was common to all concerns and to all factions, however, was a moral fervour and a belief in progress or perfectibility or national destiny. Such fervour and beliefs centred, ultimately, upon some vision of the family, the ultimate source of good and profit and order. And the heart of this family was woman, defined as the ideal mother. Nonetheless, this unanimity at the level of rhetoric and platitude broke down at the detailed and practical levels. The white race, the family, and the ideal mother were all hollow icons, appealed to from all quarters, allowing everyone to hold different notions about the specific content and uses of the ideal. Contradictions abounded, and had to be lived through. The attempt to be an ideal mother became woman's ever changing, never ending and never successful task throughout adulthood.

In the decades around the turn of the twentieth century, population ideology was directly involved in the construction of modern Australian femininity through five campaigns: for public health, infant welfare, social purity, education, and child welfare. (A sixth campaign, for protective labour legislation, was discussed in the previous chapter.)

Public health

In general terms, the public-health movement was concerned with improving the physical and moral environment of the cities. Australia's population at the time was the most highly urbanised in the world, but its cities were new and did not suffer from the historically accumulated problems of Europe, or even America. Nonetheless, Australian reformers imported ideas from these old worlds and began to see the existence of present urban evils and to project future ones. In particular, they focused upon the urban home, on the threats to society that emanated from its practices, and on the threats to it that derived from its physical setting.

From the 1880s, members of the public-health movement—doctors, moralists, philanthropists, engineers, town planners, educators and the pursuers of national efficiency—attempted to prevent industrial and domestic pollution of water supplies by ineffective legislative penalties and by more effective sewerage schemes (Hunt & Bolton, 1978; Boyd, 1978:244–9; Davison, 1979:144–51, 171–3). In the early twentieth century, the adulteration of food and the nature of secret ingredients came into question, with Pure Food and Drug Acts as a consequence (Mendelsohn, 1979:239–41; McCoy 1980, 54–69). Other reformers were concerned with housing. European-style slums might not have existed, but inadequate housing was certainly the lot of many working-class families, especially in the inner cities. Unsanitary conditions and disease were blamed for the increasing degeneracy of the population. They reduced the birthrate, affected the strength and abilities of workers (and potential soldiers), and threatened middle-class well-being through contagion. Consequently, reformist concern was exercised from the mid-nineteenth century into the twentieth against epidemics and plagues, including smallpox in the 1880s and 1890s, bubonic plague in the 1900s, venereal disease during and after the first world war, pneumonic influenza in 1919, poliomyelitis in the 1930s, and pulmonary tuberculosis throughout the period until the second world war (Mendelsohn, 1979:231; Connell & Irving, 1980:126; Thame, 1974:1–146). Legislation dealing with public health and environmental hygiene was passed throughout the period, with varying, and usually limited, degrees of effectiveness. Considerations of political expediency and of cost meant that change came slowly, with little disruption of vested interests.

Nonetheless, changes were induced in all classes of Australian family life. Cleanliness—of people and clothes and habitations—became a civic good as well as a moral virtue as education in public health spread ideas of germ contagion and antisepsis, and as the means to achieve greater cleanliness became slowly available. Such slowness should not be underestimated. A South Australian Parliamentary Inquiry in 1940 revealed that more than one-third of all dwellings in the City of Adelaide were substandard, with such common faults as defective privies, lack of amenities (95 per cent of substandard houses did not have a kitchen sink, 48 per cent were without a bathroom), rat and vermin infestation, and lack of gas or electric light (Building Act Inquiry Committee, 1940). Belief in both the necessity and the possibility of domestic hygiene underpinned new standards of cleanliness expected of and imposed upon mothers of all classes.

Through exhortation, education and legislation, public-health reformers drew some of the parameters of desired domestic cleanliness: for clean surfaces where babies played and where food was prepared, for scrupulous sanitation and rubbish disposal, for antiseptic and quarantine measures in the case of illness. The very nature of domestic dirt and the methods of its removal altered. Paving of streets reduced the dust and dirt that entered the house. Important here, though not contrived by the public-health movement, was the demise of the horse as the main form of transport and the consequent change in pollution from manure on the streets to petro-chemical fumes in the air. The provision of internal plumbing and of cheap gas and electricity entailed vast changes in household comfort as well as in standards of safety and hygiene. The increasing availability of prepared foods of guaranteed purity affected the housewife's methods of feeding her family. In addition, with the discovery of vitamins in the years between the wars, nutrition developed both as a science and a social issue, and the notion of the balanced diet was widely publicised, with sample diet sheets establishing some sort of expected standard.

Infant welfare

Inextricably intertwined with the public-health movement was the specialised campaign for infant welfare, which aimed to reduce the high infant-mortality rate. (The statistics of infant mortality were documented in chapter 3.) This campaign introduced even more changes in the standards of Australian femininity by recasting the meaning of motherhood.

In the early 1900s, infant-welfare reformers—doctors, nurses, women from charitable organisations—embarked upon campaigns to encourage maternal breastfeeding and to discourage wet-nursing and artificial feeding. At the same time, they sought an improvement in the quality of the public milk supply, a regularisation of appropriate for- mulae for the supplementary feeding of infants, and a greater dedica- tion to the cleanliness of the baby's total environment. All these efforts were significant in reducing infant mortality from diarrhoeal and re- lated conditions (Lewis, 1980:207; Mayo, 1960). By the end of the first decade of the twentieth century, a more direct assault on infant mortal- ity was launched with voluntary agencies setting up a number of clinics in the major states. Their task was the education of mothers and the surveillance of their mothering (Thame, 1974:200–39; Lewis, 1976).

Through these campaigns, a 'privileged alliance' between mothers and doctors was established (cf. Donzelot, 1978:18–21). To some ex- tent, the authority of the woman in the home was increased. She became a medical auxiliary, the agent through whom the prestige of medical science entered the home. On the other hand, she became weighed down by the imposition of ever increasing responsibility for her own and her infants' health, responsibility which drew from her an ever increasing sense of guilt. Illness and death were no longer consi- dered the common accompaniments of maternity and childhood, but were avoidable through knowledge and close attention to diet and cleanliness. Intense campaigns against both infant and maternal mor- tality were conducted in the various names of population politics throughout the first three decades of the twentieth century. The condi- tions necessary to prevent such deaths were not yet fully established but the campaigners nonetheless placed the blame firmly on the ignor- ance and carelessness of mothers (Thame, 1974:203–10; cf. J. Lewis, 1980:61–113). Mothers were urged to place themselves under medical surveillance throughout their pregnancies by attending antenatal cli- nics. They were urged to take their infants to mothers' and babies' clinics for paramedical supervision for at least the first year of the child's life. From the 1930s onwards, virtually all mothers did attend such clinics at least once (Thame, 1974:219–24). From the child's birth onwards, mothers were held responsible for maintaining correct feeding habits, ensuring complete cleanliness, and observing their children for signs of illness or retarded development. They were urged on in these responsibilities by a mass propaganda campaign conducted through the radio, newspapers, magazines, country lecture tours and films. They were held to them by the continuing surveillance of family doctors, nurse inspectors, benevolent-society visitors and social workers, school medical officers and teachers (Thame, 1974: 200–39).

Babies' weight gain or loss came to be the daily judgment of mothers' care and love. When to feed? What? How much? The answers to these questions proclaimed the fashionable and ideological limits and the intensity of maternal knowledge and responsibility. The never ending battle against germs was mothers' sacred pledge of vigilance for the health of the family and the well-being of the nation. If anything went wrong, it was mother's fault. The concomitants of maternity for Australian women became fear and guilt.

Mothers' responsibility for the physical well-being of their children was augmented in the 1920s and 1930s by responsibility for their psychological well-being. The mental-hygiene movement and theories of 'normal' child development demanded changes. But exactly what changes was rather vague. These years saw the production of a plethora of childrearing books and childrearing experts (cf. Newson & Newson, 1974; Storr, 1974). The books and the experts all tended to share a general orientation: that parents (especially mothers) exercised an inordinate influence upon the young infant, and that the child's earliest experiences were of fundamental significance in forming its adult character. Thereafter, the experts' beliefs diverged widely. Many of the beliefs were contradictory, but were nonetheless advocated concurrently or consecutively.

Empirical testing of the various theories failed to establish their validity or even their effects (cf. Lomax, 1978; Skolnick, 1975). But authoritative expert declaration, and prejudice, continued to insist upon the specific responsibilities of mothers for the mental health and psychological adjustment of the future generation. If the child grew up to be bad or sad, depraved or deprived, evil or incompetent, it was all mother's fault. Since no child was ever perfect, mothering became, by definition, an impossible task.

Social purity

An insistence upon the possibility of human perfectibility was the dominant theme of the third population programme of the 1890s and early 1900s. The social purity—or wowser—campaigns sought to eliminate the social and moral evils spawned by the godlessness of city life among the poor, and to replace them with domestic virtues, with the harmony and enlightenment of family life. Woman was the target of these campaigns. Their aim was to get her into the home and to train her to be its civilising heart. The fervour of these campaigns was derived largely from Protestant social evangelism and sectarian bigotry. From the 1880s to the 1930s, a strongly prudish consciousness gained dominance in both Protestant and Catholic churches. In a situation of intense sectarian rivalry, both sets of churchmen and their lay supporters sought to outdo the purity of each other's morality by railing obsessively against sexual dangers and lapses, against the moral decadence and degeneracy of society (O'Farrell, 1977:245–91, 374–76; Bollen, 1972).

On issues such as the strict punishment of abortion, the censorship of contraceptive information, the desire to outlaw contraceptive devices and abortifacients, the opposition to divorce-law reform, the rehabilitation of prostitutes and the outlawing of their trade, and the opposition to sex education in schools—in such matters of sexual morality, the two sects tended to hold positions more compatible than either would recognise. The family was central to both of their dogmas: a family based on the lifelong monogamous fidelity of a Christian heterosexual couple whose sexuality was dedicated to procreation, ordained for the glory of God and the advancement of the nation. Sexual pleasure was eventually acknowledged by both churches, but neither, despite other considerable differences, would allow pleasure to replace procreation. Protestants and Catholics worked separately on all these issues, but because of their overlapping ethical stances, they effectively produced a monolithic standard of sexual morality that survived, embodied in legislation backed up by prudish silence and shrouded euphemism, until the 1950s (Auchmuty, 1979). Repression and priggery became, for this period, the hallmarks of official Australian moral standards, and within their limits the standards of femininity were confined.

Negative attitudes towards women's reproductive self-control, women's self-definition of sexuality, and women's economic independence were shared across the religious and political spectrums for the first half of the twentieth century. Only in the 1950s did the consensus around social purity begin to break down. It became instead a factional political programme, associated with one party in particular. In 1955, the Democratic Labor Party split away from the Australian Labor Party, setting itself up as virtually a Catholic party, against communism and in favour of the authoritian, patriarchal family (Crowley, 1973, II:322; Murray, 1970). Its claim to the monopoly on purity breached the taken-for-grantedness of the repressive consensus, thereby granting legitimacy to opposition and reformulations of sexual issues.

On other matters of social purity, the Protestant and Catholic churches and their political supporters held distinctive and often opposing views. The Protestant cause tended to be the most visible and the most effective, campaigning against alcohol, opium, gambling, desecration of the sabbath, and general criminal vice and immorality (Bollen, 1972). A number of historians have claimed a class bias in many of the specific campaigns directed by the wowsers (Connell & Irving, 1980:123–9; O'Farrell, 1977:281). It was working-class rather than ruling-class cultural activities that drew their fire, and they concentrated their rhetoric on the dire effects of vice in creating and compounding poverty. But such class bias was, in fact, a complex issue. On the one hand, it was enmeshed in sectarian squabbles through the crude equation of working-class with Catholic, and the crude causal connection that Catholicism produced poverty and crime. On the other hand, it was ensnared in gender distinctions within the working class. Apart from sexual matters, it was largely men's activity that was condemned, and suffering wives and mothers were appealed to as agents of their reformation. It is not at all clear where the interests of working-class women—whether Catholic or not—lay.

To take just one, simplified, example: temperance. The view of the Protestant reformers, which they propagated vociferously, was that alcohol was the root of all social evil, causing crime, poverty, disease and family breakdown (Dingle, 1980:239). At the other extreme was the socialist view that the poverty and brutality of working-class life was caused by the exploitation of the capitalist system, and that alcohol was but a means of temporary, individual escape. (Despite this view, many socialists were nonetheless fierce temperance advocates.) For every drunken husband who beat his wife, there was probably another who was cheerful and kindly. In a society with few forms of anaesthetic (and no aspirin), alcohol was in many ways a family medicine. On the other hand, the purchase of a bottle sometimes was at the expense of the baby's, or more usually mother's, dinner.

Cutting through the complexity of these issues, the temperance crusaders certainly affected the family life of all classes, with many intended and unintended consequences upon the definition of Australian femininity. The intended consequence of the restriction of the sale of alcohol was the enhancement of settled suburban family life, and the reformation of the working class around this ideal. Six o'clock closing of hotel bars was introduced in all Australian states in 1916 (except in Western Australia, which adopted nine o'clock closing, and in Queensland, where eight o'clock closing was adopted in 1923). Its immediate effect was to create the infamous custom, the 'six o'clock swill', and to perpetuate it for half a century and beyond—till 1954 in New South Wales and 1967 in Victoria. (Phillips, 1980).

The indirect effects, the consequences of this change in drinking habits on domestic life, are not clearly known. The suburban standard of sober familial respectability, much admired by the temperance workers, was not easily imposed in practice. Alcohol consumption as such did not decline, only its public hours, so clearly, considerably more drinking took place in the home. (Dingle, 1980:239–40, 246). How this new household activity affected the work and power of woman as the heart of the family remains to be investigated.

One explicit effect of the temperance ideology on the meaning of femininity was the denial that women—good women—drank alcohol. Early twentieth-century femininity was definitely sober. This established an obvious and extreme gender segregation of Australian social life. Any place of public drinking was taboo to women. From this prohibition was derived the classic Australian social scene: men gathered around the beer keg, women hovering at the opposite end of the room over the babies and lamingtons. Good women were refused access to hotels, which were thereby confirmed as centres of masculine social life beyond simple drinking places. Gambling, political and social meetings, exchange of information were vital to pub life. Essential elements of working-class male solidarity were constructed in hotels, middle-class male solidarity in licensed clubs and private bars.

Because this ideological prescription has been widely accepted as reality, research into drinking has been severely biased towards masculine experience. We have no idea whether or how many women drank in their own homes; we do not know if there were any feminine domestic rituals associated with alcohol. We do know, however, that those women who were caught drinking excessively were treated poorly and as doubly deviant—by legal, medical and welfare institutions—because even the model of the alcoholic was masculine.

Education

Of rather better known effect than either sexual purity or temperance campaigns in determining the nature of motherhood was the fourth major population project, the introduction of mass compulsory education in the 1870s and 1880s, and its rapid expansion and diversification during the twentieth century. The explicit purpose of this programme was the development of a literate, skilled, competitive, honest and disciplined population. Indirectly, over time, schooling altered relations between children and adults, and between women and men. Its most basic effect was to consolidate the status of children as dependents, and hence to alter irrevocably the division of labour in the family.

Each state had slightly different regulations, introduced between

1872 (Victoria) and 1893 (Western Australia). Initially, all specified that most children between seven and thirteen years were required to attend school for some 70 or so days in each half year, with fines for non-attendance. By the beginning of the twentieth century, regulations were tighter and more extensive, with many more days' attendance required, and fewer excuses acceptable. As well, such regulations had been supplemented in the 1890s by industrial legislation which denied children the right to work, defining children according to the compulsory minimum age for leaving school (Davey, 1956:116–8). The abolition of child labour was bitterly resented and opposed by certain groups of parents, employers and children. Despite their protests, however, by the second decade of the twentieth century, the notion that 'the business of childhood is to be schooled' had achieved almost total acceptance throughout Australia (Wimshurst, 1981).

Children were encouraged to stay at school in the hope of economic advancement or cultural improvement. They were compelled to stay through fear of the truant officer, and denied the alternative of work through fear of the factory inspector. They were no longer allowed to be contributors to the family economy, either working in and for the family (for example, harvesting, laundry work), or working outside and bringing home an income. They became financial liabilities rather than economic assets. They were caught in a limbo of indeterminate but dependent status, rather than being treated as young adults.

With parents no longer so directly involved in the education of their children, and with the growth and specialisation of schooling, there developed within families new forms of relations and tensions between the generations. In some ways, children and parents were pitted against each other. Parental experience confronted children's formal learning. Nowhere was this more clearly the case than in the arguments in favour of educating girls in domestic arts. Opponents insisted that such teaching was the responsibility of mothers in the home; that all mothers, virtually by definition, were good housekeepers who would delight in teaching their daughters. Advocates countered such arguments by claiming that 'many mothers are quite untrained and incapable of imparting instruction that is of value' (Matthews, 1983: 44). They insisted that, in the interests of the health and moral enlightenment and discipline of working-class family life, the transmission of misinformation between ignorant and careless mothers and their daughters needed to be replaced by scientific training from professional teachers. Bad habits needed to be replaced by scientific procedures, disordered standards by civilised ones of thrift, industry and cleanliness.

New rhythms of family life, daily and over years, resulted from compulsory mass education. School attendance broke up the pattern of children gradually shouldering familial responsibility. Children who previously helped around the house were now absent for much of each day. In particular, the custom of older children watching over younger ones was largely lost, leading to mothers becoming more significantly involved in the care of children under seven years, which, in turn, became a factor in decisions about family size. As well, the daughters gained less practical experience in childrearing, and stood in greater need of experts' advice when they later bore their own children. As far as school-age children were concerned, the hours of schooling did not fit with any other time pattern in the society, certainly not with formal work hours. This added to the pressure on mothers to stay at home and not go out to work in order to be there when the kids got home from school. Mothers were deemed responsible for their children out of school hours, with social opprobrium attaching to those who allowed their children to wander the streets unsupervised—as larrikins at first, later as juvenile delinquents and latchkey children.

With the entry of legislative prescription and professional surveill-ance into the family—of teachers, doctors, nurses, social workers, truancy officers, labour inspectors — mothering become more uniform, more circumscribed, more responsible to external judgment, more amenable to expert advice (as distinct from experience-based advice from relatives and neighbours). Schools attempted to instil in all chil-dren middle-class standards of correct behaviour: punctuality, regular-ity, diligence, thrift, sobriety, standard language, uniform dress, pat-riotism, respect for authority (Firth, 1970; Wimshurst, 1981). Mothers were made responsible by schools for insisting on the continuation of such behaviour out of school hours. The consequences of maternal irresponsibility or incompetence in such matters were spelt out in various state Child Welfare Acts from the 1880s to the 1930s.

Child welfare

Child-welfare provisions were the punitive side of the new status of children and the reform of family life envisioned by the various popula-tion politicians. The first step was taken in South Australia with the 1886 State Children's Act (Davey, 1956:57). Over the next three de-cades, the other states followed with a variety of legislation designed to protect society from what was perceived as a two-sided danger. Indi-vidual children needed to be protected from moral, physical or finan-cial jeopardy lest they themselves came to constitute a danger to society. Such legislation spelt out in detail the rights, responsibilities and restrictions of children and, concomitantly, the responsibilities of parents towards their children and towards the state.

A variety of ages were established at law below which children were to be treated quite differently from adults. The criminal law distinguished between children, juveniles and adults in its determination of questions of consent and intent, of judicial procedure, and of punishment. Other legislation specified the ages below which no one was permitted to consent to sexual intercourse, get married, make valid contracts, buy alcohol or cigarettes, operate a lift, earn money as an entertainer or street trader, become involved in gambling, view certain films, drive a motor vehicle, vote, be tattooed, leave the country. Many of these restrictions were gender-specific in practice, if not in law. For example, over the century most boys who were committed to institutions had actively broken the law in some way, whereas most girls had not but were deemed by the courts to be in need of protection from 'moral danger' (Davey, 1956; Foreman, 1975:74–83).

The focus of state concern in such legislation was the morally deficient family which allowed the child to be exposed to moral danger or to fall into improper associations (for example, with prostitutes, thieves, drunkards, prisoners, the insane, the incapacitated, or simply the 'unfit', whether or not such associates were the parents of the child). Such exposure would lead the child inevitably into a life of vice or crime. Similarly the legislation singled out the family which allowed the child to become destitute or ill, and hence liable to become a financial burden upon charitable organisations or state welfare. Also morally deficient was the family which allowed the child to truant or engage in street trading or roaming, thus inevitably escaping the inculcation of a proper work discipline (Litherland, 1940:95–9, Barbalet, 1983:187–202). The legislation proscribed a wide variety of behaviour. It did not assert a positive ideal of familial duty, responsibility or privilege, but left it implied. Child Welfare Departments and philanthropic bodies did proclaim positive ideals of family life such as honesty, industriousness, respectability, sobriety and independence. But these were middle-class moral abstractions, difficult for poor families at risk of state interference to interpret. Margaret Barbalet summarises the problem for working-class families in South Australia in the years around the first world war:

> For a poor child to escape being noticed by the police or officers of the [Child Welfare] Department... required concern and vigilance on the part of parents and a rock-like determination to avoid the temptations of drink and petty criminal activities. It required parents to have and to maintain authority over their children. (Barbalet, 1983:196)

This new concern with child welfare left open a wide field for maternal and familial confusion and guilt. Clearly, such and such was wrong; but what was right?

Any family which failed to interpret correctly the narrow confines of acceptable structure and functioning became eligible for punishment.

Its children could be removed into institutional care (including board-ing out and fostering in more suitable families). The failed family could become the object of surveillance and disciplinary measures in its own right, fined for allowing truancy or contributing to the commission of an offence, subject to visitation by probation, truancy, welfare and police officers. Once 'on the books', the so-called sanctity and the right to privacy of any family was abandoned and replaced by direct state or philanthropic intervention.

Child-welfare regulations, drawn up in each state in the years around the turn of the century, were directed towards controlling the children of families which did not conform to a particular cultural standard derived from the ideals of the population reformers. As Lynne Foreman has written in her evaluation of child welfare services in Australia,

> the law upholds a cultural view that the preferred family unit is one that is legally sanctioned, economically independent of the State and generally is able to support, maintain and develop its own internal structure along the lines of socially acceptable criteria...[T]his represents a very narrow perception of present family organisation. (Foreman, 1975:11)

In the 1900s, the preferred family unit was composed of breadwinning father, domestic mother, and dutiful children who moved only between home and school. The law, in this field as in all the others so far discussed, sought to impose this ideal upon the heterogeneity of other existing family forms. In terms of the construction of femininity, such laws established that women, whose primary duty was mothering, must do so only within this circumscribed way, or face severe financial and legal punishment, often to the extent that they were denied, or forced to relinquish, control over their own children.

Population ideology and the good woman

For the three decades from the 1890s, these five manifestations of population ideology—public health, infant welfare, social purity, education and child welfare—were vociferously argued. The many varieties of reform were opposed every step of their tortuous ways by those who sought more effective or less costly ways of achieving the same ends, or who pointed out the inconsistencies or the ulterior purposes of the reformers. There was no grand concerted plan of coordination among them, though they shared common assumptions. There was no common purpose of domesticating the working class and forging a new image of the good woman, though each group saw specific evils in working-class life and each saw woman as the focus of change. Each campaign stumbled on, dealing with the unintended consequences of the last step, coping with the actuality of the intended effects of the step before. There was no inevitability in their success, or rather, in any particular outcome. The apparent pattern of their collusion and their successes is one that is invented by looking backwards; we impose the pattern. This pattern is formed on the basis of our perception of their common assumptions and of the eventual 'spontaneous' outcome that they all appear to have contributed to.

All five campaigns were responding to a sense of social crisis: racial, individual, moral, urban, economic and familial decline and degeneration. Both their perceptions and their responses were informed by the all-pervasive population ideology. The long-term effect of their obsessions and campaigns was the establishment of new relationships among and between households and the state, the creation of a new social order. In particular, a new gender ideology of femininity, a new ideal of the good woman, was forged.

The core of this ideal of the good woman was mothering. Before the 1880s, a woman's social value was judged at least as much from her activity as wife, as sexual partner, economic assistant, companion, servant. By the 1960s, this aspect of woman was returning to high valuation. In the years between, mother reigned. And this ideal mother was a type never before known. In earlier centuries, at least in western Europe, the discipline of children after a certain age had been preeminently a masculine task. Family honour was represented in the father as head of household. Child behaviour reflected upon this honour and hence the father was the appropriate agent for disciplining the new generation for the good of both the family and the society. This form of family, however, and this pattern of the exercise of power, was reconstructed over the last decades of the nineteenth and into the twentieth century, as the new ideology of motherhood emerged. The ideal mother's decision-making and disciplinary powers increased, to the detriment of father's, until, by the 1950s, sociologists were proclaiming the overwhelming dominance of mother as the heart of the Australian family, with father's headship becoming increasingly nominal (Adler, 1965; Encel and others, 1974:40–65; Kelly, 1978). The difference between heart and head nonetheless remained, disguised but determinant. Father's power was that of masculinity, of superiority in the public, economic, social world. Mother's power was intimate, restricted by and to her family, the boundaries of which, and the extent of their permeability, were not within her control. She made more decisions, but did not necessarily determine which ones. She managed the family, but did not necessarily control it. She had authority within the family, but not necessarily the power to influence the mode of the family's integration into the wider social processes (Bryson, 1975; Edwards, 1981; cf. Safilios-Rothschild, 1970).

Before I discuss the changing femininity of the 1950s, there is one final point to be made about the turn-of-the-century population campaigns. A number of historians have taken the image of woman presented by the reformers as an accurate depiction of women's place in the actual gender order. They have presented a world of separate spheres with home fires burning brightly. It seems to me, instead, that the very strength of the reformers' exhortation and lobbying is a sign that their views were not fully accepted, were not yet taken for granted, but were confronting competing views. Libertarians, birth-control advocates, anti-censorship agitators and liberals of many varieties opposed state and philanthropic interference with private life or sought change in different directions. The ideology of the population reformers, with its specific model of the good woman as domestic, home and family-bound, pure, clean and rationalised, was an ideology seeking to be established rather than the prevalent view or practice. Its triumph of general acceptance came in the years between the wars (when there still remained strong, but defensive, opposition), not in either the 1890s or the 1950s, which were decades of extensive transition in the meaning of femininity.

During the 1920s and 1930s, population ideology held sway, becoming muted in explicit expression because it had become part of commonsense. The varieties of social concern took population issues as axiomatic, and defined their enemies as enemies of the Australian family: bolshevism, industrial militancy, sexual freedom, fiscal extravagance, non-British foreigners, population decline and degeneracy, the urban underworld, unemployment. The second world war wrought havoc upon this insular, repressive, respectable, familial ideal. Families were separated, foreign men (Americans and prisoners of war) flooded in, married women were encouraged and single women coerced into the commanding workforce, men went away and women got on quite well without them. As discussed in chapter 4, many changes in the gender order became necessary in the interests of an all-out war effort and they were endorsed, regretfully, by political and social leaders, but 'only for the duration of the war' (Hasluck, 1970:265; McGrath, 1943).

At war's end, the special dispensations were revoked, and the agents and instruments of the gender ideology sought to restore prewar relations. But it didn't work. The experience of wartime itself, the rapid postwar economic boom, the changes wrought by reconstruction policies and mass immigration—all led away from the prewar regime of population ideology towards an ideology of permissive consumerism. The emphasis on the family in Cold War propaganda, and the popularised distortion of the theory of maternal deprivation, were last-ditch stands of an increasingly anachronistic form of gender ideology. This is not to say that the family, mothering, and femininity disappeared from the scene as ideological issues. Rather, their meanings were transformed. The family, motherhood and femininity extolled by the 1980s' gender ideology of permissive consumerism are markedly different from the prewar ideals.

The ideology of permissive consumerism

In the transition decades of the 1890s and 1900s, population ideology had been made concrete in many pieces of legislation. In the transition decades of the 1950s to 1970s, much of this legislation was dismantled. A list of these changes gives some idea of the new sets of relationships that were emerging within the gender order, between individuals, households and the state. (Many of these legislative changes affected only one or a few states, and some of the old order ostensibly still prevails in others). Gambling on totalisators and poker machines was permitted in 1954 (WA) and 1956 (NSW). Hotel trading hours were extended in 1955 (NSW), and Sunday trading permitted in 1979 (NSW). Capital punishment was abolished in 1955 (NSW). The 'White Australia' dictation test was abandoned for an entry-permit scheme in 1958 (Commonwealth), and large numbers of Asian migrants were accepted from the mid-1970s. Equal pay for work of equal value was initiated in 1958 (NSW), and extended in 1969 and 1972 (Commonwealth). Censorship was slightly relaxed in 1958 (Commonwealth), followed by a second round of liberality in the late 1960s. Divorce became a Commonwealth matter and somewhat more accessible in 1959, with 'no fault' provisions introduced in 1975. Abortion was made legal under certain conditions in 1969 (SA). Single mothers became eligible for supporting parent benefits in 1973 (Commonwealth). Import tariffs and luxury sales tax on contraceptives were removed in 1972 (Commonwealth). Homosexuality was decriminalised in 1975 (SA), and in the same year, rape within marriage (by husband of wife) was made on offence (SA). Prostitution was rendered less illegal by the repeal of the Summary Offences Act (NSW) in 1979, although soliciting was returned as an offence in 1983 (NSW). The first Sex Discrimination Act was passed in 1975 (SA), and various of the states' draconian statutes concerning child welfare and mental health were amended in the 1970s.

The more important of these changes will be dealt with in later chapters. Here, I will touch only upon the general significance of 'permissiveness' for the construction of femininity. Much of this 'permissive' legislation concerned itself with the regulation of sexual behaviour: divorce, abortion, contraception, obscenity and pornography, homosexuality, prostitution, rape. In particular, women's sexuality was at issue. Since sexuality plays such a substantial part in the definition of femininity, this new focus was a sign of dramatic change in that definition.

The fundamental distinction between the old and the new gender ideologies lay in the nexus between female sexuality and procreation. Population ideology proclaimed the necessity of the link as a means of controlling the quantity, quality and morality of the Australian people. Permissiveness weakened the link, encouraging pleasure divorced from the probability of procreation. Female sexual desire became the object of ideological manipulation which tried to channel it into the desire to consume the goods and services of the rapidly expanding marketplace (cf. Hall, 1980:22–3).

Certainly, the old image of the house-bound mother continued and was strengthened, but she did move outside the home more often to do the shopping. She became the purchasing manager for the household, rather than its servant, At the same time, her sexuality, allure, attractiveness received increasing emphasis (Game & Pringle, 1979). The image of the good woman became partially detached or disconnected from her domestic setting. She was permitted personal pleasure as well as familial duty. She was encouraged to be seductive as well as nurturant.

Much of this new imagery was created in the warrens of the advertising industry, which will be discussed in the next chapter. The household as an arena of consumption had been progressively flooded with advertisements for new products since the 1920s (Stephen, 1981; cf. Ewen, 1977). In the 1950s and 1960s, with the rapidly expanding economy and with more money available for family consumption (most particularly coming from women's increasing involvement in the commanding economy), these products were actually bought rather than simply desired. A new market was then required, and created.

While family consumption remained important, it was personal life that became the target for creating needs to be fulfilled with commodities (cf. Gadlin, 1976; Ewen, 1976). The very notion of self-fulfilment was commercialised and expanded. Crucial to this process was a new understanding of woman. Her sexuality was objectified and turned into the face and body that launched a thousand products annually. Simultaneously, it was subjectified. Advertisements induced introspection and guilt, which led to the discovery of more personal inadequacies that could be overcome, or at least disguised, by purchase of a multitude of products and services: from a new dress to a face lift to a course of relaxation therapy.

Such a shift in the content of femininity was, inevitably, opposed from many quarters, by the remnants of the population moralists, by opponents of capitalism, and by feminists. Moreover, the change was also, inevitably, contradictory. While woman in the home was the target of family-consumption advertising, increasingly more women had to earn regular wages to pay for the commodities. While woman partly separated from the home was the target for personal advertising, increasingly more women took the quest for independence and self-fulfilment beyond the realm of the marketplace into political action.

6

Management of the Gender Order

*T*he economy and ideology were crucial construction sites of modern femininity. Across the twentieth century, the organisation of these sites, and the management of the building process, came increasingly into the hands of a new and specialised group. These were the skilled 'mental' workers of the tertiary sector: professionals and experts. They became the group through whom economic and ideological processes were ordered and regularised and changed. Their common expertise was the management of people, of women and men and the relations between them. That is, they became the overseers of the gender order. Through their work, the feminine ideal was rearranged to accommodate change and to become more uniform and more universally applicable to all Australian women throughout their lives. The new experts operated in three major areas: the commanding economy, consumption, and personal life.

Scientific managers

In the commanding economy, the new experts sought to reorganise the labour processes of industry, establishing monopoly control of time and space, of decision making and movement (Cochrane, 1982). Their expertise derived from the work of the American, Frederick Winslow Taylor, who developed a programme of 'scientific management' at the turn of the century. This programme was introduced into Australia in fits and starts, treated warily by both employers and workers after providing the grounds for the devastating New South Wales Rail strike of 1917. In the second world war and the decade after, a 'managerial revolution' introduced variations of scientific management into both large and small factories across Australia. Various forms of industrial psychology—or personnel practice—accompanied these programmes in the 1950s (Cochrane, 1982; Rowse, 1978:61–73).

In the factory

The aim of the system overall was to maximise output in a given time by the reorganisation of materials, equipment and labour, and to maintain this efficiency by creating contented workers, stifling collective protest at the inhumanity of the system by manipulating individual discontent into loyalty to the company. Its effect was to break down craft skills and replace the workers' knowledge of the whole production process with isolated and repetitive motions tied to the stopwatch; to remove management from the shop floor and replace face-to-face paternal relations with anonymous, centralised relations mediated by experts (Cochrane, 1982; CURA, 1976; Connell & Irving, 1980:218–9; Rowse, 1978:61–73; cf. Braverman, 1974:70–138; Herzog, 1980).

Beyond rationalising old labour processes, the new production experts organised the introduction of new technologies into industry—machinery, automation, computers, microchips. Alongside such actions in the command economy, they were responsible too for the reorganisation of production in what had been the local economy (discussed in chapters 4 and 8). As the marketplace extended into previously hidden realms, encompassing small-scale and localised production, the new experts calculated and planned ways to adapt it to capitalist imperatives; new forms of outwork and part-time work, new links between local, national and multinational enterprises (Matthews, 1982).

Central to the work of production experts in all realms was the specification and policing of the lines of gender division in the workforce. A distinction between women's work and men's work was fundamental to the continuing organisation of capitalism, and had existed, in some form or another, since Australia's British invasion. In general, it had been a customary division, open to reinterpretation in ways determined by the local workers themselves, capable of sustaining many exceptions. All such latitude was abolished in the reforming zeal of the production experts who insisted upon rigid lines of demarcation in the interests of their conception of efficiency. (The fact that trade unions and the Arbitration Court, as well as capitalists, took up this rigid system with alacrity has already been discussed in relation to the family wage.) As new types and areas of work came into existence within the expanding, reorganised economy, they were not simply opened to talent, but were immediately gender-typed, thereby restricting access and determining the status, conditions and wages of those workers who were permitted to enter (Game & Pringle, 1983; Spearritt,

1975).

Gender division on the shop floor was maintained throughout the many technological and structural changes in manufacturing industry across the century. It was crucial to management control of workers and the work process, and to power relations among workers. It was perceived as a natural state, even when formalised through the organisational and personnel practices of scientific managers. As Game and Pringle explain in *Gender at Work*,

> it would be a mistake to view the sexual division of labour as a management plot, or as a structure imposed on the workforce from on high. Male workers accept it and women workers find difficulty in initiating more than limited resistance...[E]ven when management consciously use a strategy of a sexual division of labour as a means of controlling the labour process, it is not a matter of *imposing* it. They do not have to. It is experienced as *natural*, both in the workplace, and in the so-called private sphere of life. (1983:22–3)

No work is intrinsically better suited to either women or men—it is made so in each specific situation, and is then legitimated by recourse to specious arguments about women's nature and abilities. The result has been the creation of a femininity of the workplace which is defined as inferior in relation to masculinity: women's work is lighter than men's, or less dangerous, cleaner, more boring, less mobile, less technical (Game & Pringle, 1983, 25–40). The lines of demarcation are arbitrarily drawn, but always to women workers' detriment. In general, at whatever level of the minutely subdivided labour process, men make sure that they get the pick of the jobs, and in this they are encouraged and guided by the scientific managers.

In the office

Scientific management experts not only reorganised factory production. They took their programmes as well into the office, reorganising the administration of private enterprise and state or public service. As with the factories, such reorganisation was first, and most effectively, implemented in large organisations rather than small, many of which still muddle through, directed by the idiosyncratic methods of the owner–employer. Office procedures were rationalised by strict consideration of time and space, by division of labour and specialisation of duties. Paralleling events on the factory floor, new technologies were installed over time. Typewriters and telephones were supplemented by adding and ledger machines, telexes and eventually computers. Each instrument required that work be redivided and reallocated, and that new hierarchies within the workforce be established. Standardised procedures, from bookkeeping to note-taking to filing to programming were insisted upon, ensuring a compatibility of communication within and between firms and departments, as well as providing a standard for assessment of worker performance. As in the factory, paternalism was replaced by bureaucratic distance.

As with factory organisation, office and administrative work was firstly divided and subdivided on gender lines. Until around the first world war, the office had been a male preserve, although the United Clerks' Union had been worried as early as 1909 about the replacement of male by female clerks. (Kingston, 1975: 93–4). To men in this period, clerical work was the beginning, an apprenticeship stage of a lifelong career in business and management. By the 1920s and 1930s, the expansion of markets and the growth of large business organisations induced an explosion of office work. For example, the lowest, General Division of the Commonwealth Public Service expanded by 300 per cent from 1905 to 1922, from 7000 to almost 18000 employees (Deacon, 1982b: 240–1). It became clear to employers that there was no advantage in employing men. Their training (and 'nature') fitted them no better for using the new techniques, and women's labour could be bought more cheaply. It became clear to male employees that there was no advantage to be gained by starting at the bottom, unless they could move upward by promotion quickly.

Management experts rationalised the work processes of the expanding clerical sector. Routine work was divorced from managerial work. A career structure was built into the managerial sector to encourage the required degree of incentive, discretion, trust and company or service loyalty. Careful selection procedures, specialised training, and a clear promotion ladder were instituted. From routine work there was no way ahead; it was a dead end. It was repetitive work, poorly paid, and of low status. A high turnover of workers was not a disadvantage and, in fact, helped prevent morale problems and inefficiency (Doherty, 1980; Deacon, 1982b).

Such work specialisation in the name of efficiency was not only elitist or meritocratic. Management science was a gendered ideology. Efficiency meant, in part, male superiority, and was premised on masculine assumptions: men wouldn't work for a woman boss, nor would a woman want, or be capable of exercising, command over men. By and large, therefore, women were not only herded into the routine work but were actively discriminated against, prevented from putting a foot on the meritocratic ladder to management. Men were encouraged to see office work as a managerial career by training programmes, promotion prospects, better wages and conditions, and an opportunity to treat women as subordinates. Women, on the other hand, were denied training, refused promotion and, in most offices and public services, sacked on marriage. For example, within the Commonwealth Public

Service, women were excluded from appointment examinations until 1949, and the marriage bar was not lifted till 1966. In the New South Wales Public Service in 1983, although approximately equal numbers of women and men were employed, 59 per cent of women had temporary status, compared with only 19 per cent of men (Albury et al., 1983). In the private sector, a number of studies of executive salaries have revealed exceptionally few women in high positions (Women's Bureau, 1974:101–2).

Women's work in offices, at the bottom of the hierarchy, was organised in ways similar to the automated factory's assembly line, but with enough difference to maintain the ideology of respectability. Their work on typewriters and office machines was equally manual, but industrial psychology inculcated a differential between clerical and process work, a differential sufficient to maintain a female workforce docile in its exploitation (Doherty, 1980; Deacon, 1982b; cf. Young, 1975; Benét, 1972).

Through refinement of the gender order's processes in the economy, management experts reformulated part of the meaning of femininity. According to this gender ideology, office work was the best sort of waged work for a good woman, enhancing her natural attributes of docility and respectability, her natural aptitude for boring, repetitive work, and her natural subordination and willingness to serve men.

Consumption managers

The redefinition of femininity by scientific managers in production and administration was augmented by the work of consumption managers. A consequence of the reorganisation in the first two fields was the possibility of the mass production of commodities. The task of the consumption experts was to create an equally expanding mass market of consumers. Such experts were occupied in two main fields: marketing and advertising. Their target population in both areas was women.

Marketing

Over the century, marketing experts changed the physical, temporal and monetary dimensions of consumption, creating the modern meaning of shopping, which came to be a pre-eminently feminine activity. Before the 1890s, shopping in Australia had been largely decentralised through local general stores, with some specialist shops in urban centres where custom was sufficient to support them. Both sorts of shop were generally run by family groups, and sold unbranded goods, some of which were made on the premises or locally. Such small shops continued on well into the twentieth century, but catered for a changing and decreasing clientele.

In the cities, from the 1880s, the first of the marketing experts' creations appeared as emporia or department stores, selling a wide variety of goods, store manufactured as well as imported and locally made (Wolfers, 1980, 19–22). The ideal of scientific selling was the complement of scientific management, and similar principles were employed in the same name of efficiency. Management was centralised and removed from the shop floor. Division of labour among shop employees and segmentation of the sales process were instituted. Gender polarities and priorities were renegotiated, with women employees consistently relegated to the more routine, lower status and poorer paid positions as sales work become more fragmented (MacCulloch, 1980:168–72).

Competition between department stores was intense in the years around the first world war, and pressure on them increased in the 1920s with the establishment of chain stores. This latter form of marketing involved a centralised wholesale purchasing section and decentralised retail outlets from which goods were sold cheaply by workers who had even less knowledge and involvement in the whole selling process, and were paid less, than their counterparts in the emporia. The next change in physical shopping amenities was the supermarket complex, built from the late 1950s. Labour was rationalised in supermarkets to a high degree. The customer now performed many of the tasks once offered as services by the retailer, and the employees were reduced to cashier operators and goods handlers (cf. Weinbaum & Bridges, 1976:93–4).

As well as changing the physical nature of retail outlets, marketing experts also set out to change the experience of consumption. During the competitive interwar years, shopping in department stores was made into a social occasion, attracting customers, especially women, not simply by the availability and cheapness of needed goods, but by entertainment—theatre, exhibitions, concerts—and by the promise of glamour and the aura of sophistication (Wolfers, 1980:21–5). 'Going to town to shop' became a social event, a day's outing in one's best clothes. Further, the experts attempted to change customers' relation to money, from hoarders to spenders. Saving up to buy something became only one, and the least attractive, option. Varieties of financial arrangement for delayed payment were invented by consumption experts to encourage immediate purchase and consumption. The provision of such credit—time payment, lay-by, C.O.D., hire purchase, credit card, bankcard—all altered the individual's sense of budgetary constraint and the virtue of delayed gratification. For marketing success, the customer had to be lured into one sort of shop rather than another, and be prepared to buy more than she might immediately have money to pay for (as long as she would eventually honour her debt, with interest). Competition between the various retail outlets was extreme throughout the century, with the price of failure bankruptcy or takeover.

Having got the customer into the shop, the marketing expert's next task was to encourage her to buy as much as possible, whether she had intended to or not. Art and psychology were plundered to find what was attractive, what stimulated desire, what was the key to the customer's purse, what was irresistible to small children and within their grasp while their parent was looking away. The placement of goods in a store, their arrangement and their individual packaging all became the province of the marketing experts. Their concern was with the relationship between customers and commodities at the point of purchase, and in the preparation of the commodities for that meeting.

Advertising

If the marketing expert thus played best man to the commodities, then the advertising experts played the bridesmaid to the customer, getting her ready and willing to consummate/consume. Initially, advertising was a simple matter of notifying potential customers in a certain neighbourhood of the availability of particular goods or services. This was a situation of usually chronic undersupply. Once mass production was underway, however, both locally and overseas, it was underdemand (or overproduction) that became the problem for capitalists. By another mixture of art and psychology, competing advertisers sought to stimulate the customer's desire at three levels: the desire to buy anything at all—a consumer mentality; the desire for a particular type of commodity to answer a specific need; and the desire for a particular brand of that type of commodity that would fill the need best. By the late twentieth century, there was considerable validity in the claim that the production of some commodities preceded either a use or a need or a desire for them, and that the task of advertising experts was to fashion that desire in the individual and thereby create a new market.

The new professionals' first principle of division and specialisation came into play here. The mass of consumers was broken down into ever proliferating subgroups who were linked together through largely specious common personal attributes and interpersonal relations: all those with bad breath, with dirty clothes, with the desire to appear sophisticated; all those who were brides, or school children, or young macho men (Stephen, 1981:92–4; Pringle, 1981:26–30). Maintenance and elaboration of the basic social distinction between femininity and masculinity was thus crucial to the advertising experts. It was a distinction from which all others flowed. Each woman's desire to be truly feminine, each man's to be truly masculine, could be turned to the advantage of each product that promised such fulfilment: brand Q margarine makes you the best mother; brand G car adds the finishing touches to your playboy masculinity.

Analysis of how and why and if advertising worked is a minefield of conflicting argument, as is its specific relation to the construction of femininity. Indeed, the pervasiveness of advertising throughout modern Australian society makes it most unlikely that there could be any satisfactory single explanation of its operation. What is clear, however, is that saturation advertising through every mode of communication since the second world war has created 'consumers' as a category of people who have never existed before (cf. Ewen, 1976). As specific needs or desires came to be identified by individuals, they increasingly sought to meet them by buying commodities (including services). Whereas, at the beginning of the century, children played goodies and baddies with little more than sticks and stones, by the 1980s full wardrobes and toy weapons copied from film and television programmes were demanded. Similarly, in the 1890s, unhappiness was answered with rest and comfort and perhaps a priest; by the 1980s it was assuaged by buying psychotropic drugs, therapeutic counselling, or merely, perhaps, 'going out to buy a new dress to make yourself feel better'.

Beyond engaging with all the other processes of the economy to turn the whole population into consumers, the advertising experts also singled out women as the actual agents of consumption. Women shopped not only for themselves but for their families, buying more than 80 per cent of domestic goods sold in the market (Pringle, 1981:20). Woman became the family shopper, mediator between individual desire and family budget, caught between the social meanings of consumption and economic reality. The myriad aspects of femininity were the building blocks with which the advertising experts played.

Managers of personal life

The final group of new professionals was less directly concerned with the management of social relations in the economic sphere. They constituted a heterogeneous group, which eventually came to be known as the helping professions. It is more accurate to call them the regulatory experts. Their common focus was the family and the personal life of individuals within it. Their task was the adjustment of individual and family behaviour to the ideological standards of society. Those standards were discussed in the previous chapter. Here, I am looking at the variety of agents who put them into practice. The desired effect of the regulatory experts' intervention into family life was 'harmony': the individual would benefit from the peace of mind that comes with conformity; society, or the state, would benefit from the quelling of collective rebellion that comes from the translation of social injustice into individual problems.

Regulatory experts worked in the fields of education, health and welfare. These were all fields that had begun emerging, in their substantially modern form, through the activities of the population reformers, discussed in chapter 5. For example, from the public-health movement alone came the need for sanitary and pure-food inspectors, nutritionists, health and quarantine officers, nurse inspectors, statisticians and registrars of vital statistics, town planners, building inspectors, and the ubiquitous welfare or social workers.

Before the 1890s, the main component of the gender order's definition of the good woman was as wife. The husband was head of household, and she was his helpmate. His authority was paramount in law; he represented the family in all its external dealings. The internal dynamics of the family were the wife's concern, free from all outside considerations except as mediated through her husband. (This was an ideal prescription, of course, not to be confused with reality). With the strengthening of the perception of social crisis in the 1890s, discussed in the previous chapter, these internal family dynamics suddenly came under scrutiny by the state, its agents, and population moralists. For the first time, the wife's position became a public affair. Any perceived failure or breakdown of the family—especially the working-class family—was her responsibility. She was exhorted to make the home attractive, to lure her husband back from his socially disruptive activities in the pub. She was enjoined to encourage him in diligent and devoted breadwinning, and was denied the possibility of sharing that task with him.

In the campaigns to remedy the turn-of-the-century crisis in its many manifestations, a long-term perspective came to predominate. Many of the reformers accepted one sense or another of the evolutionist argument, and through it they were directed to look to future generations. The focus of public concern shifted from the working man and his family, to the relationship between husband and wife, to the wife herself, and finally settled on woman as mother. Mother, the public authorities and moralists determined, was the heart of the family and hence the target for reformist intervention. Through the mother's relation to her children and to their father, the whole group could be influenced and regulated.

Between 1900 and 1930, a competitive hierarchy of regulatory officials emerged to direct the processes and gender relations of mothering. Private medical practitioners established themselves at the top of the system, setting standards of maternal behaviour according to the medical model which established the patient-client as essentially ignorant and passive, and the doctor-regulator as scientific and humane (Clark, 1974:34; Parsons, 1952:436–47). Beyond this, doctors were only marginally involved in the actual behaviour of mothers (Thame, 1974:226). Suggesting, imposing and policing these general standards, and a host of more particular ones, was an army of state and volunteer regulatory agents. The following discussion elaborates upon the outline of the infant welfare movement in chapter 5.

Parents had to notify a registrar of all births. This provided a list for the home-visiting nurse-inspector. As well, or alternatively, the mother would be contacted to bring her baby to the mothercraft nurses at the local baby clinic. Although ostensibly run by voluntary organisations, such clinics were subsidised by state authorities from the 1920s. The purpose of such nurse–mother contact was to advise the mother on the best way of mothering. Here she was taught bureaucratically devised medical standards of infant feeding and the signs of ill-health and abnormality ('how much weight has baby gained this week?'). She was informed on the acceptable standards of parent–child interaction (under Truby King's theories in the 1910s and 1920s, mother should never pick up the child if it could be helped, while under the regime of Benjamin Spock in the 1950s, she was directed to enjoy playing). She was drilled in high standards of cleanliness—a standard which dove-tailed neatly into the enormous advertising campaign for soap in the interwar years, resulting in an increase in annual Australian soap consumption of three pounds per head in the 1920s (Stephen, 1981:90; cf. Newson & Newson, 1974:53–82, Mechling, 1975:44–63; Gordon, 1968:578–83).

As the child grew, other officials kept an eye out for maladjustment or deviation from expert standards. Welfare officers could be called in if neighbours or police reported neglect of an infant or child, while in the 1970s family violence emerged as a public issue and child abuse brought down regulatory state intervention (O'Donnell & Craney, 1982:176–85). At the age of five or six, the child was compelled by law to be enrolled at school for the next nine or more years, during which time her or his teachers were expected to act upon or report any apparent family malfunctioning. From the 1930s, the teacher's role was complemented and extended by the employment of child guidance experts and, in the 1970s, of school counsellors. Should the child not attend school, truant officers were employed to insist that she or he did, backed up by punitive sanctions against both child and family. If the child was caught doing something or being somewhere that con-travened the experts' standards, she or he could end up in the hands of a penal or parole officer, a social worker, psychologist, or psychiatrist. Usually, the family would be accused of some complicity in the child's deviance and also punished or placed under the surveillance of some regulatory official. The child and family were thus kept under scrutiny from the day of birth (and often earlier). Good mothering came to be defined negatively as meeting the approval of all the regulatory officials involved in family personal life to the extent that such officials need not intervene directly in family relations.

In the decades after the second world war, this group of regulatory experts expanded dramatically in size. They became, in particular, the agents of the welfare state, promising the state's protection to all citizens, claiming that all sources of structural inequality would be abolished. The standards of personal life that they had imposed and extolled in the prewar years had become widely diffused and accepted. Or rather, not necessarily the specific standards as such, but the experts' right to establish them was accepted. Their expertise and status were secure (cf. Larson, 1977).

As distinct from the production and consumption experts, the regulatory experts were disproportionately employed by state authorities rather than private enterprise. This also distinguished them from the old professionals who generally engaged in private practice. However, even doctors and lawyers tended to become state employees, or combine state service with private practice, when they embarked upon work that was more directly regulatory of individual behaviour as, for example, school doctors, court psychiatrists, community health practitioners, legal-aid lawyers. The significance of this employment status lay in its power to camouflage the manipulative aspect of the experts' activity under the guise of helping.

Professionals were generally presumed to look out for the interests of those who paid them. (Whether this presumption was correct or not is not the issue here.) Thus, a doctor in private practice was presumed to be dedicated to the patient's well-being. A doctor employed by a corporation was generally accepted as being on the corporation's side when the issue arose of a worker's compensation for ill-health caused by occupation. When a doctor was employed by the state, however, a confused set of ideological presumptions came into play. Such a doctor was the tax-payers' servant; was part of an uncaring bureaucratic machine; was provided by a benevolent body in the interests of each individual and of the whole society (both sets of interests were presumed to coincide). Central to most of these views was some notion of the state being neutral in the power dynamics of the society, especially the dynamics of class, gender and race.

The general social understanding of the state's neutrality was reinforced by the occupational ideologies of the regulatory professions, which proclaimed their work to be scientific, universalistic and value-free; or, rather, not quite value-free because dedicated to the ideals of rationality and efficiency, defined in some combination of harmony, consensus and progress. Regulatory officials employed by the state thus saw themselves, and were generally seen by their clients, as objective, scientific representatives of an organic, potentially conflict-free society. As a consequence, they could and did, by and large, convincingly present all aspects of non-conformity—from illness to unhappiness to unemployment—as individual problems, caused either by faulty personality or unfortunate accident.

Feelings, thoughts and behaviour that did not fit with the model of normality held by the particular profession were judged as individual sickness rather than signs of resistance to the oppressiveness of that normality. The expert was thus granted legitimacy to single out any 'deviant' individual and persuade or coerce her or him into conformity with a specific ideal. Clearly, here was a group with direct interest in the construction of femininity and its translation into practice by the women of Australia. Unfortunately, but as usual, the various professional groups held somewhat different standards of such female normality or femininity, many of which did not fit with each other and were also internally inconsistent. Moreover, each profession tended to see the others as competitors, and conflict could and did arise not merely over theoretical questions of best method of adjustment, but also over the actual bodies of those to be adjusted.

Education and status

Whether they worked in production, administration, consumption or personal life, the task of all these experts was the management and mediation of social relations. They monitored and directed the processes of the economic and gender orders. They inserted themselves and their skills between workers and bosses, between consumers and the market, between social groups and the state, between individuals and their own sense of inadequacy. Increasingly, they intervened in all areas of human life. Over the century, they built up elaborate networks of counselling, guidance, advice, instruction, management, supervision and restraint. Sometimes their skills were imposed—as with scientific management programmes or truancy procedures. Sometimes they were invited—as in sexual harassment cases or individual therapy. Their expertise was a commodity, sold in the marketplace to the state, to business and to individuals.

Amid their great diversity, these new professionals were united by one common thing. Their expertise was derived, in the first place, from education, and they all saw themselves as skilled mental workers, not manual. (The ideological mystification of this view is, however, clear: the advertising copywriter and the science teacher use their hands as much as the welder and packager, the brain surgeon as much as the electronics component assembly worker.) Such an ideological view meant that education was a fundamental criterion of self and social worth for these experts. The rapid expansion in the size of this caste of experts from the 1940s can thus be seen as closely related to the

postwar economic boom and the education explosion.
In the ten years from 1945 to 1955, the number of university under-graduates almost doubled to over 30 000. In the next ten years, the number leaped to 83 000 (Crowley, 1973, II:210). Various types of state subsidy made this expansion possible. Although dispro-portionately fewer than men, the number of female undergraduates increased substantially. From 1918 to 1950, it has been estimated that only about 20 per cent of those enrolled in universities were women; by 1979, 42 per cent of all bachelor degree students were female (Encel and others, 1974:192; ABS, 1981:263).

In the postwar years, these educated women poured into the market-place as new professional workers. However, one of the results of this rapid expansion was that education became devalued. When degrees were in short supply, having one meant that one was virtually assured of a good professional job and acceptance into the best circles. When, however, degrees became more common, from the 1950s, room at the top did not expand correspondingly, and many middle-level profession-als were sent away from its doors with no place to go. Over time, they created their own place.

The ideology of the old professions—claiming for them esoteric knowledge, disinterested and monopolistic use of that knowledge, and independence from both state and clients—had begun to come into contradiction with the working conditions of the new professionals as salaried employees. Their knowledge was shared by many. Their disin-terest and independence was compromised by their employers' in-terests (Larson, 1977:178–244).

Most of the new professionals were not themselves in control of the processes within which they worked. At the simplest level, they per-formed the tasks set for them by their superiors in the workplace. More significantly, the guidelines, the occupational ideology, the very defini-tion and meaning of their work was not under their control but had been established, over time, by the collective processes of the upper echelons of each profession. To be an advertising expert, or a social worker, or an industrial psychologist, was to be trained to adhere to the discipline established by those professional superiors. Moreover, be-cause one was an expert of one kind did not prevent one from being under the supervision of other experts. The industrial psychologist shopped; the advertising expert had to register her child's birth and send it to school; the social worker had to fill in the same forms for workers' compensation as everyone else.

Under such conditions, the ethic of professionalism began to crack because it could not deliver the rewards it promised to its adherents. The upper ranks of each profession, inevitably male, remained secure and tried to maintain discipline. Many of the lower ranks, increasingly female, became insubordinate. Professional associations regrouped as industrial labour organisations, rather than the privileged social clubs they had been between the wars (Williams, 1968; Rawson, 1982). From the 1960s, some professional groups even engaged in occasional strike action in pursuit of their economic interests. Some teachers, nurses and doctors, once the most fervent believers in the ideology of professional service and the respectability of mental workers, came to act in ways similar to manual workers (Connell & Irving, 1980:300–1; Ryan & Prendergast, 1982).

Apart from their upper ranks, the new professions were disproportionately female occupations. With the development of industrial organisation within the professions, the claims of these women workers began to be heard and acknowledged. On the crucial issue of equal pay, the 1930s campaign was revived and the first stage won by the New South Wales Teachers' Federation in 1959 (Ryan & Conlon, 1975:146–7). In the next two decades, women in the professions and the white-collar unions began to stretch the old masculine definitions of what constituted industrial matters. Beyond wages and work conditions were issues of discrimination, childcare, maternity leave, sexual harassment, contraception and abortion. These issues were of concern to all women workers, and had been raised periodically by various women's groups and committees. Within the increasing organisation of professional workers and growing strength of women in all unions, a concerted campaign was launched under the banner of the working Women's Charter. The demand for gender equality in the economy at last took its place alongside the traditional demand for class equality (Hargreaves, 1982).

The new professionals and femininity

The self-interest of professional workers went beyond these industrial matters, however broadly defined. In the postwar decades, the new professionals, both women and men, saw themselves as the architects, or at least the overseers, of the welfare state, and as harbingers of universal affluence. The maintenance of the welfare and affluent society was in their self-interest. In the heyday of that society, in the 1950s and early 1960s, the upper ranks of the new professions developed new and self-aggrandising ideologies. They advanced political theories that proclaimed the end of ideology, economic theories that extolled the virtues of technocratic rationality, welfare theories that declared structural inequality abolished. From among the lower ranks, however, some murmurings of dissent were heard in the late 1950s. They were becoming slowly aware of the underbelly of the lucky country (Horne, 1964). They began to hear the protests of the dispossessed minorities. Their first achievement was the rediscovery of poverty (Higgins, 1978;

Roc, 1976: 316–22; Kewley, 1973:384–93). As with all discovery and exploration, the natives knew about it all the time; the credulous imperialists came late.

The newly audible minorities of the 1960s and 1970s—the poor, Aborigines, youth, non-British migrants, the disabled, the aged—were groups whose long-standing and increasing resistance and demands were taken up by the new professionals. Their needs and demands were guided through the social information and lobbying systems by these young experts, eventually re-emerging as promises from one or other of the political parties, as policies by governments, and finally as programmes run by professionals. (This, at least, was the successful process. Many desired reforms became lost in the machinery.) Central to the professional and public attention given to the whole package of demands for social justice was the issue of women. Women composed at least half of all disadvantaged groups, substantially more in the case of the poor. Women were also disproportionately employed in the welfare sector, and their livelihood depended upon their clients' claims being met. Increased government spending on health care was good for the sick, and better for nurses and doctors. Likewise, government funding for programmes to alleviate poverty may have aided the poor and certainly provided more employment for social workers, economists, statisticians and clerks.

This is not to say, by any means, that such professional workers were solely motivated by economic self-interest. Much of their concern was genuine humanitarian, political or professional outrage against social injustice and inequality. As well, there was no clear-cut line between providers and recipients of services in many cases, especially for women. The nurse needed childcare in order to work, so too did the migrant factory worker. The social worker needed contraceptive advice, as did the Aboriginal teenager. The right of married women to work and to obtain maternity leave was not specific to class.

Beyond and as important as the fact that many recipients and providers of professional expertise were women, concern with the issues of women and social justice was generated in the late 1960s from the very logic of the work of the new professionals. The new professionals were organisers of economic life and managers of ideology. They had overseen the expansion of the marketplace and the development of the ideology of permissive consumerism. In all their operations, gender differentiation had been a central principle, and women had been their special target. In other words, the content and method of their work made women visible as a group, instead of invisibly incorporated in the false universality of masculinity. The very fact that the processes of the gender order could be seen to be consciously manipulated—on the shop floor, in marketing strategies, in welfare provision—meant that the gender order itself could at last be understood as a social, not natural, system. The fact that the meaning of femininity could be seen in the process of construction—in redefinitions of women's work, in the fantasies of advertising, in the demise of anachronistic discriminations and the creation of new ones—meant that not only the naturalness of women's subordination and inferiority, but the whole process of such construction itself could be challenged.

Part III

Living the Impossibility of Femininity

In PART II, I have been weaving a pattern of the main social forces which gave femininity its changing meanings in twentieth-century Australia. The expansion of the capitalist marketplace, the rise of an ideology of population and its transition into one of permissive consumerism, the rise of the new managers: the detail of these phenomena is both foreground and background to the meaning of woman. Women have been both agents and subjects of the changes.

In the following section, I look more closely at the process of becoming a woman in twentieth-century Australia. Here I introduce the captured biographies of the women of Glenside Hospital in order to provide an individual focus to the preceding history of femininity. This section retraces some of the points made so far, concentrating less on the general patterns themselves and more on their effects in individual lives. The women of Glenside Hospital were mad, their life stories often extreme. They are not representative of women in general. But from their lives we can pick out some of the contradictions of the gender order that affect us all. Their failures in the pursuit of femininity are writ large. But they point to the inevitability of some such failure in all our lives because of the idealised nature of femininity and its internal contradictions.

7

Sexuality

*I*n the late 1970s, a new feminist slogan appeared on the walls of Australian cities: 'a woman without a man is like a fish without a bicycle'. It was brave graffiti, not only because it was long, but because it repudiated the feminine condition. It denied the naturalness of the symbiosis or complementarity of man and woman; it asserted woman's independence. It denied the hegemonic view that a woman without a man was an anomaly; it challenged the compulsory heterosexuality of the ideal of femininity (Rich, 1980).

The gender ideology that was in process of constructing modern femininity from the 1890s throughout the twentieth century held as its unchanging core the belief that it was woman's sexuality that marked her as different from man. The ideology was flexible as a belief system: one could believe that the consequence of such sexual difference was the inferiority of woman to man, or their complementarity, or—rarely—the superiority of woman to man. It was, however, rigid as a system of behaviour. The maintenance of the specific Australian gender order, the relations among and between women and men, demanded that woman's sexuality must be severely limited. The gender ideology allowed only one legitimate expression of feminine sexuality: in heterosexual, monogamous marriage.

From the 1890s, this standard became explicit and inflexible. It was regressively embodied in the legislation and regulations of the state, in the morality of religion, and in the science of medicine. The state was concerned to create and shore up a particular vision of the family as the chief agent of individual discipline and welfare; the churches concentrated upon regulation of fertility; and medicine became fascinated with sexual practices. Between them, they established a regime of great severity which lasted virtually unchallenged until the 1960s. From that decade there began a gradual loosening of the impossibly tight bonds regulating the expression of feminine sexuality. The old populationist mentality was challenged by permissive consumerism and a New Left (involving libertarians, the counter-culture, and the student, women's and gay movements). In consequence, women's sexuality became the cause of ideological battle, and women's bodies became the battlefield, as the old populationists regrouped themselves as a New Right (Sawer, 1982; cf. Gordon & Hunter, 1978). Campaigns for and against a host of issues turned women's sexuality from a natural essence into a political subject within the gender ideology: censorship and pornography, prostitution, divorce, contraception, abortion, lesbianism, sex education, masturbation, orgasm, sadomasochism, rape, wife battering, incest, nude swimming, all came out of the secrecy of the confessional and on to the pages of glossy magazines and popular radio and television shows. The terms of the debate were changed, and the boundaries of sexual behaviour permitted to women were widened. Nonetheless, the combination of the three ideals of heterosexuality, legality and monogamy (in that order of priority), still remained at the centre of the feminine ideal. Throughout the century, feminine sexuality and marriage remained virtually synonymous.

This confinement of sexuality into marriage as the legal, permanent and exclusive commitment of a woman and a man to each other, was extolled by every Australian social agency. On this, and perhaps this alone, was there universal agreement. Various groups might dispute about whom or when it was appropriate to marry, about the legitimacy of particular sexual acts, about the number or the rearing of children, about the forms of family life. But the first step, marriage, was deemed an essential part of every truly feminine woman's life plan. And most women agreed. The single state became progressively less popular as the century rolled on, marriage becoming an almost universal experience. (Approximately 15 per cent of women born in the 1880s–1890s never married, whereas less than 5 per cent of women born after 1930 remained single (ABS, 1980a:21; Ruzicka & Caldwell, 1977:34, 204).) Moreover, the unpopularity of the single state was such that it was abandoned at progressively earlier ages. (The average age of women at their first marriage fell from 24 years at the turn of the century to 21 years in the 1970s (Krupinski, 1978:9; McDonald, 1974:140).) There were exceptions, but for every girl child born in Australia in the twentieth century, marriage was both a desire and an expectation, and to miss out on it led to some sense of failure to be suffered or brazened out or compensated for.

Marriage, however, was not only a good to be devoutly wished by each individual woman. It was more importantly the cornerstone of femininity. Even if an individual woman did not desire marriage, she must come to accept it as a necessity. Further, although an individual might once have desired marriage, having experienced it she might wish to leave it. She must then be persuaded either to stay in the old or to find a new marriage. Walls of necessity were built around the institution of marriage and the rest of the landscape was blasted so that no feminine living could be had from it.

The three elements of feminine sexuality expressed in marriage—heterosexuality, monogamy and legality—provided the standards against which women's failure to achieve the ideal were measured. The extremity of failure in the dimension of heterosexuality was lesbianism. The definition and punishment of this failure was left largely in the hands of the medical profession. The opposite of monogamy was prostitution, dealt with by law, which also, with religion, policed legitimate marriage and its dereliction—divorce and irregular unions.

Heterosexuality

From the middle of the nineteenth century in the western world, an extraordinary fascination with sexuality emerged, taking a wide variety of forms. Sexuality became endowed with new meanings and new powers that needed to be harnessed and controlled by those in authority (Foucault, 1979). The means by which this appropriation of control was attempted was science, as defined and ordered by the medical profession. Medicine at the time was just emerging victorious from the struggle with religion over the right to interpret, correct and control personal behaviour. Divine will was ousted by the laws of science; wickedness became illness; morality emerged as medical normality (Foucault, 1967:270). That is, in matters of personal behaviour, social control came to be exercised under the direction of a new discipline with a new ideology. Having appropriated the field, medicine sought to harness the power and truth of sexuality as a 'cause of any and everything' (Foucault, 1979:65). Medicine proclaimed monogamous heterosexuality to be the scientific standard of normality (without any prior questioning or investigation), then began to categorise, theorise and attempt to cure all forms of feelings, thoughts and relationships that did not conform. In the process were born the modern meanings of 'normal' feminine and masculine sexuality, with their accompanying failures: sexual deviance, perversion and pathology.

In other words, the medical profession fed its scientific knowledge into pre-existing models of social behaviour and used it to confirm both the models and its own power. More rigorously than had ever occurred before, medicine named and codified sexuality and gender behaviour into two mutually exclusive categories, and deemed any variation sick. But the categories of femininity and masculinity were not equivalent. Rather, superior normality, the status as 'adult,' was reserved for heterosexual men, and a considerably inferior normality was attached to femininity. Man (the masculine gender) was and is still the measure.

Barbara Ehrenreich and Deidre English have argued that, with the rise of the medical profession in the late nineteenth and early twentieth centuries, the theories which guided doctors' practice 'held that woman's *normal* state was to be sick. This was not advanced as an empirical observation, but as physiological fact. Medicine had "discovered" that female functions were inherently pathological' (1979:99). Since that time, while medicine might have toned down its notion of 'femininity as a disease', many researchers have shown that a patient's gender significantly affects the diagnosis and treatment they get from doctors (Roberts, 1981:10). Studies since the 1970s have revealed that practitioners of psychological medicine are especially prejudiced, considering normal women as distinctly inferior to normal men. Psychoanalyst Lester A. Gelb lists the characteristic view in his profession:

> Psychoanalysts have contributed to the view of women as weak, inferior, passive, fragile, soft, vacillating, dependent, unreliable, intuitive rather than rational, castrated, and handicapped. Men have been polarized as aggressive, controlling, strong, superior, proud, independent, venturesome, competitive, hard, and athletic. (1973:367)

A series of surveys undertaken by psychologist I.K. Broverman and her co-workers came up with similar results. Their project revealed, firstly, that psychologists held a double standard of health and normality according to gender which was not more scientific but was identical with that held by 'the man in the street'. Secondly, they showed that the characteristics both groups attributed to a normal woman identified her as less capable than a normal man. Thirdly, their studies indicated that, while the masculine ideal was different from the feminine ideal, it was the same as the ideal for the normal healthy adult. Further, these masculine, adult characteristics were believed to be undesirable in women. In other words, not only is masculinity the norm, but it can only be achieved in the male body (Fransella & Frost, 1977: 41–54, 186–7; Gatens, 1983. 154). The list of attributes of a healthy woman form a powerful negative assessment of women:

> Clinicians are far more likely to suggest that healthy women differ from healthy men by being more submissive, less independent, less adventurous, more easily influenced, less aggressive, less competitive, more excitable in minor crises, having their feelings more easily hurt, being more emotional, more conceited about their appearance, less objective and disliking math and science. This constellation seems a most unusual way of describing any mature, healthy individual. (Broverman and others, 1970:4–5).

The significance of these various lists of attributes defining the normal woman lies in the extreme conflict that they create for women. If a woman conforms to the prescribed behaviour, she is by definition inferior when compared to the universal adult (that is, male) standard. Should she challenge this inferiority and exhibit the positive characteristics considered desirable for a competent, mature adult (man), she places her femininity in jeopardy.

It is here that the category 'lesbian' becomes relevant. In both popular and scientific usage, the word or its numerous derogatory synonyms was and is used to describe a 'mannish' woman: not feminine in appearance, in temperament or in behaviour. For the woman who displays independence, competes with men in their own sphere, succeeds, rejects subordination to the wishes of men, is not married and refuses to see this as failure, declines gratuitous sexual advances from men (including her husband), wears trousers—the list is endless and motley—the consequence is to be labelled 'unfeminine' and eventually 'lesbian'. As the 1974 New York Radicalesbian pamphlet, 'Woman-Identified-Woman', declared,

> Lesbian is the word, the condition that holds women in line. When a woman hears this word tossed her way, she knows she is stepping out of line. She knows that she has crossed the terrible boundary of her sex role. She recoils, she protests, she reshapes her actions to gain approval. Lesbian is a label invented by the Man to throw at any woman who dares to be his equal, who dares to challenge his prerogatives (including that of all women as part of the exchange medium among men), who dares to assert the primacy of her own needs.

Within medical practice, from the end of the nineteenth century, lesbianism was scientifically categorised as a sexual deviation—a mental disorder. Nonetheless, it was rarely mentioned by the psychiatrists of Glenside Hospital. Even on these rare occasions, the term was not used as a major category of diagnosis but as a behavioural symptom of broader mental disorder. In these instances, lesbianism was interpreted by psychiatrists to mean not positive and loving relationships with women, nor sexual object choice of women, but rather, negative relationships with men, most particularly male psychiatrists. May Carter, who was sixty seven and married when admitted, did not like her male doctor:

> She is negativistic and hostile in the extreme and absolutely refuses to allow me to come near her...She always gets up and walks away whenever I go around saying good morning to the patients. She seems unduly aggressive towards men (doesn't mind the nurses at all) suggesting that there may be an unconscious homosexual basis for her psychosis.

This, however, was in 1955. There were six doctors for 1700 patients, and all the doctors were male. May's doctor did not distinguish between himself as an authority figure and as a man, so he could not imagine that she might have been reacting against his institutional power over her, not his personal masculinity. Instead, her refusal to accept her position of subservience as a woman and as a patient meant yet another sign of her madness.

The ideological use of the designation lesbian is similarly revealed in Katie Allen's casenotes. She was admitted to a psychiatric institution in 1959, suffering from depression. While there, she 'had the added complication of forming an attachment with an ex-patient'. (She later had 'tormenting dreams about...ex-boyfriend'.) She was transferred to Glenside Hospital where she stayed for about a month and a half. By this stage in the notes and, indeed, throughout their whole length covering eight years of out-patient treatment, there is no mention of Katie having any close association with women. Nonetheless, the label lesbian was suggested by her psychiatrists because of her hostility towards her husband: 'He feels his wife is in part repelled somewhat by sexual intercourse yet she "wants" him but seems to lose interest? Latent Homosexuality.' The medical reaction was an instant diagnosis of disease. That Katie's 'repulsion' might have been a normal and rational response to an unpleasant situation was not contemplated. Katie's own explanation was not recorded for some years (after two miscarriages, indicating at least some continuing heterosexual activity):

Sex life—'only one climax in my married life, but that is not his fault, he's been very patient in that respect' [1966]...Still finds is frigid with husband, feels it may have started when she was working, was tired and husband would not help—resented this. [1967]

In this case, lesbianism was clearly a scientific label applied to a moral judgment. It was a derogatory label to indicate Katie's lapsed femininity through her failure to live up to a masculine standard of marital intercourse.

Lesbian, then, is an epithet used to keep women complying with the norms of femininity. But what of the 'real' lesbian, the female homosexual, the woman who disobeys the gender ideology's compulsion to heterosexuality, the woman who cares for, loves, has sexual relations with other women? 'The Lesbian is one of the least known members of our culture. Less is known about her—and less accurately—than about the Newfoundland dog.' (Abbott & Love, 1973:13) It might truly be said that the only people who know, accurately, anything about lesbianism are those who accept the label, and this self-conscious knowledge has only begun emerging in the last 60 years. Until women began self-consciously identifying themselves as lesbian in the 1920s, and in much greater numbers in the 1970s, 'it is likely that most women with lesbian inclinations fitted inconspicuously into the general world of women' (Weeks, 1981:94; Smith-Rosenberg, 1975). The polarity lesbian/heterosexual was virtually meaningless. There was, rather, a line of continuity between all women (incorporating class differences), based on their common existence in a female world constructed of shared physical and social conditions, and shared subordination (Rich, 1980).

With changes in the meaning of sexuality and gender behaviour in the early years of this century, lesbians became more visible, and required to be understood. Up till then, the little literature that existed about lesbians had been pornographic, written by men for masculine titillation. Medical science took up the challenge, and failed. The literature it produced was sparse, highly contradictory and confused. Emphasis was mainly on male homosexuality, and specifically effeminate homosexuals: those who were judged to have fallen away from or abandoned normal masculinity and seemingly embraced aspects of femininity. Female homosexuality, apart from the 'symptoms' of unfeminine behaviour discussed above, has gone largely unnoticed, or has been tacked on as an afterthought. There is no medical agreement about what lesbianism actually is, how prevalent it is, what causes it, how to treat it, nor, indeed, whether it is curable. The same can be said of female heterosexuality: the profession's failure to understand that phenomenon is at the basis of its failure towards lesbianism. In other words, for doctors, female sexuality in general is an issue of intense moral concern, about which they have very little scientific knowledge. Most of the profession's research and practice has been premised on ideological standards of femininity, thereby blinding it to the reality and variety of women's sexual desires and practices. Only in very recent years has female sexuality been recognised both as qualitatively different from male sexuality and as different from, though affected by, the overt prescriptions of the gender ideology (Brake, 1982). Little of this new knowledge has been accepted by the profession.

As an aspect of female sexuality, lesbianism thus remains a confusing and contentious issue for doctors. The only consensus they have ever reached has been that lesbianism is some sort of illness. (It had to be, since illness was the generic term that established the boundaries within which the medical profession could claim its monopoly.) And even that consensus has broken. In 1972, the Australian and New Zealand College of Psychiatrists declared that it 'strongly condemns community attitudes and laws which discriminate against homosexual behaviour between consenting adults in private' (ANZCP, 1972). A year later the College produced a Clinical Memorandum surveying studies of current psychiatric opinion on the nature of homosexuality, which ranged from the traditional view that it is a neurotic disorder, through to the radical view that it is a normal variant like lefthandedness. They concluded that '[m]any psychiatrists consider that homosexual feelings and behaviour are not necessarily or commonly associated with neurotic symptoms and are compatible with good adjustment and a useful and creative contribution by the individual to society' (ANZCP, 1973). (Despite such liberality, 'many GPs and sections of the professional specialties have retained perspectives not in accord with "official" policy' (Human Relationships, 1977, II:143).)

A major reason for lesbian invisibility and medicine's failure to understand the phenomenon lies in the masculine bias of the gender order. For most male doctors and legislators, as much as for the man in the street, the positive aspects of lesbianism, love between women, were considered insignificant, and sexual relations between women impossible. To them, sexual intercourse by definition required a penis, therefore women must merely comfort and caress each other, perhaps excessively, but still within the understood boundaries of femininity. In terms of this ideology, execration, ridicule or pity were reserved for the woman it classified as a 'true' lesbian; the woman who tried to be a man; who dressed as a man; whose clitoris ('vestigial penis') was abnormally large, or who resorted to a dildo in order to emulate male heterosexual intercourse. Understandably, the numbers of these women were infinitesimal, and were more correctly classifiable medically as female transsexuals, not lesbians. To a large extent however, they were a figment of masculine fantasy. During and after the 1920s, it was this reservoir of masculine prejudice that was tapped and used to attempt the drowning of any self-proclaimed lesbians or of any women at all who sought independence from men within either their public or private lives, and who sought release from adherence to the strictures and failures and subordination of the feminine heterosexual ideal.

The prejudicial consequences of declaring oneself or being suspected of being a lesbian were many. Because lesbianism was formally classified as a mental illness, lesbians could be subjected to medical persecution: incarceration in psychiatric institutions—often against their will; treatment—on the basis of unsound and unproven theories—by a variety of horrific therapies ranging from clitoridectomy through psychosurgery, aversion therapy, hormone therapy, hypno-therapy to psychotherapy (Human Relationships, 1977, III:114; cf. Ehrenreich & English, 1979:111; Weeks, 1981:31) In other areas, wherever discretionary power was granted to others, suspected women were liable to severe discrimination. In terms of employment, lesbians were refused jobs for which they were suitably qualified, or peremptorily dismissed without adequate reason—as if the employers were afraid to utter the word (Human Relationships, 1977, V:108–9). They were especially vulnerable to this treatment in jobs which required security clearances. Both government and private employers claimed to fear the possibility of blackmail. They therefore victimised women believed to be lesbians on the grounds that they were vulnerable to victimisation. In the case of the armed forces, police and institutional officers, the discrimination was even more pronounced. Homosexuality somehow posed an extreme threat to the normality of highly disciplined and hierarchical organisations.

Similarly, lesbians appeared as a threat in jobs that required contact with children, especially teaching. The gender ideology declared that, in the lesbian woman, true femininity, with its fundamental instinct for nurturing the young, was apparently turned unnaturally to the opposite, an instinct for preying on the young. This view also had consequences for child custody. Lesbians tended to be defined as unfit mothers, as placing their children in moral danger. (In the past few years, some few lesbians have been granted custody after savagely fought battles in the Family Court, but usually stringent conditions have been imposed (Lesbian Custody, 1980; Harrison, 1980).) For those lesbians who attempted to live out the ideal of monogamous and permanent coupling, they were denied the legal endorsement, as well as the financial benefits of marriage (superannuation, probate, income tax). In general, they were treated publicly as strangers, unable to claim the status and access of next-of-kin. As well as such specific acts of discrimination, lesbians were also subject to general social revilement, ridicule and physical assault. Although not as well publicised as poofter-bashing, lezzy-baiting and bashing are similarly Australian national sports.

Such acts of discrimination, victimisation and violence against lesbians are the punishment for violation of the norms of femininity. Looked at another way, they are the exorbitant price demanded of women who seek independence from their subordination as women. The effect of defining lesbians as sick, as ostracised deviants, is to deny other women the possibility of viable alternatives. The existence of real lesbians, as exhibits in a human zoo, is useful, though probably not necessary, to this aspect of repressive gender ideology. The probability that rigorous definition is not ideologically necessary is indicated by the fact of the social invisibility of lesbians, and by the absence of clear definitions in the legal codes and medical vocabularies. In both law and medicine, the category 'homosexual' normally excludes consideration of 'female homosexual' and neither that term, nor 'lesbian', has appeared in any Australian legislation. Precision of definition is not important. What does matter is the way in which the gender ideology encourages use of the concept of lesbianism. It establishes a sliding scale of synonymous epithets directed at an enormous range of behaviour that does not comply with the feminine norm of lifelong, legal, exclusive devotion to one man and subservience to all others (cf. Cowie & Lees, 1981). Women's experience of the subordination, of the oppression, of the unequal relations between the sexes is defined as natural and normal, and any expression of opposition is individualised and deemed pathological.

Throughout the twentieth century, the gender ideology has presented lesbianism as the anathematised end of the fall from feminine grace in the dimension of heterosexuality. It also designated stations along the way to indicate to any particular woman that she was going in the wrong direction and hence placing herself in jeopardy. These stations existed in large number throughout adolescence. Two of the major ones were conditions known as tomboy and wallflower. These conditions were permitted, even indulged, in young girls as a 'phase' they were going through. Persistence, however, was a sickness.

By the second half of the twentieth century, adolescence was a clearly identified stage in the lifelong pursuit of femininity (Connell and others, 1975: 214–6). It was a period of transition between being a good girl and a good woman. In early adolescence, the girl was expected to be a member of a small, all-girl group. The next step, after puberty, was participation in a mixed group, within which developed a dating pattern—pairing off with a sequence of boys within the somewhat protective shelter of the group and with the close support of other young women (Connell and others, 1975; cf. McRobbie, 1978). By late adolescence, the group began to break up as the heterosexual pairings became more intense and exclusive. Not to have a boyfriend at this stage generally meant extreme loneliness since seemingly everyone else was paired off. The young women who were in such pairs tended as well to become isolated, cut off from their own female group friends, each one being reduced either to the sole company and support of her man, or to being tacked on to the edge of his peer group.

Adolescence came to be seen as a crucial period of transition to adult femininity, requiring the young woman to pass through a new terrain and time of young, competitive heterosexuality. Throughout this transition, her parents usually remained a strong influence on the girl's behaviour. Most young women lived in their parents' home until marriage (Stephenson, 1970:46; Young, 1980:44). There was little economic possibility of alternatives. Thus, her parents' emotional reactions and moral stance set the broad parameters of each girl's pursuit of femininity (Connell and others, 1975:198–205). Her behaviour and reputation and femininity reflected upon her parents, who were their creators and guardians until such time as they passed on the responsibility to a suitable man, a husband. In other words, the femininity the young girl pursued was not her own, but was a social construct in which many others had an investment.

In the pattern described here, the first sign that a young woman was on the correct path to the acquisition of a husband was for her to find a boyfriend. In this, Fay Johns was a failure. At seventeen, she was scared of men. Her fear of them was such that she became addicted to drugs in order 'to get enough courage to go out'. Over five admissions to Glenside Hospital from 1965 to 1969 she attempted suicide on a number of occasions.

Her over-riding concern is one of being able to meet people and face them without 'being liverish inside'...Fay told me that she realises the reason she takes drugs is because 'outside the hospital, when I'm with other people—like boys—my nostrils flare out and I get self-conscious about this and feel inferior—I've never told a doctor about this before—but that's why I take drugs—when I'm on drugs it doesn't happen' ...She can relax and mix with her own sex quite well, although this is harder with people in authority such as the ward sister. She says she cannot mix with men or boys of any age and cannot relax or think of what to say.

Fay's anxiety distorted her appearance—or so she thought—and physical attractiveness was a crucial element in feminine popularity. (The fear of unpopularity through unattractiveness was the basis of much advertising directed to both female and male teenagers in the postwar years: for products to remove or hide body odour, bad breath, pimples). Fay's anxiety made her tongue-tied. The relatively protected world of childhood, made up of family and small peer group of girls, was being invaded by strangers with whom she had little in common and whose strength and obvious power frightened her into silence.

If we step back from its exaggerated form, what Fay's story represented is the unhappy life of an adolescent wallflower: the desperate desire to be popular counteracted by excessive self-consciousness. Adolescence for girls, even in the best of cases, tends to be a stressful and anxious time. Each girl leaves behind the relative freedom of childhood, where she has picked up and been taught the rudiments of feminine behaviour. Now she must put it all into practice. She must establish her heterosexuality and exercise her charm, that is, get a boyfriend. Involved in this process is the breaking of her childhood self-confidence. Since adult femininity requires the acknowledgement, in personality and behaviour, of inferiority and dependence on males, the teenage girl learns to behave in a more self-effacing manner, to become less confident in her sense of self-worth. Compared with boys, she lacks assurance and self-acceptance. (Connell and others, 1975:38, 67–8). This adolescent depression of self-esteem can go too far, with the consequent creation of a tongue-tied, shy, fearful wallflower. Such a situation is a sign of failure in the young woman's pursuit of femininity. In the transition from girlhood to womanhood, she has got stuck. She is unable to take the first step into the world of strange men that will eventually take her from her father's to her husband's house.

Among the psychiatrists at Glenside Hospital, such inability to take the necessary steps along the path to adult heterosexuality was a sign of mental illness if it continued for too long. Their very definition of feminine normality emphasised that young women should enjoy heterosexual social pleasures. This blatantly ideological position was clearly expressed in the notes of Eve Innes, who was admitted at the age of 24 in 1965. 'To judge by her story...was always schizoid; no boyfriends, no dancing, didn't want to go, etc.' Not only was heterosexuality compulsory; specific cultural manifestations of it were mandatory and must be enjoyed.

Even worse than the girl who got stuck was the girl who refused to move. Such a girl—who would not relinquish her girlhood self-confidence, who did not show an interest in boys (except, perhaps as friends in adventure) who did not cast aside the sexual freedom of childhood and groom herself to feminine attractiveness—was initially labelled as a tomboy. If her refusal persisted, the category shifted in seriousness to suspected lesbianism.

In the case of Joyce Norton, lesbianism was imputed because she had not attempted to make herself physically attractive to men and 'resents authority'. Running through her notes is the theme that to desire to attract men is a sign of feminine normality. That is, the psychiatrists seemed to be applying moral standards of the gender order rather than medical standards of madness when commenting on how a normal woman should look and act:

> Joyce is a dark complexioned girl with pleasant features. She has shiny black-brown hair which is uncut and uncombed. She wears no make-up and partly because of her blue shirt and trousers, has an unfeminine appearance.

This was 1968, and Joyce was only fifteen. Her psychiatrist seemed to be laying down a standard: dresses and make-up were necessary to be feminine, a healthy and good woman. Anything outside this standard was liable to be seen as part of the woman's problem. In Joyce's case, deviation from the standard of feminine appearance put the psychiatrists on the alert for lesbianism: 'Relationship with Nurse Jones?' There was a tone of relief expressed later in the notes: 'Joyce dressed in feminine clothes to attend ward social'; 'a developing young lass with heterosexual feelings'; ' "belle of ball" at ward dance'.

Monogamy

Having acceded to the standard of compulsory heterosexuality, each young woman was still confronted by the two other imperatives of feminine sexuality; monogamy and legal marriage. The extremity of failure in the monogamy test was prostitution, with its way stations of 'a reputation' and promiscuity.

For the adolescent girl, the period before she was safely married was fraught with the danger of 'getting a reputation'. She was required to make herself heterosexually attractive and pleasant to the group of appropriate men among whom she was eventually expected to find a husband. The complex standards of femininity ordained that she must not be fearful of men but, on the other hand, she must treat both men and herself with 'respect'. That is, she must be both respectable and respectful in terms of the gender ideology: she must not be too free with her favours. Her passage through the dangerous period of dating and pairing was an anxious time (Cowie & Lees, 1980). Sexual desire, pressure of peer competition and conformity, the sometimes anachronistic gender standards of her parents, the danger of pregnancy, the fear of social rejection—all must be juggled with day by day over several years. As she reached late adolescence, some degree of heterosexual intercourse seems to have been tolerated, but not promiscuity. Birth statistics indicate that sex outside marriage, while seen as a breach of the ideal standard, was condoned if it took place in a serious, monogamous heterosexual relationship that was likely to lead to marriage. Pregnancy was allowed, though not encouraged, to decide when the wedding took place. Such latitude meant that heterosexual intercourse was often made into the test of the seriousness of a relationship, of the couple's commitment to each other as permanent partners. This form of sexuality often meant different things to the young man and the young woman involved. She thought they were serious, he thought they were just having a good time. If she made this mistake too often, or didn't care about the standard, such a woman acquired the infamous 'reputation'.

Gwen Kirk was judged by the Glenside Hospital psychiatrists as being a text-book case of the fall from the pursuit of true femininity through a reputation, to promiscuity, to prostitution. At the age of 13, in 1961, she came to the notice of the Women Police and 'was questioned about alleged indecencies with youths'. She was pregnant at the time to a married man. Although there is mention in the casenotes that maintenance proceedings were instituted against the putative father, there is no indication whether he was prosecuted for carnal knowledge, since Gwen was well below the age of consent (sixteen). That is, at law, Gwen was in no way responsible for her behaviour whereas the man committed an offence against her. Nonetheless, it was Gwen who was punished, despite her technical innocence. She was charged before the Juvenile Court with being uncontrollable, and was committed into the custody and control of the Child Welfare Department until she turned eighteen. (See chapters 5 and 6 for a discussion of this process.)

Gwen bore her baby, and she and her mother cared for it for about two years, after which it was adopted. But the stigma of Gwen's fall from feminine grace remained to haunt her. Not only was she still under legal surveillance by welfare and probation officers, but she endured continuing social punishment. Her father died after a long illness and

Gwen overheard a remark made by her mother to a friend that 'worry had killed him and that Gwen was the cause of all the worry'. Gwen felt guilty about his death although she could not put her finger on any reason apart from the worry caused to him by her illegitimate pregnancy.

She left home at sixteen and lived briefly with a series of relatives and friends, then moved in with her 17-year-old boyfriend and his parents.

She claims that since the illegal pregnancy she has had no sexual relations with any boys. She and her boyfriend are both Sunday School teachers and take an interest in the Church... Then her girlfriend decided to tell the boy's family about her illegitimate child and they became cold towards her... The boyfriend's parents decided that she should leave and not see him again.

After a 'terrible argument' Gwen attempted suicide and was admitted to Glenside Hospital. She was only just seventeen. She had already fallen a long way from the feminine tightrope, and it was clear to her that she was being punished rather than helped back up for another try.

By the age of 21, in 1968, she was pregnant again, and again committed to hospital. After a short stay, her behaviour was causing her doctor considerable frustration and anger. She broke hospital rules and continued to have sexual relations without the intention of marriage, or even commitment. While under minimum surveillance, when allowed out on day-leave to look for work, she instead engaged in 'prostitution'.

Whilst she is not prepared to submit herself to the inevitable regimentation which goes on in any institution, she has also flouted the question of honesty with men, remaining unprepared to honour promises... I do not think that this hospital can tolerate to be made the vantage point for illicit love activity. Because of it, and because of her contention that she has no more to lose anyhow by a more rigid adherence to social convention, there is but one remaining option which is to allow this woman to leave this hospital... It was thought fit to recommend her admission to jail on remand [for insufficient means of support] rather than a return here, in the hope that this may perhaps drive home a lesson. [Her attempt to seduce authority figures] underscores the lethal nature of her acquaintance... The overall outlook unfortunately is that this young woman may not be able to stop short of becoming a virtual public prostitute, or a good-time girl at least.

Her psychiatrist judged Gwen to be exploiting men. She was not using them legitimately, in pursuit of femininity, to get safely from childhood to adulthood, but was placing her own immediate pleasure foremost. She was active in seeking sexual gratification, not passive; she would not pay the price of dependence which was possession by and submission to one man; she was not deferential to masculinity. Gwen's behaviour towards men was judged not simply a failure in her pursuit of femininity, but was rather a sign of deliberate refusal to follow the true path, and hence of conscious immorality. A clearly ideological judgment of Gwen by one of her doctors reveals how thoroughly in his eyes she had lost all claims to true femininity:

Therapeutically it is to be hoped that the remaining 'grain of goodness' in this person may prevent her becoming 'wholly' bad. But the chances are that her impulsivity and inability to put time between thought and deed will carry her further to the precipice of disaster... A picture of apparent innocence, her exterior has so far belied the core of her personality, devoid of emotional attraction, despite her superficial charms. A 'femme fatale' to most oncomers. I likewise have to beware.

An unromantic notion of sex, judged by many to be appropriate to masculinity, brought outrage when expressed by a woman. Gwen's 'superficial' charms and 'apparent' innocence promised conformity with her psychiatrist's ideal of true femininity: subservience, dependence and romantic love directed towards one man. It was breach of this implied promise of exclusivity that was called dishonesty.

Gwen was not asking men to pay for her sexual involvement with them, and presumably she made decisions as to which men she wished to have sex with. This lack of payment and the element of discrimination removed her activity from the technical definition of prostitution. But the downward slide was clear to her psychiatrist. Moreover, to him, Gwen was solely to blame. The gender ideology considered women unilaterally responsible for prostitution, ignoring the men, the customers. To this psychiatrist, such men were victims, not collaborators. These men could have refused Gwen's attentions, foiled her seductions. What the psychiatrist seems to be complaining of so bitterly was Gwen's arrogation to herself of supposedly masculine attributes: initiation, responsibility for her own sexuality, and wilfulness with regard to others' involvement. She was not keeping to the social conventions of femininity and must therefore be cast out.

As with lesbianism, the gender ideology presents prostitution as the end of a fall from femininity, the extreme transgression against the standard of monogamy. Depending on the specific social circumstances, any woman who has sex with men or even merely displays her heterosexual attractiveness and attraction outside marriage can be tagged with a label that indicates that she is slipping towards that end. A woman who has sex with a man without loving him, with her boyfriend before there is any stated commitment, with her fiancé if wedding-night virginity remains highly prized, with any man who is not her husband of the time, even with a rapist in the eyes of some judges—each one of these women may be called loose, easy, a dog, a moll, a slut, a whore. The extraordinary range of synonyms allows every social group an epithet for all female heterosexual behaviour outside marriage, all female behaviour that does not measure up to specific gender expectations. The words can be stated or implied without proof, used as jokes, abuse, threats. They are in themselves a punishment and a demand that the woman conform to gender expectations (cf. Cowie & Lees, 1981).

As with 'lesbian', 'prostitute' is a label of deviance, used by the gender order to keep all women in line. As with lesbianism, prostitution is also an activity or life style with positive meaning adopted by some women in defiance of the gender order's insistence on monogamous feminine sexuality. There has been little direct investigation of prostitution in Australia, and what work has been published has generally followed European and American precedent in being heavily biased in legal, moral and psychological directions. Thus, little is known by researchers about prostitution as an occupation which, seemingly, is how it is known by the women concerned.

As with most women (and men), prostitutes work for the money. Prostitution, as work, requires little training. The only qualification required is femaleness. (Male homosexual and male transsexual prostitution do exist, but are minor and different phenomena.) The desired age range is apparently twenty to thirty five, but work at a lesser rate is available for women much older than this (Golder & Allen, 1980). Given the limited opportunities for women in Australia to earn a living wage, win promotion, achieve a secure career, and be economically independent of men, prostitution has appeared to some women as a suitable career, initially more exciting and certainly more remunerative than most other unskilled female work (see chapters 4 and 8). For other women, it has been seen as desirable or necessary part-time or occasional work, when other work is denied or when money is needed urgently.

In effect, prostitution as an occupation involves the selling of a form of heterosexual femininity producible as a commodity or service by all women. Indeed, it has been argued by many analysts (James, 1951:1– 12; Smart, 1976:79–93) that the uses prostitutes make of their sexuality are really little different from those of respectable women. Given the dependent status of women, the respectable use the lure of heterosexuality to contract advantageous marriages; thereafter, 'marital duties' become part of the payment for their husbands' continuing economic support. The main sexual difference between prostitutes and wives lies in the nature of the contracts they undertake with men: short-lived versus lifelong, with a succession of men versus the one man, payment being immediate and strictly monetary versus diffused and honorific.

Nonetheless, throughout the past century in Australia, prostitution has been anathema to most public authorities. These authorities have proclaimed as natural a form of femininity that domesticates woman as a dependent within the home, that demands that the adult woman commit herself legally, exclusively and permanently to one man, who will support her economically at his discretion. The prostitute's promiscuity and demand for direct and immediate payment, her exercise of non-monogamous heterosexuality outside marriage and without the justification provided by 'being in love', mark her as unnatural within this gender ideology. On the other hand, the same ideology establishes a double standard by proclaiming that masculine sexuality is different from feminine: men naturally need more sex than women and most are incapable of restraint. (cf. McIntosh, 1978:53–64). Thus, to restrict masculine sexuality to monogamous marriage would be impossible, and the attempt to do so would be harmful both to men and to the legitimacy of the gender order. Following logically from this, the ideology cannot insist absolutely on the feminine virtue of monogamy for all women. Hence, the creation of a special class of deviant women becomes a necessary evil. Following this tortuous gender logic are three propositions. First, prostitution itself should not be proscribed or penalised. Second, a woman of the so-called deviant class must be marked as such and kept in her place by denial of access to the correctly ordered respectable society. Third, women not of the deviant class must be denied knowledge of this underworld lest it shock their correct feminine sensibilities or, more importantly, lest it attract or dupe or coerce them into its depths.

This gender logic and its propositions are entrenched in the legal codes of the Australian states. Nowhere—since the 1870s at least (Evans, 1975:16)—is prostitution as such illegal. But the woman who 'offers her body commonly for acts of lewdness for payment' (cf. Wolfenden Report, 1957:82) can be labelled as a 'common prostitute'. Thereafter, she is liable to prosecution for a variety of acts deemed to be connected to her occupation which, if performed by anyone not so stigmatised, would not be offences, notably soliciting, loitering, vagrancy, disorderly behaviour and other such 'street offences'. (In 1979, the New South Wales government abolished these offences by the repeal of its Summary Offences Act. In 1983, soliciting was again made illegal.) Further, a common prostitute commits an offence simply by being in certain places even if she is not working at the time: premises habitually used for prostitution or soliciting, hotels, bars, gyms, saunas, massage parlours, photographic studios (Human Relationships, 1977, V:112–3; cf. Wolfenden Report, 1957:67). As well, at various times, prostitutes have been subject to compulsory arrest, detention and medical examination for venereal disease, while their customers, equally transmitters of disease, have remained untouched by law (Murnane & Daniels,

1979).

The significance of all these legal prohibitions lies in the fact that they apply against any woman who has been labelled, on police initiative, as a reputed or known or common prostitute. That is, they establish status offences, and the prostitute's status is carried with her always, whether or not she is, at any particular time, engaged in her occupation. Thus, her non-working life is as regulated as her actual work time. By such legal status, reinforcing the gender ideology, a woman becomes a disreputable and immoral person, whose word is significantly less worthy than anyone else's, and who is less eligible for any of the benefits or protection that society provides its citizens. A prostitute finds it virtually impossible to prove that she has been raped or subjected to indecent assault. She is liable to have her children taken from her as being neglected or in moral danger (Foreman, 1975:74–9). She cannot adopt children, and her contact with other women, especially young women, is curtailed under laws against procuration (although this offence is now rarely charged) (Wolfenden Report, 1957:112). She is denied all the discretionary welfare benefits available to other women of good moral character. She is limited by her reputation as to where she can live. Respectable landlords disdain her, and those who accept her demand exorbitant rents.

In terms of her working life, the prostitute is similarly penalised. She is subject, without any form of legitimate relief, to considerable work-related stress, the possibility of violence (from customers, bludgers or hoons, criminals and, allegedly, police), and occupational illness (venereal diseases and vaginal infections). She is not eligible for any of the work and welfare provisions available to other workers, such as clean and safe workplace, unemployment and sickness benefits, holidays, long-service leave or worker's compensation (Aitken, 1978:10–2; Golder & Allen, 1980).

She is further denied one of the essential conditions of femininity: a relationship with one man. Both law and morality mete out severe punishments to men who live off the earnings of prostitution. Ostensibly, this is to protect the prostitute from undue exploitation. But, as with other 'protection' for women, it is double edged. The prostitute is not allowed to share her life and living with a man of her own choosing. Having chosen an occupation that makes her sexually available to all men, she is denied the emotional benefits that the gender ideology holds out as the reward for heterosexual pairing.

In general, both the work and private lives of a prostitute are hedged around with a series of laws and regulations that deny her ordinary civil rights and leave her vulnerable to extreme exploitation and personal violence. She is seen as blatantly flouting the norms of femininity and must be denied any of the compensations it offers as the price of subservience. She has fallen, been pushed or, in certain cases described as pathological viciousness, has jumped from the realm of socially ordained virtue. She gains economic independence, freedom from the subordination of domesticity, and a limited freedom of movement—at night, in the streets and public places. She pays by being stigmatised as a pariah and made a victim to the repressive aspect of the gender order. Her work is necessary, for the benefit of the masculine ethos, but she herself is condemned.

Within the Australian gender order over the past century, both prostitution and lesbianism have been labels applied to, and lifestyles adopted by, women acting against the restrictions of femininity. They have been defined as sins and diseases, unnatural deviances taken up by or inflicted upon individuals. Against that definition, however, they have been political stances, whether taken involuntarily or consciously. Both lesbianism and prostitution are methods of relating to the power of masculinity. They are attempts to render that power either more beneficial or less harmful. Whether men's power is legitimated by the gender order simply because they are men, or whether it is supplemented by hierarchical position (as with the Glenside psychiatrists), this power is seen both by the men themselves and by others to be a personal element or consequence of their masculinity. Thus, women's hostility to the exercise of any power over them by men brings accusations of lesbianism because it is a challenge to the supremacy of masculinity, a denial of its legitimacy. On the other hand, any woman's attempt to gain access to masculine power by seducing it, employing it in her own interest, is called promiscuity or prostitution. Such was Gwen Kirk's appellation. An even clearer case was that of Eugenia Radetzky, who was labelled 'over-sexed'.

In 1949, Eugenia was admitted under certification to Glenside Hospital from an Immigration Centre. She was a displaced person, a refugee, and had presumably been in Australia only a few months.

> She appears to be divorced from reality and is indifferent to her position. She brings flowers to the Senior Staff Officers and has delusions regarding their attention to her...She is a source of worry and annoyance to the Centre by her behaviour. Her husband believes she is pregnant. Appears to be 'oversexed'.

At the hospital, a nurse interpreter was available to translate between Eugenia and the Admissions doctor, but much the same statements and judgments of her behaviour were made:

> A big, strong looking, untidy woman of Polish birth...Appears very poorly educated and her general intelligence is low. In Austria she did forced housework on a farm under German control. Married after defeat of Germans to man she had only known a week and he put her in a mental hospital in Austria not very long after their marriage...She is childish for her years and thinks every man is in

love with her and is going to marry her. She says she likes many men, but thinks the Aussies the best. Formed unwelcome attachments on the ship, particularly for the officers, so that she had to be placed in seclusion and the same happened at the immigration camp. She appears to be strongly oversexed and does not attempt to exercise any control.

The symptoms of Eugenia's madness were that she lavished sexual attentions upon officers on board the migrant ship and at the Immigration Centre, was oversexed and suspected of pregnancy. In other words, she was a 27-year-old, married, foreign, sexual delinquent. We can only guess at what underlay her behaviour. Eugenia had lived through a savage war in Europe as a forced labourer. Her value to her Nazi masters had been as an embodiment of an aspect of femininity, houseworker, thereby suggesting that she may have come to believe that other aspects, for example, seductiveness, could also stand her in good stead and lighten the burden of her enslaved state. This conscious or unconscious use of sexuality for material advantage is further suggested by the fact that the main objects of her flirtatious attention were senior officers both on ship and in camp. Her casenotes assert that she thought 'every man is in love with her and going to marry her' so, with the entire field to choose from she went straight to the top levels of the masculine hierarchy, well outside her own refugee group. She was attempting to use feminine sexuality to gain access to power while in a powerless position. This was madness because it did not work, and was instead seen as highly incongruous promiscuity. 'She is indifferent to her position'—as a stateless, penniless refugee, as a married woman.

This sense of incongruity, of Eugenia's failed femininity, would have been exacerbated by two things peculiar to her social circumstances. Firstly, the Immigration Centre was situated on a section of an army camp, and the Centre was run on army lines. It was a world for men in uniform and its authorities expected visible adherence to strict standards of masculinity and to the norms of the gender order. Secondly, there was a considerable imbalance of the sexes, with 141 men to every 100 women over the whole period of the Displaced Persons Scheme (1946–1952), with a greater imbalance in the early years. This imbalance was significant because the hostility of the Australian population towards the 'Balts' and 'reffos' and the continuing camp life of the DPs reduced their possibilities of intermixing and intermarrying. One consequence of this imbalance and isolation, combined with the DPs' sense of insecurity and with the general masculine perception of women as property, was intense anxiety and jealousy among the male refugees. (In 1953, Jean Martin conducted a survey of DPs in a New South Wales country town, called Burton in the study, in which she reported that the imbalance between the sexes among the displaced persons and the inaccessibility of Australian women produced a good deal of anxiety about getting and keeping a woman in the early years of large scale immigration. Quarrels and fights over women were common in Burton at the time of the first study in 1953. Men watched their women jealously and were quick to suspect them of philandering, and some of the women certainly enjoyed being in such demand. (Martin, 1965:55).

Eugenia Radetsky, however, overstepped the mark. In the context of army-style life and intense jealousy her behaviour was too threatening to be accepted, so she was certified, and sent to hospital for six months. Over that time, her diagnosis changed considerably, largely because 'a precise diagnosis is impossible without an interpreter'. At first she was said to suffer from melancholia, then schizophrenia hebephrenia, and later, depressive psychosis. The final note of her case record reads, 'at present I tend to the view that this is an affective disorder seen in Continentals in the U.K.' This diagnosis seems to mean: 'this woman's behaviour does not conform to the standards of subordinate, passive and sexually demure femininity suitable to Australian life and to the particularly fragile gender relations of a refugee camp where all that the men have to hang on to from their past lives is their sense of masculine superiority. This deviance is caused by a temporary mental illness which will be cured in the course of time rather than by an irredeemable viciousness which would reduce her to the permanently outcast status of prostitute.'

There was a difference between viciousness—or a woman's deliberate renunciation of the pursuit of femininity and her conscious transgression of the gender ideology's precepts—and incongruity or failure—a woman's inability to cope appropriately with the contradictions between the standards of the gender ideology and the particular circumstances of her life. Eugenia Radetsky failed because she sought heterosexual relations with powerful men well above her own social class and status. Annabelle Nehler failed merely because she sought heterosexual relations and legal marriage with a man who rejected her. It was his prerogative, within the gender ideology, to initiate such relations, to establish and retain control of his relations with women.

Legitimacy

Annabelle Nehler was thirty six when she was admitted to Glenside Hospital in 1957. She lived at home, in between live-in housekeeping jobs in her country district.

States that she has a right to marry Tom X in spite of his opposition and cannot be convinced that she has no such right... She is 36 years old and considers it is the 'natural and lawful thing' that she should be married. Accordingly, she chased after Tom [constantly breaking into his house and refusing to leave him alone] and says she loves him. When asked whether he has said he loves her, she says, 'you don't have to say those things you just know' ...It puzzles her that there should be no sexual attraction felt by Tom because she has done 'everything right for him'... She cannot appreciate that her attitude and behaviour in relation to [wanting marriage and family] is at all unusual. 'You don't get anything if you don't persist, do you?'

Over fifteen years and nine admissions, the recorded snippets of Annabelle's distracted conversation indicate the strength of her belief in the ideology of marriage, and her desire for it. 'Her mental content shows a preoccupation with the thought that her trouble is "all due to not being married".'

Annabelle Nehler had taken up the clichés of the 1950s ideology of romantic love and strung them together into a programme of single-minded action. Strung together in another way, the clichés ordering her madness could easily form the content of a *Women's Weekly* short story or a Mills and Boon novel of the period. What she was speaking of and acting upon were the postulates of a specific aspect of the gender ideology of femininity: the naturalness of the state of marriage, the intuitive understanding of love, the need to work hard at romance. She was even able to speak the negative aspects of this ideology of youth. 'I said, "How old are you?" She replied, "Too old—old enough to know better".'

Annabelle here was trapped into incongruity because she was unable to adapt this ideology to her particular circumstances. She was unable to compromise with the impossibility of achieving in reality the ideal of femininity in its abstract, ideological representation. Such discrepancy was and is common to the lives of all women, not just mad ones. Nor does successful achievement of any of the objective conditions of feminine sexuality—heterosexual, monogamous and legal marriage—prevent most women sensing their failure both to be independent and autonomous, and to be truly feminine.

For every Australian woman throughout the past century, her sexuality has always been central to her femininity, both to herself and others. Man is the measure of all things. Woman's status is dependent on the nature of her relationships to him, and fundamental to all these relationships is sexuality. In the Australian gender order, women's sexual attractiveness should be confined to catching a suitable husband, and sexual activity confined to marriage. In this scheme of things, the single woman was an anomaly, and a range of labels were available for her deviance. If she retained her sexuality for her own benefit, she was a prostitute or a lesbian. If she sublimated her sexual-

ity into maternal caring outside her own family, she might be eligible
for a simple occupational title, as nun, teacher or nurse. Such titles,
however, have tended to carry more or less pejorative connotations for
many people. If she denied her sexuality, she was a spinster, an old
maid. Or if she retained caring contact with her family of origin or her
siblings' families, she might be a dutiful daughter or a maiden aunt.

Among these latter women who repressed their sexuality were many
who were considered 'good' within the gender ideology, and occasionally allowed the description 'feminine'—but only in a token way, in
pity or surprise. ('She's such a good woman; what a shame she's never
married.' 'She's so attractive; I wonder why she hasn't got a husband.')
Lack of a husband was interpreted as a critical absence in the life and
being of an adult woman. She had failed against the third standard of
feminine sexuality: legal marriage. Such a failure could be the result of
misfortune, sin, or sickness. It was manifested in singleness, adultery,
irregular unions, and divorce. The gender order made all of these
experiences undesirable and subject to severe sanctions. Since the
1960s, there has been some relaxation of the standard and its punishments, some flexibility and variation allowed. The meaning of marriage
is in the process of change. But essentially, legality is still generally
accepted as an important element in the feminine expression of sexuality. The good woman is a married woman.

In almost every circumstance of her life, without a husband to
protect and mediate for her, an adult single woman was vulnerable.
Without a male guardian she was restricted in when and where and
how she might move. To be out at night, to be in public places,
especially the streets, was to fear rape or sexual violence. Other places
were difficult to enter without a male escort. Hotels and restaurants
frowned upon 'unaccompanied' women, claiming to fear that they
might harass their customers by soliciting. As well as restricted movement, the single woman was restricted in where she might stay. Many
landlords saw her as a bad risk: who would pay the rent, who would
keep the house repaired, or perhaps she meant to set up a brothel.

As for supporting herself, the single woman was faced with yet more
obstacles and restrictions. As discussed in chapter 4, women were faced
with an extremely limited range of occupations. Throughout the century, the majority of women in the waged workforce were concentrated
in only eight occupations. Women were trained to want and to expect
to be supported by a husband, and hence to be satisfied with these few
choices. As well, they were discouraged or even prevented from entering other jobs through legislation, trade union restrictions and employer prejudice. 'Women's jobs' paid substantially less than the wide
variety of jobs open to men, and such discrimination was judicially
sanctioned through the Arbitration Commission's award-wage system.

Beyond such discrimination in direct earning ability, single women were also denied equal access to the benefits of financial institutions. They could not establish credit or take out loans simply on their own behalf, but required a male 'guarantor'. They were denied the right to participate in certain insurance and superannuation schemes, or could participate only under discriminatory conditions. Loans for housing were hedged with special conditions, and government housing was reserved for married couples. (In most of these areas of discrimination, married women were no better off than single, and were sometimes even more disadvantaged. But it was expected that through their husbands they would have easy, though indirect, access to all benefits.) From the 1960s, some of the legislative restrictions against single women were removed, and new legislation sought to outlaw the most blatant forms of discrimination (Ronalds, 1979). But many areas have not been covered, and so many wide loopholes still exist that the gender ideology is still able to present marriage as the safest and most economically secure, though not independent, state for an adult woman.

Until the 1960s, the most severe restriction placed by the gender order upon the behaviour of the single woman was its refusal to allow her to exercise her sexuality without the prospect of marriage. This refusal was effected not only by the threat of social ostracism through labelling her a lesbian or prostitute. Single women were also denied the means to control their own fertility, to take responsible action to determine the consequences of their heterosexual activity. They were then punished should they become pregnant, and that punishment was extended to any child born out of wedlock.

Throughout the century, contraception was difficult and harmful. Until the 1920s, forms of available contraception were unsatisfactory and unreliable, and 'nearly all were suited chiefly to use within marriage where prolonged and careful co-operation and planning could take place and where improvement could be achieved with practice' (Ruzicka & Caldwell, 1977:25). The medical profession, with its ideological monopoly over the control of sexual activity, insisted that its assistance was scientifically necessary for the provision and correct fitting of new devices available from the 1930s—Dutch cap, rubber diaphragm, Gräffenberg ring. Hence, these devices were virtually denied to single women because of the almost universal moral indignation shown by doctors (Ruzicka & Caldwell, 1977:28–9; cf. Lewis, 1980:203). From the 1920s to the 1960s there were only three birth-control clinics operating in the whole of Australia, and they provided information and devices only to married women, and only suitably 'eligible' ones at that (Summers, 1975:407; Daniels & Murnane, 1980:75–6).

Although there were no specific laws dealing with the actual use of contraceptives in Australia, many obstacles were placed in the way of women seeking information about or access to them (Whalley, 1972;

Coleman, 1974:60–1). During the 1930s and 1940s, all states except South Australia passed legislation forbidding the advertising and display of contraceptives. In South Australia, similar restrictions were imposed under voluntary agreements among newspaper proprietors and pharmacists. Supporters of such bans argued variously about public morality and decency, or about population growth and defence. Further controls were imposed by Federal legislation. Advertising was banned under the Broadcasting and Television Act, distribution through the mail was curtailed under the Posts and Telegraphs Act. As well, from 1901 to 1959, the importation of contraceptives and advertising matter relating to them was forbidden on grounds of indecency and obscenity. With the gradual emergence of the less repressive standards of femininity in the 1960s, this ideological moral stance was replaced by the profit motive. In 1966 import tariffs of between 7½ per cent and 45 per cent were imposed on contraceptives. These duties were finally abandoned in 1972. At the same time, sales tax on contraceptives, originally introduced in 1930, was also abolished.

State and federal legislation forbade the advertising and display but not the sale of contraceptives. Before they could get them, however, women were confronted by the moral stances of the professional gatekeepers, doctors and pharmacists. Some devices, especially the pill after 1961, could only be bought on prescription, which could be flatly refused by a doctor or provided only after parental or husband's consent had been produced. Some chemists refused to stock any devices at all. Alternatively, they charged exorbitant prices. (Norman Haire reported in 1943 that contraceptive pessaries were sold for 1/6d. in English clinics, whereas Australian-made pessaries were sold for 15/- in Australian clinics, or for as much as £1-1-0 by Australian chemists (Haire, 1943:290).)

As well as financial and legal impediments to fertility control, factions within the Christian church proclaimed their ethical opposition to contraception. Throughout the period, the Catholic church adamantly condemned the practice. In 1930, Pope Pius XI's Encyclical on Christian Marriage declared that, 'Each and every marriage act which in its exercise is deprived by human interference of its natural power to procreate life is an offence against the law of God and of nature' (Lawler and others, 1976:329). Before 1930, the Anglican church had also condemned birth control, but in that year the Lambeth Conference gave the practice its qualified approval. The other Protestant churches held opinions of varying liberality on the subject.

Much the same variety of ethical opinion was proclaimed by the churches on the question of abortion, a last-resort method of birth control. The Catholic church holds the foetus to be an 'innocent human life' upon which 'any direct attack...in whatsoever condition it is found from the very first moment of its existence, is wrong' (Lawler and others, 1976:321). The Lutheran church holds a similarly strong line, although permitting as a possible justification abortion to save the mother's life. The other churches add progressively more justifications and recognise more ethical complications (Human Relationships, 1977, III:150–1).

At law, there are similar complications and varieties of interpretation. Until the late 1960s, abortion was illegal in every Australian state, with a possible exception allowed in the case of preserving the life of the mother. In 1969, legislation was passed in South Australia allowing abortion to be legal in certain situations, while almost simultaneously in both Victoria and New South Wales the law came to be much more liberally interpreted by judicial decision. In the remaining states there has been neither legislative nor judicial liberalisation.

For most of the century, then, Australian women were denied access to legal, safe, cheap and socially approved methods of fertility control. Many women, both single and married, therefore resorted to home-made, patent and often illegal devices and methods for both contraception and abortion, the consequences of which were extremely harmful if not fatal. Other single women became pregnant, bore the illegitimate child, and suffered the punishment meted out by the gender order to those who transgressed the feminine standard of legal marriage.

Deidre Quilper was one single woman who was denied the right to control her own fertility and was then punished. She was a member of the Catholic church, which maintained one of the most repressive stances against women within the gender ideology, claiming spiritual sanction for marriage, and against divorce, adultery, fornication, masturbation, homosexuality; contraception and abortion. The existence of such sanctions did not mean, of course, that all Catholics adhered to the approved behaviour. What it did mean was that they were likely to suffer additional guilt over transgressions. In other words, for Catholic women, for Deidre, femininity held an extra and precise dimension of standards to be lived up to.

In 1950, aged thirty, Deidre was admitted to Glenside Hospital.

She states she has no friends now as she has dropped them. She was born in Western Australia, with 6 sisters and 2 brothers, herself being the 4th girl. Her father died last year; her mother is alive at Pt Augusta. The former was a Protestant, the latter a Catholic (she herself is a strict Catholic)...She was good at school and reached the Sub-Junior. She had to think when I asked if anyone ever proposed to her—'Yes, but it was Religion'. She is stated to have come to Adelaide on her own about 9 years ago and to have been here for the majority of time since then working first at munitions and then other light factory work and living at the YMCA Hostel. She became pregnant by a married man whom she had been going about with in 1949...Last May she had a baby (a boy), the father was a married

man but 'he did everything possible and the Solicitors handled it'
...Deidre went to a Catholic Refuge in Adelaide, where she stayed for
several months until shortly after her child was born. The nuns state
that while she was with them she seemed relatively happy and was
well liked at the home. They did not know very much about her but
understood that it was her first lapse and that her family were not
oversympathetic. The baby was weaned and placed for adoption
almost immediately and Deidre went with her mother to Pt Augusta.

Deidre's story is a labyrinthine one. Pursuit of Catholic femininity was
obviously full of pitfalls and dubious choices. The gender norms of a
variety of institutions stood as a complex network of obstacles to its
achievement. The endogamy of her religion had prevented an earlier,
legally legitimate marriage, whereas, presumably, the loneliness of nine
years' factory work and living in a women's hostel had led to adultery
with a (presumably) Catholic man, against the precepts of both church
and law. Denied the means to control her fertility by both law and
religion, Deidre became pregnant, then was further denied the possibility of abortion, again by law and church. As mentioned above, the rate
of pre-marital intercourse was high among young Australian women
throughout the century, and pregnancy often decided the timing of
marriage. But again, Deidre was denied this solution. Her man was
already married and she was caught in competition with his existing
wife. The man could have divorced his wife, or rather, been divorced by
her on the grounds of adultery—a long, expensive and distressing
experience under the law as it stood at the time. But if we presume the
marriage to be Catholic, neither husband nor wife would readily have
taken the option for divorce. Moreover, even though divorce was
possible both in law and religion, remarriage was not, according to the
latter.

The man in question 'did everything possible', but essentially, there
was little that could be done within the gender ideologies of law and
church. Deidre was trapped. Her child was illegitimate, she was a
scarlet woman, and there was no other man she could depend upon or
marry. She could have tried to bring up her child alone, but financial,
as well as moral, legal and religious forces would have been against her.
Factory wages would have made it impossible for her to be both mother
and worker, since there were no good, cheap, childcare facilities available.

In 1950, Deidre would not have been eligible for any state welfare
benefits. From 1912 to 1941, she would have been eligible for a £5.0.0
lump-sum payment on the birth of her child, since the Commonwealth
maternity allowance legislation discriminated on residential and racial,
but not marital, grounds. From 1951, child endowment was made
available for first children, and Deidre would have been eligible for 5/-
per week. From 1973, she would have become eligible, six months after

the birth, for a supporting mother's pension of $32.00 per week. But in 1950, as an unmarried mother of her first child, there was no financial help available (Kewley, 1973:103–9, 190–210; Human Relationships, 1977, IV:82–4; Poverty in Australia, 1975:208–12).

It is highly unlikely that the man involved would have been able to afford maintenance. As well, this would have increased the likelihood of his offence being discovered by his present wife who had rightful claim over his resources for the maintenance of their legitimate family. Deidre's own family was unsympathetic, denying her the final option of bringing up her child within an extended family arrangement. Her only solution was thus to have the baby adopted, try to forget about the whole business, and start out again in pursuit of femininity, with the knowledge of her major 'lapse' always there to be held against her. This was indeed the course she took, but with extremely harmful consequences.

As well as seriously transgressing against the gender ideology through single motherhoood, Deidre offended against another of its precepts by conducting an adulterous relationship. Strictly speaking, adultery could be committed only by a married person, but an unmarried person in a heterosexual relationship with a married one was also condemned. The security and discipline of marriage was threatened, and the gender ideology's insistence upon monogamy and legality ensured the suffering of all parties, including the 'innocent' spouse— especially the wife. Discovery of her husband's adulterous relationship commonly brought about intense anger from the legitimate wife, whose own security was based upon dependence on her husband, and was put in jeopardy by her rival.

Seventeen-year-old Heather Lawson was caught in this situation in 1965.

> Since being in Adelaide, she teamed up with a married man and had intercourse several times but claims that this had never happened before. Just prior to her admission to hospital, this man's wife found out about the 'nigger in the woodpile' and there was a great showdown at which this man's wife, Heather and Heather's sister were present. Following this heated argument Heather took [an overdose of pain-killing tablets]. She is frightened that her father might find out about this and begged her sister not to tell him. It would appear that her overdose was a manipulation to prevent her sister from telling her father for she freely states that she would kill herself properly if her father is told. Also she was rather worried about the possibility of a pregnancy and V.D.

Heather's relationship with a married man led her into conflict with important social values held by the various actors in this drama, values that associated true femininity with legitimate marriage, and considered adultery as offensive to society or to God, as well as seriously damaging to the innocent spouse. The two major sources of these values in twentieth-century Australia were the law and Christian religion, both of which held that marriage was 'at the root of all social relationships, essential to the preservation of society and sacred in nature' (Joske, 1952:8). The minimal definition of marriage for these two institutions involved 'the union of a man and a woman to the exclusion of all others, voluntarily entered into for life' (Joske, 1952:119).

In terms of Australian law, the seriousness of Heather's activity had only just been increased. Since 1929 in South Australia, adultery had been admitted as a ground for either a husband or a wife to petition for divorce equally. (This was also the case generally in all Australian states except Victoria, where various forms of aggravated rather than simple adultery had to be proved by the wife but not the husband (Joske, 1952:156).) But before the 1959 Commonwealth Matrimonial Causes Act, only a husband was eligible to claim damages against the male co-respondent. After 1961, when the new Act came into force, petitioning wives gained equal rights and could claim damages from the female co-respondent. Wives were no longer mere chattels of their husbands, nor the receptacles of their honour, and female lovers were no longer exempt from legal responsibility. Heather's complicity in activity that could legally lead to divorce was clearly seen as justification for moral outrage and 'a great showdown' on the part of her lover's wife. (We know nothing from the notes about the judgment on and treatment of the man involved.) Femininity required dependence on a man, and so a competitive situation became established among women in terms of both acquiring and keeping one.

The second major source of values associating true femininity with the sanctity of monogamous marriage was Christian religion. Differences existed among the various denominations as to the exact status of marriage—whether or not it was a sacrament, whether or not there were any grounds for dissolution, what was its spiritual purpose. All denominations, however, valued marriage highly and condemned adultery. As mentioned in the discussion of Deidre Quilper's case, the Catholic church held the most extreme views, condemning adultery as sinful, denying the spiritual legitimacy of divorce, and refusing to allow a divorced person—even the 'innocent party'—to remarry (Lawler and others, 1976:511–2).

Both the law and religion proclaimed adultery an offence against marriage and hence a bar to true femininity. But in the cases of both Heather Lawson and Deidre Quilper neither of these institutions directly condemned the women, as far as the casenotes reveal (although, since Deidre was a 'strict Catholic' and since she entered a Catholic refuge, it is likely that she went to confession and undertook penance). Rather, the direct sanctions were applied by the women themselves and by the families most affected. The specific terms of these personal interventions are not revealed by the casenotes, but the actors are. Heather was confronted by the outraged wife and her own sister, but feared most of all her father being told of her offence. That is, her sense of transgression was less one of shame, of failure to achieve ideals she accepted for herself, and more one of guilt, of being caught out in violation of externally imposed norms held by others close to her. In Deidre's case, there is little evidence of either shame or guilt. Rather, there is a sense of being trapped. Her lover was incapable of changing her situation; her family was unsympathetic; to the nuns from whom she sought assistance she was a sinner to be helped back on to the true path. Deidre attempted to 'laugh off her troubles with little success'. She had 'ideas of persecution', of 'people standing over her bed'. She was truly trapped.

The gender ideology severely condemned and punished all modes of heterosexual expression for women except within marriage. The ideology of marriage was deeply embedded as a desire in all women. But the ideology could not provide the conditions and means of fulfilling such desire for all women. Many women thus found themselves trapped by the contradictions between the ideology and their personal circumstances, desiring marriage to a particular man but denied its reality. Some of these women compromised and adhered to the ideology as best they could, living in monogamous, longstanding heterosexual unions that were not legally or religiously legitimate. Such de facto wives were usually denied legitimacy because either they or their de facto husbands were still married to someone else and unable or unwilling to be divorced.

In general, these irregular unions were socially ostracised and denied the state's and the law's financial and contractual benefits (NSW Law Reform Commission, 1981; Wade, 1981). Children of the union were illegitimate, and the woman had few of the legal claims on the man's maintenance, or even their shared property, that were available to the lawful wife. Legal distribution of property by courts in the event of the de facto husband's desertion or death was, and still is in large part, decided on the basis that the parties were legal strangers, and hence basic contractual formalities must be observed.

> In so deciding [distribution of property], the courts can not give any value to romance nor to housewifely duties nor to children. Nor will the de facto wife be able to rely on the presumption of advancement that, where a man purchased property but put it in the woman's name, the property was a gift to the woman. (Sihombing, 1979:289)

The only recognition of de facto wives' needs was in the provision, from 1947, of a widow's pension for those women who had been dependent upon a man within a de facto relationship for more than three years immediately before his death.

In the 1970s, condemnation of irregular unions lessened somewhat. In 1975, the South Australian parliament passed the Family Relationships Act which introduced the concept of 'putative spouse', which allowed the de facto spouse a very few of the rights and benefits of legitimate spouses. Other states have also begun investigations informed by more liberal or pluralist views of gender relations.

For the century before the 1970s, the lot of most de facto wives was a pitiful one. Such women conformed to the imperatives of feminine ideology in being dependent upon a man, bearing his children and maintaining his house. But they were not eligible for the material and status rewards necessary to compensate for their lack of autonomy and necessary for their survival should they be left manless. Marriage has often been viewed as a property relation, and the plight of dependent wives within it seen as inequitable. For the de facto wife, her dependence upon her spouse's good will was magnified, and her material and emotional insecurity doubled.

Denial or refusal of the legitimacy of marriage, and hence of the possibility of true femininity, was experienced by some women as unhappiness or shame. Thus, Claire Masters thought that 'she would be happier if the legal side of her domestic life were settled'. She was admitted to Glenside Hospital in 1955, at the age of 39, claiming that her husband, who was later revealed as her de facto spouse, 'was going to kill her'. She had twelve children, and there is no mention in her notes as to why she was not legally married. It is likely, however, that either she or her de facto had been previously married and were not legally divorced. This was the case with another woman, Doris Quennall, admitted in 1955, who 'at first...said she was married, then contradicted this statement and said her husband was separated from his first wife'. Both Claire and Doris called the men they lived with husbands, and wished to be thought of as legitimately married. Not being so was recognised by the hospital doctors as a cause for anxiety. Of Claire Masters, the doctors agreed that 'her large family with her marital state appear to be too great a strain on her'. The importance placed by psychiatrists in the 1950s on adherence to the strict standards of the gender order is further revealed in comments concerning Rosalind Hughes, admitted to Glenside Hospital in 1950.

> She dismisses major issues as being of little importance, such as her marriage (she never lived with her husband after the war for which she blamed her parents), and the fact that her daughter is living with another man and her own children while separated from her husband.

Marriage and femininity

The social and psychosocial sanctions against women's sexuality, economic independence and safety outside marriage denied women viable alternatives. These same sanctions kept women within marriage, often against their own best interests. In 1972, the American sociologist Jessie Bernard pointed to the differential effects of marriage on men and women. Marriage is good for men:

> There are few findings more consistent, less equivocal, more convincing than the sometimes spectacular and always impressive superiority on almost every index—demographic, psychological, or social—of married over never-married men. Despite all the jokes about marriage in which men indulge, all the complaints they lodge against it, it is one of the greatest boons of their sex. (Bernard, 1972:17)

Married men have superior mental health to unmarried men; their careers and earning power are advantaged; they live longer and report themselves significantly happier. On the other hand, marriage is destructive for women. Compared to both married men and unmarried women, married women suffer poor mental and emotional health. They are more likely to commit suicide and in general die relatively earlier; they are more anxious, depressed, and psychologically disturbed. They also, paradoxically, report themselves happier than unmarried women (Bernard, 1972:54).

If marriage is a health hazard for women, who do they believe themselves happy and why do they choose to stay? Partly because the gender ideology has convinced them, against all evidence to the contrary, that in this state they must be happy. Only a truly feminine woman can be happy and a truly feminine woman must be married. Therefore, marriage brings women both femininity and happiness. More importantly, once married, and especially once she has children, there is no alternative, no escape that could be conceived in any way as an improvement on her lot.

Throughout the casenotes of the Glenside women, there is one constantly reiterated theme: home is where a good woman should be, and there is nowhere else to go. Only three highly undesirable alternatives presented themselves: divorce, madness and death. Divorce reduced a woman to the single state, without the protection of a man, an anomalous and vulnerable position. Hence, it was not an easy step to take, apart from the extreme difficulty of obtaining one before 1976. Helen Vane, after seven years in and out of hospital, and after a psychiatrist had suggested that she and her husband were incompatible and should consider divorce, was reported as saying:

> We drifted apart years ago, but I cannot find a new life, all I had was

a home and children for 6 years when the actual break occurred and I've hung on for no other reason than being faithful to marriage. I know there is no future in hospital, but I shouldn't harm my husband's business... Why isn't there another life for me where I can build my character again.

Paralysed by indecision induced by the conflicts of the pursuit of femininity, many women stayed in hospital, and the longer they stayed, the harder it was to leave. Iris Wentworth at sixty tried suicide as a way out of her hostile family environment. The attempt failed, and she found instead that Glenside was a pleasant enough place—'she has a depressive illness but seems to enjoy it at Glenside'. Her condition was not acute enough to warrant her staying in hospital very long on any of her four admissions, but eventually she refused to go home and was discharged to a psychiatric hostel. 'I doubt if she will be able to function outside of a hostel in the foreseeable future. She says she does not want to return home.' Katie Allen at thirty four also tried suicide.

Two days ago felt as though she didn't want to go on, 'had no interest in home or children...love them very much... I shouldn't have gone home feeling as I did...my husband had been in...had an argument...took about 50 tablets, all I could find.

After a short stay in hospital, Katie did in fact go home, but kept the hospital outpatient clinic as an escape route, returning regularly over eight years. Jean York also yoyoed from hospital to home between the ages of thirty six and forty seven, not happy in either place and despairing of ever being so.

I want to be out of here but I want to be well...My life is just draining away and I am losing my family...I must go home to establish myself but being in here so much has ruined that for me. Unless my feeling comes back.

For some women, the despair was complete and insoluble. Both divorce and suicide were ruled out by legal and religious sanctions. The hospital was an alien and terrifying environment. Their home lives were insupportable, but the sanctity of marriage and the straitjacket of femininity demanded their constant capitulation. In early 1970, Carmella Gniada was dropped at the front door of Glenside Hospital by her husband who said he wanted her to have immediate treatment and then left for his home in the Riverland without further explanation. Carmella's English was almost non-existent. The doctors were puzzled. An interpreter was called in, but Carmella denied having any symptoms of nervous disorder, any marital problems, or any knowledge of the reason she was there. The doctors concluded that there appeared to be no evidence of instability and no reason for her to remain in hospital. She was therefore to be kept overnight, then put on a train back to the

Riverland. That night, an entry in the notes read:

> to keep her really sedated, esp. tomorrow morning as she had
> expected to go home. She is to stay in hospital. Certification papers
> will be sent—about 3 days. Apparently tried to harm her children.

Carmella's local doctor sent in the certification papers eventually, but
they did not comply with the legal specifications. Ten days later,
Carmella was discovered to be missing, and it was learnt that she had
returned home. Nothing could be done legally to have her returned as
she had always been, technically, an informal patient. But three days
later, she was back in hospital under order of a Justice of the Peace.
This time she had been driven the several hundred miles by the police.

> Medical Certificate. Doctor: during examination sits in chair rocking
> from side to side, either whimpering or whispering unintelligibly.
>   Brother: says that somebody is trying to take her children away
> and kill them. Also says that everything is red.
>   Police: has been picked up wandering along the roads at all hours
> of the day and night about once or twice a week for the last several
> months.

Nurse interpreters and an Italian-speaking doctor were called in, and
her relatives were contacted by phone. She stayed in hospital two
months, then returned home, where she was periodically visited by a
Mental Health Visitor on country circuit from Glenside. After two
years, however, she was returned to hospital, again under certification,
and stayed six months. Over all this time, her diagnosis ranged from
depression with schizoid features, through paranoid schizophrenia,
atypical depression dating from a puerperal psychosis after the last
child, borderline mental retardation, to 'a very unsuitable marriage'.

Carmella Gniada was born in 1935 in southern Italy. Her brother
and sister migrated to South Australia at some stage and established
themselves in an Italian group settlement in the Riverland of South
Australia. In 1960, it was arranged that she should marry, by proxy, a
Yugoslav settled on an isolated farm in that district. Seven months
later, at the age of 24, she migrated to Australia and met her husband
for the first time. From that very first day, her husband was 'disappointed' in her. She 'could not find her way around the house, even
confusing the bathroom and w.c.' He thought her odd, and they began
having 'quite a few arguments as she would not agree with him'.
Within a year she had a son, then eventually two others. After the birth
of this third child, Carmella began to neglect the house and children.
She couldn't manage. She took to walking seven miles into the local
township where her brother and sister lived. She was restless, depressed, could not sleep and was very lonely and homesick. Her brother
reported: 'too lonely in the bush—pain in head—go mad there.' During

this period, Carmella's mother was brought out from Italy for a visit, financed by the brother and husband. Then came a nephew for a visit. Mr Gniada complained:

nephew was better looked after than husband, 'the best for him'. Then he found out Carmella had a relationship with nephew, went to dances with him, leaving the children alone, etc., gossip. He did not want nephew, but all Italians got on his back, led to quite a big scandal.

Mr Gniada found all Carmella's family 'odd'. He mixed only with the Yugoslavs of the district.

It was at this time that both Carmella's brother and husband had her admitted to hospital. According to Mr Gniada, what was wrong with Carmella was:

(1) she is unbearable
(2) she couldn't cope with her family
(3) she was crying all the time
(4) her affairs with 2 men
(5) she didn't like him
(6) he feels overpowered by the Italians of her family.

The final entries in the Mental Health Visitor's report indicated Carmella's situation in 1973:

At home alone. No improvement in housework, etc., but seems better when she talks. Husband has not encouraged her in any way. Hard to live with—I would not be surprised if she relapses again and that he may not want to take her back... Keeping fairly well. Her mother died in Italy. Not so much homesickness now.

Carmella suffered from an unsuitable marriage. Such unsuitability was not merely an idiosyncratic failure on her part, but was part of the social and ideological failure built into the centre of femininity and the institution of marriage. Her case is an extreme one, since she was trapped into an extraordinary number of the possible contradictions of living out the ideal of femininity. It is the piling on of so much suffering that makes up the extremity. Each one of the traps of femininity into which she was ensnared had caught many other women.

As a proxy bride, she was pushed into legal marriage, although she was perhaps saved from some of the anxieties of adolescence inherent in the ideals of romance and individual attraction. She was also denied any control over her own sexuality by becoming a commodity exchanged contractually between two sets of men.

As a migrant, she had to live through the discrepancies existing between at least three different ideologies of femininity. She had to accommodate in her behaviour the meanings of being the good Italian woman of her childhood belief, the good Yugoslav woman of her husband's expectation, and the good Australian woman of her new country's standards of femininity. She was held to each of these ideologies by the complex groupings of people among whom she lived, as well as by the institutional sanctions of Australian society.

As a Catholic, she was denied any possibility of leaving her unsuitable marriage, which the church held to be indissoluble. Divorce and remarriage were banned. Separation was theoretically possible (Lawler and others 1976:512), but would be materially impossible without the support of another man, which would be sinful.

As the wife of a hard and jealous man, her every act of independence was an insult to his masculinity. His standard of femininity entailed her total passivity and subservience to his will. Her sexuality must be exclusively directed to him, her time absolutely at his disposal and her work at his direction. 'Mr Gniada is aware he wouldn't get another woman to live in the circumstances he provides.'

Carmella's submission to all these ideological injunctions was ensured by making escape materially impossible. She could not support herself economically, because the only skills in which she was prepared and trained were those of marriage. She had no money because her husband controlled the family income and she had no legal claim to it while she remained married. ('Carmella resents helping husband make more money that she would never see any how... She is sick of living in a primitive fashion now that he's established.') She had no possibility of making her way outside her censorious migrant community because she had been denied opportunities to learn English. (The language problem she confronted was enormous. In the hospital she was isolated. 'Group Activity: mental condition plus language barrier make her impossible to communicate with, therefore not involved in any ward activities.' But even in her home she was isolated as her children became assimilated through compulsory education: 'the children are finding it more and more difficult to communicate with her in her dialect'.)

Carmella had forced upon her the contradictory demands of true femininity, and could not escape. Many other women chose marriage freely, but still found that they were denied the comfort and happiness promised for conformity. Many suffered gravely from the contradictions within the ideal. All suffered from the suppression of their independence and autonomy. Only a few were able to escape, and they were made deviants or outlaws, to be pitied, ostracised, victimised and punished.

Over the century, desire and necessity drove women towards marriage. Severe punishments were exacted for deviation from the narrow path leading into and through lifelong, exclusive, legal subordination to one man. As discussed above, some leniency developed in the late 1960s and 1970s—in relation to fertility control, married women's participation in the commanding economy, irregular heterosexual unions and divorce. The nature of marriage and of relations between men and women within marriage have been opened to public scrutiny. The previously accepted superiority of the husband has been challenged in public debate. Issues of violence within marriage—husbands battering and raping their wives—issues of financial inequity and of married women's general subordination and vulnerability in relation to their husbands are coming to be seen as unjust and insupportable aspects of the gender order. Women's refuges, health centres and rape-crisis centres have been established by feminists to offer help to the victims of the gender order and to point to the need for alternatives to the oppression of marriage and its consequence of violence directed against all women. The inferior status of single women, of prostitutes and of lesbians, the discrimination they suffer in public life, the restrictions placed upon them and the violence directed towards them by individual men and by social institutions, are no longer occurring without notice or concern. Marriage, sexual relations and sexual power have been politicised, and heterogeneous forces are ranged on many sides.

But, to a large degree, the old standards of femininity still prevail. Feminine sexuality is still bound within the triple standard of heterosexual, monogamous, legal marriage. Indeed, marriage has never been so popular as during the 1980s. Nonetheless, the meanings of marriage for women have changed over the century. The important struggles at the present are to encourage recognition of marriage as an ideological form, to overthrow the social sanctions against alternatives to marriage, and to create places of safety for all women who flee from its confines.

8

Work

A woman's work is never done—or recognised, or paid for. An early women's liberation cartoon pictured a harried, many-armed woman: one hand holding a baby, another a broom, another on a typewriter, pushing the office tea trolley, working a sewing machine, pushing a supermarket trolley, stirring dinner. In this chapter, I will be looking at some of the experiences of Australian women caught in the contradictions between the ideology of femininity and the material circumstances of their working lives as they struggled to be good women.

The most significant economic trends affecting Australian women's work in the commanding, local and domestic economies over the past hundred years have been discussed in chapter 4. Throughout the century, the gender order demanded a system of gender apartheid, and proclaimed women's place to be in the home. As with racial apartheid, however, the economic order contradictorily demanded the integration of women's and men's work into a profitable whole. The resulting compromise encouraged the gross exploitation of women's work by men—husbands and fathers—and by capitalist employers: all in the name of femininity. The gendered economic order devised a differential algebra, in which masculinity = public sphere = marketplace = waged work = economic justice (or class struggle) and which did not equal femininity = private sphere = home = labour of love = paternalistic protection (or masculinist oppression). Under this algebra, women's work was systematically segregated from men's ideologically if not always physically. It was circumscribed, downgraded and disguised.

House work

From the last decade of the nineteenth century until well into the second half of the twentieth, adult women were primarily classified as dependents within the home. Only here could true femininity be pursued. Truly feminine work, acknowledged only as a labour of love, was house work. As with all women's activity, little intellectual energy has been spent in analysing it, and the housewife herself has knowledge of her own work only in isolation (Berk, 1980:7–27). Not until the late 1960s did women begin investigating and writing about house work, seriously challenging the accuracy of the gender order's characterisation of the world of work (Gavron, 1966; Benston, 1969; Mainardi, 1970; Lopata, 1971; Oakley, 1974 a & b; Leghorn & Warrior, 1975).

Some form of house work has existed as long as there have been houses. The housewife, however, is a modern category of worker. She emerged, as was shown in chapter 4, out of the demise of the domestic-service economy in the years between the wars. For the first time, house work became an isolated activity. No longer could the woman of the house buy the assistance of servants nor commandeer the services of daughters and unmarried female relatives. The specialised division of labour within the household collapsed into specialised tasks performed by one woman.

These tasks can be divided into three general categories. First of all, house work entails the physical maintenance of an abode: a house, flat, room, caravan, hut. That is, a shelter of some sort must be kept clean, tidy and in repair. Some of the labour entailed in this maintenance, and the maintenance of the equipment used, must be bought commercially, but that involves more work of supervision. (The difficulties of such supervision are manifold without a person on the spot. A tradesperson will come 'sometime on Wednesday. No, sorry, can't give a more definite time than that. Someone will be there?') Much of the work of maintaining the house is routine and daily or weekly, and is essential for safety, hygiene and comfort. Standards of performance vary widely, but sometime, some of the work must be done.

The second dimension of house work is the physical maintenance of people, family members. The specific details of this work depend upon the age, health, and activities of family members, and upon the economic resources of the family. Daily feeding is all-important, entailing buying food and preparing it for consumption, taking into account any specific needs of individuals, for example, the food required by the very young and the ill differs from that needed by healthy adults. If any food is grown by the family, it needs tending. Clothing needs to be bought or made, kept in repair and kept clean. The personal cleanliness of family members needs to be supervised. Again, the very young, the frail aged and the ill are incapable of cleaning themselves, and it must be done for them. This personal physical maintenance is required, as with the house, for safety, hygiene and comfort.

In both kinds of maintenance, the standards of performance vary widely, but have been constructed over the century by the practices and rhetoric of various external agencies and adapted by individual housewives. The new regulatory professionals emerging at the turn of the century took a particular interest in the housewife, focusing their manipulative skills upon each aspect of her work (see chapter 6). Inflexible standards of cleanliness, nutrition and cooking were presented to her as necessary in the interests of the health of the race and the survival of new generations. The time and money and physical environment necessary to achieve these standards were not provided. After the second world war, industrial expansion and technological innovation created a mass of commodities—to eat, to wear, to use— and the new consumption experts took the housewife as their target, exhorting her to shop and buy. Under such onslaughts, the range of meanings and standards of safety, hygiene and comfort of the modern housewife was constructed.

Inextricably linked with these two physical dimensions of house work is a third, psychosocial, aspect: the construction and maintenance of personality. There are various theories that attempt to explain, firstly, how, over the generations, newborn infants come to be social beings, how they acquire the heritage of ideas and laws of human society; and secondly, how, over her or his life, each individual is appropriately fitted for her variety of socially specific activities and is daily able to go about them. These theories—varieties of psychoanalytic, socialisation and reproduction theories—have created a minefield of conflicting and contentious concepts. But on one point they agree. Whatever the processes by which we become human and members of specific class, gender and status groupings, they begin in the family. In particular, it is woman, as centre of the family, who is the primary agent involved in the process. All the theories accept the centrality of woman in her aspect of mother. None of them, however, sees her activity as work. Bringing up baby, looking after and teaching the children, servicing husband—all are part of the housewife's job. As with the physical components of her work, this task of constructing and maintaining the personality has been influenced by the whole range of regulatory and consumption professionals.

A further dimension of this task, generally unacknowledged by the various theorists, is the housewife's creation and maintenance of her own personality through her work. That is, house work is not simply the application of labour power to objective tasks, but is incorporated into the personality structure of the woman who is the housewife. British sociologist Ann Oakley expresses, in the language of socialisation and role theory, the results of the processes that create the feminine identity:

> preparation for housewifery is intermingled with socialization for the feminine gender role in the wider sense. Neither in theory nor in

practice is one process distinguishable from the other...Through the integration of feminine role learning with self-definition, housekeeping behaviours tend to be developed as personality functions.
(Oakley, 1974a:113–4).

To be a housewife is part of the very definition of true femininity in modern Australia as in most western societies. Although many house-wives see their work as work, most also see it as a 'natural' part of being a woman.

Beyond the question of what is house work, we need to enquire next into the conditions under which the work is carried out. Since the 1920s in Australia, as mentioned in chapter 4, domestic servants have been available as houseworkers only in ever decreasing upper-class enclaves. Thus, it has been the wife and mother who performs house work. Again since the 1920s, 'labour-saving devices' have become increasingly available for her to work with, and since the second world war they have become fairly universally employed: gas or electric stove, washing machine, hot-water system, vacuum cleaner and refrigerator being the most important. In 1946, only 13 per cent of Australian homes had a refrigerator, while only 2 per cent had a washing machine. By the 1970s, ownership of these commodities was seen as a necessity, not a luxury. (Game & Pringle, 1983:26) As well, changes in the geography and economics of shopping have been significant, particularly the demise of corner shops and their home-delivery services and the rise of suburban shopping complexes and supermarkets. These changes in technology have altered the specific nature of house work over the past several decades. What they have not done is reduce the time spent in doing it.

No extensive studies have been done in Australia of the time spent in house work (Blackburn & Jackson, 1963:12–4), but data from a num-ber of other western capitalist countries seems applicable. In general, it seems that little change in the hours of work has followed from changes in the techniques of house work. The housewife's hours are among the longest of any category of workers. A series of studies undertaken between 1929 and 1974, and commented upon by Ann Oakley (1974a) and by Alva Myrdal and Viola Klein (1968) indicated house work time (including shopping and childcare or supervision) ranging from 48 to 105 hours per week, with most workers spending between 60 and 80 hours per week on the job. Joann Vanek's comparison of hours spent in house work in the 1920s and 1970s in America revealed that, in both periods, full-time housewives worked 52–55 hours per week, while familied women with full-time jobs in the commanding economy de-voted another 26 hours per week to house work. Differences existed between rural and urban homes, with country housewives spending less time at work (Vanek, 1979:500–502). Generally, it seems that the use of domestic technology has raised the standards of performance of housekeeping as well as rationalising them. These higher standards have been imposed on the housewife not only by her own sense of the appropriate, but by other family members, relatives, and by the standards embodied in the ideology purveyed by the mass media and social institutions.

Two other points emerged from these surveys of house work. Firstly, there was no direct correlation between hours spent in house work and number of children in the family. Secondly, there was a very low level of participation in house work by husbands. In the later surveys, there was some general agreement among those interviewed that men should help in household tasks, but that this assistance would be given voluntarily and not under any sense of obligation. Thus, not only is house work one of the most time-consuming occupations, but it is a gender-specific job, exclusively allocated to women rather than to adults of both sexes (Oakley, 1974b:1).

Apart from its hours, house work is generally carried out under appalling industrial conditions. This situation springs mainly from the status of house work as non-work, as opposed to economically productive work or, more precisely, to work in the commanding economy for which wages are paid. Wages are not paid for house work, nor are any of the other financial benefits accruing to 'real' work available: overtime payments, sickness and holiday pay, superannuation, unemployment benefits. Housewives are not covered by any industrial award, are not eligible to join any union, do not receive holidays or sick leave as a right, nor, indeed, can housewives easily resign their jobs. The work is repetitious, monotonous, fragmented and boring. The one clear satisfaction from the work, as reported in the surveys, is that housewives are their own boss. But even this autonomy is undercut in two ways. Firstly, there is the obligation to get the work done according to deadlines provided by husbands' and children's needs and expectations. Secondly, although there are no institutionalised standards, or rather, because there are none, housewives are subject to the imposition of contradictory and idiosyncratic standards by husbands, children, relatives and neighbours, as well as those of external social agents—teachers, doctors and the mass media.

Over the last 80 years of the development of these working conditions for housewives, there have been a variety of attempts to improve the situation. Advocates of scientific home management or home economics tried from the turn of the century to raise the status of housewifery by associating it with the prestige of the physical and social sciences and of scientific management in the workplace (Matthews, 1983). They succeeded in having domestic arts or science taught in Australian state schools where various certificates for proficiency were offered. But there was little hope of ensuring that housewives would be employed, that is, married, because they held a certificate. The education may have been helpful in a practical sense for the future housewife, and it may have helped provide entry to a range of other, waged occupations, such as domestic servant, milliner, seamstress, dietician, textile consultant. But it did nothing in a collective sense to establish objective standards or to improve the status of housewives as workers.

Another attempt to rehabilitate housewifery began between the wars, when Housewives' Associations were formed, attempting

> to support, protect and raise the status and interests of the home, women and children, and to instil into women and, through them, into the children that 'housewife' does not necessarily mean scullery maid. To make them understand the dignity of the word 'housewife' and all it means in relation to the interest of the home, and to create a wider understanding of what home life may mean. (Housewives' Association, 1930).

The dignity, efficiency and selflessness of housewives were foremost in the rhetoric of the Association, but year after year it admitted that their status was depreciated. In the long run, the Housewives Association was much more effective as a consumer protection and advisory service than as an advocate for housewives as workers.

In the past decade, a new campaign for 'Wages for House Work' has emerged. The common argument behind this demand is that within capitalist society, everything has a money value to judge its worth. Work is popularly defined as that activity for which one receives a wage. Consequently, the work of the housewife is not acknowledged because she receives no payment for it. The Wages for House Work campaigners therefore seek to raise the status of housewives by having their work incorporated into the general structure of the economy through payment. But the campaign has been supported by women holding otherwise contradictory political views: by revamped population moralists in the guise of, for example, Women Who Want to be Women, as well as by socialist feminists (Windschuttle, 1974; Ryan, 1984; Webbly, 1982). The slogan itself is the only point of unity, and the campaign is floundering in a morass of contradictory answers to a series of economic and political questions. Who benefits from house work and hence who should pay: husbands, capitalists or the state? How much is a housewife worth: should payment be token, based on replacement costs, or on work-value or productivity criteria?(cf. Ferber, 1982; Warrior & Leghorn, 1974).

All these attempts to have house work acknowledged as work, and to raise the status and improve the conditions of housewives have been remarkably unsuccessful. All have foundered on the rock of the family; specifically, on the private, isolated, emotional and ideological nature of the family, and of woman's identity with it. The ideal of femininity centrally involves the equation of woman = housewife = wife = mother. Whether justified by recourse to biological or evolutionary arguments, to religion or to nature, this ideology of equivalence is granted popular legitimacy regardless of countervailing argument or evidence. Woman's identity and her work in the home are inextricably bound together in her own eyes and in those of her culture. Over recent decades there has been some slight recognition that woman may be and do more than this, but her place remains, finally, in the home.

From the casenotes of one of the women admitted to Glenside Hospital, we can see some of the effects on an individual of this dual nature of house work, as work and identity. Ada Norris entered hospital voluntarily in 1962, complaining of 'lack of interest in housework and family matters of several weeks duration'. She admitted herself another five times over the next four years, suffering from depression as well as many physical illnesses. Ada's immediate problem was that she had too much to do and too many family worries. She constantly strove to achieve the domestic ideal of femininity, and the attempt took its toll.

Born in 1904, Ada had married in the late 1920s or early 1930s. She was living in the country at the time, and within a few years had her first 'nervous breakdown'. No explanation is given for this except that she had 'always been tense and anxious'. During the 1930s, Ada bore her seven children, and during the 1940s she brought them up alone while her husband was overseas at the war. When the husband returned he was seriously incapacitated. So Ada continued on alone with, in fact, one more helpless dependent. The family's income was apparently only a war pension, at least until the children were old enough to work. The family did, however, own their own house. Throughout the 1940s, then, Ada Norris's life would have been one of extreme difficulty and total devotion to her family, but it would have met with social approval. She would probably have been seen as a good woman bearing up under all vicissitudes.

By the late 1950s, Ada's children were grown up and five of them married. She may at this time have had some slight respite from her responsibilities as wife and mother, but then more troubles came. 'The eldest and youngest boys were not married and lived at home. Two other boys were parted from their wives and expected Ada to be able to look after them and their children.' The broken marriages were 'the cause of great anxiety to her'. Moreover, 'she herself has had a lot of sickness'. Then Mr Norris developed diabetes. 'He was a very sick and helpless man who wasn't even well enough to potter around in his garden. He was very deaf and would just sit about quietly doing nothing.' The husband was unable and the sons were unwilling to help either themselves or Ada.

The family seem to expect too much from Mrs Norris and were not prepared to do anything for her. When she is ill she gets up and prepares their meals then goes back to bed. The boys never asked if she would care for any food, and just left her lying there.

The only assistance Ada did receive was from her married daughter who visited once a week, and from her brother, an age pensioner who was formerly a hotel manager. 'He lives there from time to time and at times like the present when she is away he carries on for her.'

Ada Norris strove to be a good housewife–wife–mother. What she was not good at, however, was coping with the continuous and heavy demands for her physical and emotional services over 40 years. To a certain degree, the hospital psychiatrists recognised the legitimacy of her seeking temporary escape from these demands. 'Present admission is really to afford some relief from domestic worries.' She stated on a number of occasions that 'she is unable to continue at home any longer, although she realizes that her husband, who is older than her, is unable to manage unaided at home'. Here Ada was coming up against the contradiction of the meaning of good wife and mother as both work and also an aspect of her identity. She had a job to do: to care for her husband in sickness till death. But she also felt that she should be wanting to do so and enjoying it. 'Worried about husband...Not wanting to go home at weekend but worried.' These two aspects fitted together relentlessly. Domestic work being integral to her sense of femininity, there was no access for Ada to the mechanisms that existed in public working life for bettering conditions or rationalising work loads. She had no holidays to take as of right, nor could she resign. The only way out was to abdicate responsibility for her personality. This was achieved by becoming ill, which relieved her, temporarily, of the guilt at abandoning her family. But soon after each admission, brought about because she could cope no longer, the guilt would return, she would worry, become 'uncooperative with treatment', demand her discharge 'too soon', and she would return to the unchanged domestic situation.

Nonetheless, Ada's illnesses did allow her to take a rest from being a good woman by transforming her into a good patient (Parsons, 1952:436–7). This temporary transfer of roles meant as well that relations within her family were not severely disrupted. Her husband and children were relieved of the necessity to consider the situation in which Ada was unhappily existing. Rather, they could put their faith in medicine, in external expertise, to counteract the apparent disease that was causing her to act strangely. Mr Norris, in 1965, 'was going to make sure that she did not come home too soon this time, and asked the doctor to have her locked up so she couldn't return before she was better'. For everybody concerned, to define Ada as ill meant that her illness could be cured or helped. Her record as a devoted wife and mother need not be spoilt, nor need the internal dynamics of family relations alter.

By mid-1966, Ada was about to be discharged again, and it was recorded in her casenotes that she

> was not thrilled at the idea of returning home to look after her invalid dementing (*sic*) husband — but this morning when due to leave, her son rang to say that her husband had died last night.

The next entry, three weeks later, recorded that she was 'relieved re death. Looks much brighter, has put on weight, sleeps well if she takes sleeping tablets and tranquillisers'. She was referred to her local general practitioner for continuing supervision, but she did not attend. After 20 years of nursing an invalid as a good wife, and after 40 years of being a good mother, Ada Norris disappeared from the records.

Other aspects of the meaning of house work are revealed in the notes of another woman admitted to Glenside Hospital. Irma Weiman's story exemplifies particularly the economic dependence of a housewife upon her husband. As well, it shows the conflict that can arise over standards of work. Because of its private nature, there are no objective standards for house work, only individual ones, and because of its status as non-work, a housewife's standards are able to be considered as an aspect of her personality. Irma's story also exposes the isolation of the housewife, magnified in her case because of her being a migrant.

Irma Weiman migrated to Australia, probably under the Displaced Persons Assistance Scheme, in the late 1940s or early 1950s. She was in her mid-twenties at the time, and bore two children in the first few years after her arrival. Nothing is known of her previous life, except that she was born in Poland. Money obviously had come to mean a lot to both Irma and her husband, a common enough situation among refugees, whose material goods were usually destroyed or left behind, and for whom reaccumulation came to mean security in the new land. Within ten years of arrival in a foreign country, an assisted refugee migrant with few possessions and little money to his name, Mr Weiman had saved money from his wages on the railways (and possibly from overtime or another job), bought a block of land in a country town, and built a house with his own hands. Irma remained at home as the frugal housewife, caring for their two children. She never worked for wages, and it is likely that her husband, if not Irma herself, held strongly the view that it was man's responsibility to provide monetary security and the woman's to tend the family and the domestic hearth. Many European migrants to Australia held strong views about the gender division of labour, and often found them in conflict with what they saw of Australian domestic life and the relations between the sexes. This was especially so with the apparent freedom of Australian women from male control in the ways that male migrants were used to seeing such control manifested (Martin, 1965:55ff). The probability of such conflict between the Weimans emerges from the psychiatrists' reports of the opposing stories told by Irma and her husband.

In 1960, Mr Weiman had his wife certified and admitted to Glenside Hospital. He claimed that Irma

> will not speak to husband or neighbours. For some time has refused to prepare meals. Gives children tinned food only and will not prepare fresh meat or vegetables. Frightens children so they will not go near their father.

In this statement as to why he thought his wife mad, Mr Weiman indicated clearly the identity of work and personality in the housewife. Irma's failure to live up to his standards of a good housewife meant not simply that she was a poor worker, but that something was wrong with her that must be cured. (I am not necessarily suggesting that Irma was not mad, merely pointing out the specific behaviour that her husband believed sufficient sign of madness).

Irma denied her husband's charges, both as to her madness and as to her failure to care for her family:

> Says she has been looking after the home and children and was brought away by the women police in the middle of doing the washing. Says she cooks good meals for her family and denies only living on tinned food. Cried over the children coming home from school and finding her gone...She does not know why sent to hospital. Always fighting with her husband. Her children don't have enough clothes and her husband won't give her the money to buy them. Her husband won't tell her how much he earns each week. He does all the shopping for food. She only goes shopping when she gets family endowment. Their troubles are always over money. They own their own house. It is nearly paid off. Husband built it himself. He buys enough food but she doesn't know how much it would cost. He buys meat—chops, braising steak, sausages—and she cooks it. Her girl and boy are aged 10 years and 9 years and they are both well... She denies the accusations of her husband given in the schedules. She likes Australia. 'It is beautiful. I like it better than Europe because everything is the right price' and they can buy things that they would not have had enough money for in Europe...Husband says she 'is not a very good wife' but does not say why. She has refused to sleep with him for the last year but she 'has not had one other man' during that period. She sleeps with the girl. She does not know whether he had other women. 'I don't think.' He gets drunk very often—about once a week. His friends come sometimes and stay very late and they drink. She told one of his friends to leave the house and go home and her husband gave her a 'hiding' because of it.

This story was found to be 'connected and plausible and will need investigating' by the examining doctor, who could not find 'any mental abnormality'. Nevertheless, this was Irma's second admission (there were no details in her casenotes of the first, which was said to have been occasioned by a similar situation), and 'in view of the home situation will need a longer stay in hospital this time'.

What emerges from these accounts is Irma's desperation to do a good job of physical maintenance and emotional nurturing of her family. It would appear, however, that Mr Weiman held very strong views on woman's proper place and proper behaviour, views that were not clear or agreed to by Irma. He tried to hold her to a performance of his values, which focused on the home and house work and their rigid separation from the public world. Irma's life was circumscribed by his power. He controlled the family purse and, more than that, he controlled access to the outside world. The only visitors to the house were his male friends. The usual means of housewives breaking their domestic isolation, shopping, was denied Irma. One consequence of her housebound situation was that, after ten years in Australia, she still 'could not understand some directions because of language difficulties'. Irma was not allowed out, and presumably, on the few occasions when she did venture forth, she would still remain cut off from others because of her limited grasp of English. This appears to be an extreme instance of the process by which many non-English speaking migrant women remained aliens in their adopted country. Such a situation was created by the inevitable loss of emotionally supportive relationships through a migration process in which women were largely adjunctive to men, combined with the social expectation of good women being wives and mothers within the confines of the family home (see chapter 3).

Mr Weiman's power over Irma was that of mediator between her life and the wider society, and ultimately this was expressed in his ability to have her certified as mentally ill. The examining doctor reported, 'does not present any fresh symptoms of [illness] at present, however the family must be disorganised at present. Duration of present attack is given [by husband] as 12 months, so must be important'. Mr Weiman was requested several times to come to the hospital for an interview, but he did not. The last comment in Irma's notes reveals the continuing clash of standards about house work and its integration into the housewife's personality: 'Says she is getting on well with husband and children...Husband says [she] shows little interest in home and housekeeping or family but this has improved slowly'.

The home as workplace

A central tenet of the gender order was segregation. It proclaimed that the social world should be, and was, divided on gender lines: home for women, the marketplace for men; the private sphere for women, the public for men. This segregation established the domains of the correct pursuit of femininity and masculinity. But these ideological realms did not square with reality. There were substantial contradictions between such illusions and the world experienced by both women and men in twentieth-century Australia. Certainly, it has come to be accepted since the 1970s that women, even married women, have always had a place in the paid workforce (Ryan & Conlon, 1975). What has been less well recognised is that the home and the marketplace have never been as separate as the ideology has pretended. The home has not been distinct from, but has itself been a domain of paid work. Women moved between the home and the ideologically defined masculine world of work throughout their adult lives. They moved at times out of their own homes into others to undertake paid work. Alternatively, they brought into their own homes paid work that was compatible with their family domestic work.

Domestic service

The home as a domain of paid work rather than a sheltered haven can be most easily shown in the case of domestic service. As discussed in chapter 4, in the latter part of the nineteenth century and the early decades of the twentieth, domestic service as a paid occupation was considered by the state, potential employers and population moralists as the most suitable employment for young women of the working class who could not be supported by their families in the period between leaving school and getting married. The work was not seen as contradictory to the correct pursuit of femininity—for working-class women— because it was performed in the home. The approved life pattern was thus: the young working-class girl lived in her father's home, helping and learning from her mother while acquiring her compulsory state education which included, preferably, training in domestic arts. Upon leaving school, she took up employment as a servant in a 'suitable' home, relieving the middle-class mother of some of the burden of house work and childcare, and learning from her the proper, civilised way to run a household. After a suitably late marriage, which allowed the middle class an extended use of her services, and she and her fiancé time to acquire savings for a down payment on a house, she settled into her husband's home, bore his children, and conducted her own household in a proper manner, thereby bringing the light of middle-class respectability into a small corner of the working class. Should she later find herself bereft of her husband's income through dire misfortune not of her own making, she could always return to some form of service (living out or part-time, of course, if she had children), since good women were hard to find.

Everyone benefited from working-class women following this pattern.

The women themselves were kept from poverty, the middle class gained domestic service, and the state ensured compliance with the gender order since the injunction that a woman's place is in the home was not violated. Of course, 'the home' thus became manifold, the boundaries between each were made permeable and the relations within each variable, but the woman herself was always bound there. She was bound by filial obligation, by employment contract or by marriage contract. It could also be mentioned here that, should she 'fall' sexually in her pursuit of femininity as she passed through these homes, she would then be sent to a Home—for Unmarried Mothers or Wayward Girls—where she would be bound by obligation to a charitable organisation or by law to the state, and still required to do domestic work.

That a woman could perform domestic work in a place defined as a home, yet move between private and public, state and institutional spheres is revealed in the casenotes of Catherine Parnell. Catherine was first admitted to Glenside Hospital in 1937 for a stay of four months. She was a nun, and stated that she felt 'unfit to live because she was not performing her religious duties properly'. Although the notes give no indication of the actual work she did in the convent, it seems probable that, apart from spiritual matters, she was engaged basically in domestic work.

Catherine was born in 1906 in the country, and she stayed at home after leaving school. Her mother died when she was fifteen, so more than likely she was required as her father's and brothers' housekeeper until one of the brothers married and his wife was able to take over. In 1932, when twenty six, Catherine began training as a nun, and she stayed in the convent for eight years. In the eyes of her religion Catherine became a bride of Christ. At the beginning of the second world war, she left the convent and wandered the country, taking up 'intermittent and irregular house work and nursery'. As a single, unemployed woman she should have come within the ambit of the National Manpower Regulations of 1942 and engaged in essential war work, but probably her mental-hospital record and country nomadism kept her from this form of industrial conscription. Her wandering working life continued until 1950 when she was readmitted to Glenside Hospital, where she stayed till 1961. During this time, it was reported that 'she does light ward duties in looking after the clothes in F ward during the day—her hands will not permit her to do heavy duties'.

In 1961, Catherine sought permission to live again in a convent. This was granted, and she worked in the convent laundry for a number of years, 'at least eight hours a day'. Even though she was an invalid pensioner, it was still considered necessary that she perform domestic duties, presumably in the interest of the convent as well as herself: economic value plus maintaining her pursuit of femininity. In 1975,

'Catholic home closed down' and she was 'moved to hostel' (one of a number of state subsidised and regulated homes in the community). Thus, Catherine had worked all her life in a succession of homes. In some she was paid; in others her work was a labour of love of father or Father; in yet others her work was therapy. She scrubbed her way through the domestic, religious, medical and paid realms of the economy, and never left home.

House work, wherever it was carried out, in whatever sort of home, was part of the regime of femininity. To be female was the only qualification it demanded. (Male servants did and do exist in Australia in large numbers compared to other western countries, but their job has never been housework as such, but rather such specialised outdoor or indoor work as groom, gardener, chef or valet). The social relations of house work, wherever it was carried out, therefore involved some form of the personal submission, dependency and exploitation or oppression accepted as appropriate to the condition of femininity. For the housewife, as shown above, to labour for love under such conditions was supposedly incorporated into her personality. For those who performed house work as paid employment, these conditions were incorporated into the job specifications.

Vera King, whose case was detailed in chapter 1, was born in 1900 and left school at thirteen to enter domestic service. Her psychiatrist reported her working life as follows:

Most of her employers were unkind to her, demanding a great deal and giving little reward, materially or otherwise. After the age of 15½ her employers were particularly hard, and she was treated as a drudge, again suffering threats, abuse and depreciation for all her work. 'I felt that I could never do anything right; they used to tell me I was useless and lazy'—rather pathetically. 'I used to try so hard; but I was never any good'—tearfully. (Did they frighten or harm you?) 'I thought they would hit me.' (Why? People are not allowed to do that.) 'I don't know. They used to look at me as though they would.' When aged 24 she went to work for a Mrs Grey. 'She was the best and kindest woman I have ever known; they were all good and kind to me', naming the members of the family...

Vera was thirty seven when she left Mrs Grey's employ and the paid workforce in order to get married.

Here is exemplified the feminine work situation: a close personal relationship of super- and sub-ordination that could range in quality from benevolence to tyranny because it was presumed outside the economy and unencumbered by external regulations. Private domestic service was outside most of the contractual safeguards of other public work. Covered by no industrial awards, protected by no union, domestic servants were subject to the whims and idiosyncracies of each employer. (There were a number of attempts to organise domestic

servants industrially around the turn of the century, but they apparently came to little (Kingston, 1975:51–5).) As with the housewife, no
objective standards existed. This lack of rationalisation of work and its
relationships was the most hated aspect of domestic service (Heagney,
1933: 64–5; Kingston, 1975:51–5; cf. Davidoff, 1974) and from the
beginning of the century (and before) women fled from private service
whenever the opportunity arose.

The decline in the numbers of women working as servants in other
people's homes was arrested slightly during the depression when government pressure pushed unemployed women into service. There was a
further lift in the years just before the second world war, possibly due to
the influx of central European refugees (Keating, 1967:295). Thereafter, the decline was fatal. The preferred site for house work became the
woman's own home, not a multitude of others'. The boundary between
home and marketplace remained permeable through sale of house work
only to those women who could not survive through dependence on a
male breadwinner, who were ineligible for state support, and who were
unfit or untrained for the commanding workforce. Domestic service
was no longer a feminine career. It was a stopgap or a job of last resort,
usually performed part-time.

Meanwhile, the home still remained the site of other forms of income-earning work for women. In so far as they were able to combine it
with their own family housework, married women were still able to sell
their domestic skills to others. Whether they went out or remained at
home, women worked and were paid by others for their laundry work,
ironing, knitting and needlework, cleaning, typing, cooking and childminding. To a large extent, throughout the century, such work was
part of a local economy. The women would rarely declare themselves as
workers for any census or survey purposes; they paid no tax. In the
1960s and 1970s some of this work became more rationalised and was
incorporated into the commanding capitalist economy. Some women
worked for small businesses and contractors: in public laundromats, for
private catering or cleaning firms, as family day-care workers. (Matthews, 1982)

Boarding

Another form of using house work skills within the home for profit was
that of providing board, lodgings or bed and breakfast. This was a
curious phenomenon indeed within the terms of the domestic ideology of
the gender order: women selling the privacy and comforts of the home
and haven to strangers. As with other forms of women's work, it existed
in the shadows of the commanding economy and has attracted little
attention or analysis (cf. Davidoff, 1979). Over the century, govern-

ments and local councils tried both to classify and regulate boarding as a housing matter, but, as with other aspects of the local economy, they touched upon only a tiny number of situations. A lodger could be turned into a visiting friend or a second cousin at any moment of inquiry. Large establishments might well be registered, but family homes with one or two 'extras' could easily slip from sight. Advertising of places could simply be by word of mouth in the neighbourhood. The money exchanged could appear merely a share of household costs. Thus, hard data on how many women at any time earned income from the supply of houseroom and services to non-family is impossible to get.

The supply and demand for lodging obviously altered over time, affected by such changes as the design and size of houses, the balance between home ownership and rental, the availability of cheap alternative accommodation, geographic patterns of employment, generally accepted standards of privacy. In her discussion of boarding and lodging in England, Leonore Davidoff (1979) lists the types of people who took up lodgings at various times from the nineteenth century to the 1930s: railway employees, building workers, seasonal workers, soldiers, sailors, prostitutes, clerks and shop assistants, students and holiday makers. A similiar listing would seem likely for Australia, with the addition of newly arrived immigrants. Davidoff also discusses the types of people who supplied lodgings. Two sets of circumstances apparently induced people, especially women, to engage in this form of paid work. First, there were those women who had no male breadwinner to support them and had to find their own livelihood: widows, separated women, divorcees. Second, lodgings were provided by some married women at specific stages in the family cycle: when the children were very young and did not need much house space, or while they were not yet able to make their own financial contribution to the household; and again, later, when the grown-up children left home, leaving rooms and services that could now be sold to lodgers.

It would seem from British and American analyses that lodging as a widespread economic practice declined in the years between the wars. With the establishment of the norm of the small nuclear family in its own home, there was neither physical nor social space for lodgers. It is probable that, in Australia, lodging continued into the early years after the second world war, providing for the huge influx of single men in the first waves of the mass immigration programme. By the mid-1950s, lodging probably began dying away to be replaced by hostel and rental accommodation as the housing shortage was eradicated by the building boom. Lodging as a practice persists into the 1980s, but 'as a recognised social experience it has, like residential domestic service, almost disappeared' (Davidoff, 1979:29). It has been noted recently, however, that with the recession of the early 1980s, cheap lodgings are again being sought by large numbers of young unemployed people (Williams,

1983).

For the period of its popularity, keeping a boarding house or lodgings or letting a room was a way for women, denied other access to the capitalist economy, to make ends meet. Through it, money could be earned while still maintaining the facade of femininity. The women concerned did no work different from that which they already performed for family members. They remained at home, as housewives, or as mistresses if they employed servants. But they brought the capitalist economy into the home, selling their services as commodities, violating the sacrosanctity of the domestic hearth, abolishing the ideological segregation at the heart of the gender order.

Relations between landlady and boarder were always based on the payment of rent, but less directly economic and more familial relations must often have come into existence when boarders were long-term. Such a confusion of economic and familial relations can be seen in the case of Nicola Dolci. Nicola migrated to Australia with her husband sometime between the wars. In 1945, aged 34, she was first arrested and admitted to Glenside Hospital, suffering from delusions of persecution. She stayed in hospital for about four months. In 1949, her husband left her to return to Italy for a visit. It was uncertain whether Nicola had earlier deserted her husband, in 1946, and also unclear whether divorce proceedings were underway or concluded. At this time, Nicola went to live in a boarding house run by Mrs Campbell. There she stayed for eight years, claiming Mrs Campbell as her only friend. Nicola was again arrested and admitted to hospital in 1957. Soon after, a social worker presented a report on Nicola's previous history, which included information about and by Mrs Campbell.

> Mrs Dolci was clean when she came but gradually went downhill and her room became so dirty that for the sake of the other boarders and family Mrs Campbell partitioned off part of the laundry. This became dirty also. Mrs Dolci had eaten almost nothing for about 4 weeks prior to admission. She never bothered with food anytime much and would buy 6d. worth of chips or a loaf of bread...Mrs Dolci has not worked for many years, her husband does not send her money...Mrs Campbell stated Mrs Dolci never went out and did not mix much with friends who visited Mrs Campbell. She had no men friends and Women Police have no record of men being involved with her. Mrs Campbell stated Mrs Dolci was antagonistic to the idea of remarrying...Landlady appears kind...is a widow who has a job also. She is aged somewhere in her 50s, has a mentally defective or crippled son who is aged 34 and is an invalid to care for so probably would not be willing to take on any care of Mrs Dolci. However, no mention was made to her of this.

Two years later, Nicola's casenotes record, 'prospects of discharge are not good as there appears to be nobody who takes an interest in her'.

After another two years, a couple of previously unknown brothers turned up, who took Nicola home on weekend leaves. Shortly after, she was discharged into the care of her single brother. 'Going along well. Helps in the home and does cooking and washing and ironing.'

Concentrating on Mrs Campbell rather than Nicola in this story, we can discern something of the work and relations of a landlady. Mrs Campbell had no male breadwinner to support her, and had an adult invalid son who was economically dependent upon her. Running a boarding house provided her with money. The notes say nothing of the other job she held, but presumably, with her responsibilities in the house, it would have been part-time. Mrs Campbell became a friend to her boarder, and tried to involve Nicola in her own network of friends. She put up with behaviour and dirt that went well beyond the call of economic obligation and would have put her at risk in relation to her other boarders. There is even a suggestion that Mrs Campbell may have waived or at least reduced Nicola's rent. In other words, over eight years, the relations between Mrs Campbell and Nicola moved from an economic to an almost familial basis. The crucial difference, however, was that no one expected Mrs Campbell to maintain such family-type obligations forever. Whereas, in other cases, the hospital put considerable pressure on direct family members to take back into their homes patients who were not cured but were fit to leave hospital care, such pressure could not be and was not placed on Mrs Campbell. In the end, it was the economic nature of Nicola's relationship with Mrs Campbell (over eight years) and her kinship relations with her brothers (who had had no dealings with her for years) that were weighed against each other. The hospital determined that support of a dependent woman could only be asked of family, and presumably Mrs Campbell agreed. Ultimately, a boarding house was not a home—for the boarder.

Home business

Apart from domestic service, doing a bit of ironing for somebody else, and having paying guests, there were three other forms of work that have linked the home and hence women to the capitalist economy: running a small business from the home, helping in the husband's business, and outwork. Running a small business from the home was possible for those women who had acquired saleable skills beyond general housework. They avoided all the legal and other costs and regulations of keeping a separate business establishment and, most importantly, they were able to organise their time so as to be able both to earn money and to care for their families.

The case of Karen Arndt exemplifies the situation. Karen was born in 1909. At the time of her first admission to Glenside Hospital in 1945 she was a full-time housewife, married to a schoolteacher, and had two children, the younger of whom was eight months old. There is no record of her working outside the home before marriage.

[Husband left] soon after he admitted her to Glenside in 1945. Went away with another school teacher and took two boys with him: sent Tom back to her a few years later. During this time she boarded in the city, music teacher. Worked hard to make a home for Tom and herself.

Karen was readmitted to Glenside some 25 years later, after her son had married and her skills were dissipating with age. In the intervening years, she appears to have been moderately successful in her ambition to make a new home. Deserted women with children had always been considered unfortunate because their dual tasks of economic self-support and domestic work seemed necessarily to cut across each other. Karen, however, with a semi-professional skill as a music teacher, could work from her own home. She had a certain limited freedom to organise her time so as both to earn money and care for her child.

Skilled married women ran small businesses from their homes in order to integrate earning an income with their family responsibilities. Single women also ran small businesses from their parental homes for the same reasons and because, in the years before the second world war, it was more respectable than working outside the home. The gender ideology demanded apartheid, and proscribed the commanding economy for truly good women (except, perhaps, for some professional women). But many respectable women were poor, so they sought to earn an income within their proper place, the home.

The most common form of home business among women was dressmaking. How prevalent it was is impossible to tell. Registration as a 'women's garments factory' was only necessary when the owner employed at least one person in manual labour. Self-employed seamstresses were unsurveyed and unregulated. Sewing was not a capital-intensive industry. With a sewing machine, a sign in the front window, a notice at the local shops and a good reputation, a woman could gain at least a small income as well as making her own family's clothes and performing her requisite household duties.

Such activity, however, did require as well both a well-trained and well-recognised skill and a good address. It tended to rely on clients with money in the immediate neighbourhood, and the respectability of the worker had to be unimpeachable for such clients to be willing to cross the threshold. In the case of seamstresses, the clients had to be willing to undress for fittings; in the case of music teachers, their domestic circumstances and relations had to be fit for small children to visit. For women without these qualities, and who needed a more regular income, the solution was outwork.

Outwork

Outwork was the edge of the feminine economy closest to the commanding masculine economy. Therefore, more is known about it—it has a history. Outwork was a system where materials to be made up were supplied by factories or workshops to workers at home who turned the materials into finished goods which they then returned to the factory or shop (Fry, 1956:77–8) For this work they received a rate per piece, a rate usually much lower than that obtained by the piece or as a wage by workers employed directly in the shop or factory. The clothing trade was the one with which outwork was most commonly associated from the late nineteenth century to the present day. Outwork also developed in the footwear and paper trades and, in the 1970s, in clerical work (Red Fems, 1980).

Throughout the century, the place of outwork was ambiguous, caught as it was at a confluence of the economic and gender orders. Outwork was poorly paid, and an unreliable and insecure source of income. Its competitive existence forced down the wages of women employed in factories. But it was work done in the feminine sphere of the home. Writing of the debates over the 1884 Factories and Shop Bill in the Victorian Parliament, Anne Marie Lynzaat has argued that

> The spectre of the poor widow and the single daughter of aged parents seemed to haunt the thoughts of both Houses...While alive to the impoverished circumstances of the sweated worker the Members saw her in a traditional womanly role: she was a brave, struggling person, supporting and caring for her sick, disabled, aged, young or unemployed relatives—and, most importantly, she did all these things in the home. This image can be contrasted with that of the factory girl, generally thought of as a young woman, or girl, unmarried and with few responsibilities beyond her own support. (Lynzaat, 1979, 87)

Because outwork was done in the home, legislators were loath to let the regulative powers of the law of the land intrude. In the commanding economy, legislation was passed to protect women (and preserve men's superiority), but in outwork, the iron law of profit was allowed to run riot, to exploit the economic vulnerability of women caught in poverty but still in pursuit of femininity.

Throughout the twentieth century, outwork remained an important means of support for a large but unknown number of women, the overwhelming majority of whom are now migrants, disabled or handicapped, and mothers of young children (Owen & Shaw, 1979:51). With the continuing assumption that woman's place is in the home, little has been done either to improve the wages and conditions of the home as a place of work, or to increase the possibilities of women working outside it. Outwork has been the only way in which many women can combine their household and childcaring responsibilities with paid work. Answering the question why are women homeworkers, Mary Owen and Sylvie Shaw declared:

> Although faced with poverty-line wages, insecurity and the lack of protection, women homeworkers have little option. Because of inadequate community-based childcare centres, lack of community support facilities and society's attitude that 'women's place is in the home raising children', mothers with young children have the choice of earning nothing, farming out their children to unregistered, ill-equipped child-minders at approximately $27 per week [in 1979] in order to take a fulltime job, or of doing work at home.
>
> Migrant women are faced with the added hurdles of language and cultural constraints which make fulltime work difficult in factories and impossible in offices. Childcare centres are seldom adapted to migrants' needs; nor do they employ multi-lingual workers...The pay is low and the women don't feel that they get paid what the job is worth. However, many homeworkers consider this is the price they must pay for an otherwise ideal situation. (Owen & Shaw, 1979:52)

As with the other forms of women's paid work associated with the home, outwork probably decreased in the years around the second world war. As mentioned in chapter 4, the war itself, by removing men from economic production, opened up places for women, both married and single, in the commanding economy, wages for women increased, and state-regulated childcare facilities were provided. After the war, married women were driven from the male jobs they had held efficiently during it, the childcare centres were closed down, and home was again extolled as woman's place. Unions began a new campaign against the sweating of outworkers, but were concerned with its economic consequences for their members in factories rather than the economic survival of women at home (Allport, 1983). As well, the post-war suburban boom meant that women who left their inner-city homes to take up poorly serviced residence far from the inner-city factories were cut off geographically from their traditional part-time outwork. This, however, was only a temporary phenomenon. In the mid-1950s, many clothing and other factories were relocated in suburban areas, and suburban women were again able to find outwork employment. (Allport, 1983). By the late 1970s, the expansion of the commanding economy began to provide new forms of outwork for women, in clerical work with a home word processor linked by telephone to a central computer, as well as in light assembly work and packaging (Red Fems, 1980; Hargreaves, 1982: 173).

Unpaid helpers

The final form of work women could undertake from their homes was not strictly paid work, but it was certainly integrated into the capitalist economy. Helping in their husband's business—as an unpaid helper—was a means of increasing the economic viability of the family economy. Obviously, this option was open only to women married to self-employed men. Small family shops and family farms relied on married women's work; clergymen's, politicians', doctors' and tradesmen's wives were physically involved to various degrees in the husbands' work, if only as telephone minders (that is, as secretaries and counsellors). There was also the less material but equally important social work performed by the wives of capitalists and executives, providing entertainment and psychological support while husbands clinched deals or consolidated contracts.

To be one's husband's helper was, however, once again to be invisible in the commanding economy and invisible to its survey-takers. Such women were rarely recorded in censuses, by the departments of industry, or in taxation records. (Over the past two decades, more of these women have become visible because legislative changes have made husband-and-wife partnerships a means of reducing tax liability (Jones, 1983:427).) The conditions of helpers' work were not regulated or rationalised, and the social relations of their work were governed more by familial than capitalist considerations.

Helen Vane was born in 1924. She left school at the end of her primary years, and took up work as a domestic, moving from there to nursing, probably as a nursing aide. During the war she joined the Women's Auxiliary Australian Air Force. She married a mechanic at the end of the war, and they eventually moved to Adelaide where Mr Vane took over management of a garage. By the time of her first admission to Glenside Hospital in 1963, she had three children, the youngest of whom, a 10-year-old girl, was mentally defective.

> Husband has a service station. Helen did cleaning. Husband had a woman bookkeeper. Helen was jealous of respective positions. The woman left to have a baby. Subsequently Helen became pregnant. 'I didn't deliberately get myself the same way, it was just one of those slips'. Says jealousy is a feeling of inadequacy; also says husband didn't want her to do the books as he didn't want her to know how much money he had...Husband states: Is not carrying out home duties he would normally expect. She has tantrums with him and with children. Husband says that he has sent a boy away and wishes to send girls away because of mother's irrational behaviour at home.

Although her children were of school age, the fact of one being mentally retarded would have increased Helen's domestic responsibilities, making it difficult for her to undertake a full-time job in the commanding economy. The family lived near the garage, and Helen's cleaning of it seems to have been taken both by herself and her husband as a mere extension of her housework. Helen was willing to do more, thereby reducing Mr Vane's wages bill. But a line was drawn at her having knowledge of his financial affairs. It was not the case that Mr Vane considered women in general could not or should not handle financial matters. Rather, it was an issue of keeping home and family life and work distinct. There was little physical separation possible since wife and husband shared both premises of home and work. Therefore, to keep it clear, at least in his own mind, that his wife was a housewife, not a co-worker or owner, Mr Vane kept control of the crucial symbol of the segregation: money.

The Vanes's personal relations, which will be discussed in more detail in the next chapter, were violent and hostile, but in their attitude to money they were similar to many other Australian couples. There is generally a dearth of information on internal family financial relationships, but, 'one of the best-known results from studies on family finances is the discovery of the wife's lack of knowledge of her husband's income' (Edwards, 1981:103). The ideological separation of work and home is reinforced by such ignorance. The oppression of femininity is entrenched even deeper by the assumption that money, the mediator of most interactions between the home and the public world, should be controlled by men. Women as managers of family consumption usually have some control and decision-making power over money. But men as breadwinners tend to set the boundaries of the total family budget. Women's lack of knowledge and lack of control over family finances has been related by some analysts to women's general subordination in economic matters. Once again, the home and marketplace can be seen as intertwined, this time at the symbolic, psychic level. Meredith Edwards, concluding her study of financial arrangements in Australian families, claimed:

> The disadvantages which women face in obtaining equal
> opportunities with men outside the home can have an impact on
> their financial arrangements within the home. It is difficult for
> women to share equally with men in the control of finances inside the
> home or more generally in economic power outside the home, when
> they have no income they can call their own, and so long as the
> labour market disadvantages them. The relationship between the
> market place and the domestic economy and its effect on women
> deserves closer examination by researchers. (Edwards, 1981:133-4)

Work and femininity

The final area of women's work, in the commanding economy, is the area that has received the most attention, from a few masculine economists but mostly from feminists. Since the late 1950s, women, especially familied women, have become increasingly visible in the economy, and discussions of the nature and conditions of their work have led to the beginning of an understanding of the interrelation of the economic and gender orders in the construction of femininity. Books such as those by Ryan and Conlon (1975), Kingston (1975), Hargreaves (1982) and Game and Pringle (1983) have been vital to this process. Rather than repeating their work, I have in this chapter looked instead at the more hidden realms of women's work. My purpose has been to shift the focus of analysis away from those areas in which women can be directly compared with men using concepts derived from masculine experience; to challenge some of the canons of orthodox masculine interpretation; to argue for a continuity as well as a change in women's economic experiences that are other than men's.

Gender segregation of the economy is one of the most remarkable features of Australian capitalism, but its wider ramifications have rarely been noted. The ideological imperative that woman's place is in the home has likewise been narrowly interpreted. Within such a restricted framework, a number of analysts have, as mentioned in chapter 3, attempted to interpret the dramatic increase in the numbers of married women entering the commanding workforce since the 1950s as a sign that the old gender order is changing and that women are entering upon a freer and more equal relationship with men, less oppressed by the trammels of a circumscribed femininity.

I would suggest that such changes are largely illusory. The economy that is segregated is not just the commanding realm, but includes the domestic and the local economies. For Australian women since the end of the nineteenth century, the ideological segregations between home and work, between work for love and work for money, have not been the fundamental lines of gender division. Rather, the crucial segregation between women and men has centred on patterns of organisation of the time and space of work. Some single women have experienced, for the usually short time of their singleness in the commanding economy, masculine patterns of work. But their expectations—and others'—of the organisation of their whole working lives have been different from men's. Most fundamentally, familied women throughout the century have retained the work of the household and of childcaring, and this work has been embedded in the meaning of femininity. All and any other work has been seen as secondary to these basic concerns.

The physical circumstances in which housework and childcare have been performed have altered substantially. Domestic servants and mistresses in large households have given way to single housewives and their domestic appliances in small households. The work combined with house work has altered. The local economy has largely been supplanted by women taking up part-time work in the commanding economy. But in whichever economy she works, the familied woman needs waged work whose hours are flexible enough to allow her to continue her domestic work, and whose wages are sufficient to allow her to employ other women to care temporarily for her children and house. In the current definition of femininity, whether she works part-time or full-time, she still does the housework. She still must cease work if there is a family crisis such as illness. She still must put the welfare of her home first. In other words, there may have been a structural shift in women's work, beginning in the 1930s and consolidated in the 1960s and 1970s, but it has been a shift in location, not in either quality or quantity. Woman's responsibility for, if not so strictly her place in, the home, has remained the fundamental defining aspect of her pursuit of femininity.

9

Mothering

[Katie Alleń. Born 1926, England. Roman Catholic. Five children. Voluntary admission to Receiving House, 1959. Transferred to Glenside Hospital, 1960.]

[March 1960] She is prone to blame most of her difficulties on her in-laws, whom she says came from U.K. to stay with them a year ago. '...things not the same between husband and myself since they left.' She expresses considerable hostility towards her mother-in-law, whom she describes as a 'very dominant person...no one could live harmoniously with her...' [Attempted suicide two days ago.] She lacks confidence in her ability to care for her household and children, and in recent months has had the added complication of forming an attachment with an ex-patient of Receiving House. Added factors exist in her inability to adjust to present environment, which even after five years 'seems so strange to me'.

[May 1960] Outpatient Clinic. Her eldest son—an epileptic boy—gets very miserable and upset and this upsets the family. Advised to take child to Children's Hospital.

[August 1960] Occasionally screams at the children...Still occasionally broods about her 'in-laws' and the shoddy way they treated her in the past.

[September 1960] Fed up with being a housewife.

[October 1960] Crying, tense, 'nothing has any meaning any more—there is not a little thing that I enjoy'. The children are the only things that keep her alive—'they're such sweet good children, they don't deserve this'. She feels a recurrence of her old bitterness against her mother-in-law. 'No-one wants to talk to me. I'm just a burden to everybody.' Husband says she has hardly been at home with his mother since the age of sixteen. Feels there is fault on both sides. He went out of his way to be offhand with parents when they were here. When they went to live with in-laws just after marriage it was only for six weeks and after that saw them only once a month.

[March 1961] Fears she is pregnant. Period is overdue. Husband

used sheath but it came off. She is tense and depressed.
[June 1961] Had miscarriage two months ago. [Still having
nightmares, depressed.]
[1963] Still attending as Outpatient. At present working in a
factory.
[August 1964] Some improvement, but unfortunately is to return
to work [as day-nursery attendant] next week. Parents and
parents-in-law coming to Australia in near future. Katie exhibits
hostility towards husband.
[October 1964] One child has 'epileptic' fits which are now
controlled but he has developed nightmares instead.
[1965–66. Series of illnesses and family crises: pneumonia,
hepatitis, pyelitis; nephew ran away from home; son failed at school
and went to work at a supermarket; two children apparently
epileptic; financial problems.] Also miserable about her sex
life—finds husband revolting and can't bear to be touched.
[December 1966] Confused about her children still—is almost
totally pre-occupied with tests of intelligence, etc., on children. Can't
imagine why her boy should have emotional problems. Also, she now
refuses to believe that her daughter could possibly be retarded
(I.Q.80)—'she's a perfectly normal girl'.
[March 1967] Feels well in herself but has tense and worrying
situations at home. a) Eldest son has become a fanatic about religion,
has become withdrawn and stays in his room most of the time. Cries
when praying. She thinks he is mad... b) Second son was accepted
into police force but on the night of taking his job he stole some small
article. c) Smallest child—a daughter—is an epileptic and a little
dull. Katie has stopped work [teacher in a school for retarded
children] and does not intend to go back there.
[May 1967] Miscarriage.
[August 1967] Starts on contraceptives—more frigid.
[September 1967] Parents-in-law here and Katie feels very down
in the dumps. They nag her all the time.
[February 1968. Social worker's report assessing home situation:]
Katie exerted considerable pressure on son to go to Uni., Teachers'
College. Son tries to convert everyone—until they are 'reborn' he
cannot associate with them. Katie convinced son is sick and requires
treatment. Mental Health Visitor suggests another doctor's opinion
with the possibility of certification. Katie reluctant to act.
[August 1968] She has many real family problems to cope
with...Katie is far from well but is unlikely to improve further at
present on our supportive therapy. (Edited casenotes, 1960–68)

Motherhood was the third crucial site of the construction of femininity
in twentieth-century Australia. It was the intended outcome of
feminine sexuality; it was the designated central content of feminine
work. But, as with those two other sites, the construction of feminine
motherhood was a contradictory process. The contradiction was spelt
out in the gender ideology itself. On the one hand, motherhood was

presented as a natural event, the concomitant of femaleness, every woman's potential biological destiny. On the other hand, it was also a medical, legal and religious event and process, the apotheosis of femininity, every good woman's necessary social duty (cf. Rich, 1977). The contradiction was differently expressed in the 1970s feminist aphorism: 'If it's natural, I don't want anyone telling me how to do it'. In this chapter, I will discuss three aspects of this contradictory process: the making of the maternal body; the creation of the good child; and the end of mothering.

The maternal body

Femininity is lived through the body, and that body is as much the subject of historical construction as behaviour and belief. In recent feminist literature, there has been considerable discussion of the physical images of women presented in art and advertising, in the variety of communication media. Some of the first protest actions of the early Women's Liberation Movement were directed against beauty contests, which sought to present a standardised ideal of feminine beauty and to cajole and coerce women into trying to conform to that ideal. The physical ideal of femininity was more than skin deep, to be bought at the cosmetics counter, the hairdresser and the boutique. It was also an ideal of the body itself, and its pursuit involved rigorous regimes—of dieting, exercise, counselling and medication (cf. Orbach, 1978). That pursuit was fuelled by fear and guilt: fear of not finding and keeping a man, guilt because inevitable failure to achieve true femininity was blamed upon insufficient dedication to the ideal.

The physical ideal of femininity was not only one of beauty. For adult women it was also an ideal of physical fitness for maternity. The good maternal body would produce the good child. Women's pursuit of this second physical ideal became, throughout the twentieth century, increasingly under the definition and control of the medical profession. The adult woman, before and during her pregnancy and at birth, became a walking pharmacopoeia, taking drugs for contraception, weight control, insomnia, fertility, nutrition, blood pressure, anti-emesis, purgation, anaesthesia, labour induction, milk production.

Most of these drugs had both short and long-term undesirable effects, which could affect women's general health or their ability to conceive and carry to term, and could affect the viability of the foetus or cause deformity. Many of the difficulties and failures of pregnancy were medically induced, as were many of its comforts and successes (cf. Oakley, 1979:18). By the 1970s, after the eventual revelation of the widespread and horrific consequences of certain drugs, most physicians and pharmacists offered warnings to women against taking drugs during the early stages of pregnancy—exactly the stage that women were rarely sure about, and that even doctors could not easily detect.

Apart from this heavy ingestion of drugs, the mother's body was also subjected to physical intervention, assistance and surveillance at childbirth (cf. McKinlay, 1972). By the 1970s, this entailed, routinely, shaving off pubic hair, artificial rupture of the membrane, vaginal examination in labour, bladder catheterisation, electronic monitoring of foetal heart and of contractions, forceps or vacuum extraction of the baby, with caesarian section as a possibility (cf. Oakley, 1979:17–8)— all this without mention of more recent physical manipulation of in vitro fertilisation procedures.

The construction of the maternal body was not entirely a medical monopoly. It was achieved rather through an unstable and unequal alliance between women and doctors. The demographic transition over the century, discussed in chapter 3, was the result of women's decisions to limit their families. In the early years of the century, this was in the face of fierce hostility and opposition from doctors as well as population ideologues. In this case, doctors joined the band wagon late, only slowly recognising the inevitability of the trend and seeking to control it to their own profit. Similarly, the trend to hospitalised childbirth in the 1920s, and to 'natural' childbirth in the 1970s, were the outcomes of women's decisions made within circumstances determined by doctors: firstly, to reduce the risk and pain of giving birth, and secondly, to challenge the medical conception of pregnancy as an illness.

Within the mother–doctor alliance, however, the individual woman was at a distinct disadvantage. By and large, medicine took the credit for whatever was deemed progressive and successful. Women took the blame for individual failures. The gender ideology championed the claims of the medical profession which guaranteed the health and safety of mother and child *if* the mother obeyed all the tenets of ante-natal hygiene, and followed the experts' regimes punctiliously. The contradictoriness, changeability and vagueness of these tenets and regimes, as well as the difficult social and economic circumstances of many mothers, meant that the guarantee could always be reneged on, and the blame for failure placed squarely upon the individual mother.

As discussed in chapter 6, other regulatory professionals apart from doctors also entered into variously imbalanced alliances with mothers: nurses, teachers, social workers, women police, family counsellors. The mother's body and her maternal behaviour were put more closely under surveillance, were made more open to intervention, became of more intense and direct social concern to the professions and to the state. Ideological standards of physical motherhood became firmly entrenched values in the knowledge and practices of the professions. Further, the most generally accepted of the standards were given substantive form by legislation passed at various times after the 1880s.

Thus, abortion had long been a criminal offence, but around the turn of the century, the state began to prosecute women and their abortionists much more rigorously. At the same time, the various colonies or states legislated to penalise people (in practice, mainly women) who committed infanticide; who failed to provide adequate food, clothing, nursing or medical care to children under the age of 14 in their care; who wilfully neglected or ill-treated such children; who failed to have such children vaccinated against infectious diseases (Thame,

1974; Allen, 1982; Laster, 1982). Over half a century later, from the late 1960s, some of these ideological standards of physical maternal care underwent formal change. The illegality of abortion was modified, legislatively or judicially, in most states. The notion of neglect was made more flexible and its physical dimension qualified by reference to psychological considerations (Foreman, 1975:13). Further, the prevalence of child abuse, or parental maltreatment of their children, became of public concern and legislative moves were begun against it (O'Donnell & Craney, 1982).

Through this set of alliances and interventions, the physical ideal of the good mother was built up within the gender order. Its standards became expectations internalised by women. Failure to achieve those standards induced guilt. Failure to pursue them brought down punishment.

By the second half of the twentieth century, the gender ideology prescribed a clear pattern for correct childbirth and rearing. Good married women (with some leeway now permitted to Catholic women) made decisions about how many children to have and when to have them. Once pregnant in accordance with these decisions, they carried their pregnancies to term, and bore healthy children. Any deviation from this pattern was deemed a failure of true femininity. Somehow, it was the woman's fault and to be reproved as an act of will, rather than treated as an act of God to be accepted fatalistically, or an accident to be acknowledged rationally. Katie Allen defaulted at three points in this pattern.

Katie was a 34-year-old English migrant who was admitted to Glenside Hospital in 1960 suffering from depression. She stayed only two months, but remained in contact with the Outpatient Department for the next nine years. Over that time, her failures in mothering were recorded in detail in her casenotes, which are summarised at the beginning of this chapter.

First of all, Katie failed to exercise correct control over her fertility. Although a Roman Catholic, she practised contraception, that is, made decisions about her fertility, but failed to do so efficiently. She twice became pregnant by mistake. She compounded these mistakes by failing to carry her pregnancies to term, by miscarrying. Twice before, when she had succeeded at these initial stages, she failed in a third way by bearing unfit children—two epileptics, one of whom was also mentally retarded. The consequences of all these transgressions against the gender ideology were depression, confusion and guilt.

Throughout the twentieth century, Australian women progressively achieved control over their fertility. The possibility of such control, however, was accompanied by increasing responsibility and ideological pressure to exercise it. Such responsibility, which entailed making decisions from among many conflicting priorities, meant that pregnancy and childbirth could never again be treated as simple, natural consequences of heterosexual desire. An example of the complex web of motives and priorities involved in pregnancy is revealed in Helen Vane's casenotes, previously discussed in chapter 7:

[Helen Vane. Born 1925. Married 16 years. Three children—15,
12, 10 (mentally retarded). Voluntary admission 1963.] Mr Vane
has a service station, Helen did the cleaning. Mr Vane had a
woman bookkeeper—Helen was jealous of respective positions.
The woman left to have a baby. Subsequently Helen became
pregnant. 'I didn't deliberately get myself the same way, it was
just one of those slips'...[She was denied a therapeutic abortion by
her gynaecologist.] Was told she could be aborted in Melbourne
for £100. Felt it was wrong, but went; finally couldn't make up
her mind to stay for the operation and returned to Adelaide where
she haemorrhaged spontaneously, but did not lose baby; however,
there was considerable doubt at this stage whether baby was alive.
(Very distressed at this point of the interview.)...Helen agrees her
present illness is due to uncertainties re present pregnancy,
especially in view of tablets, etc., she's had at start of pregnancy
(slimming, for URTIs, etc.) and that she has one mentally
deficient child. Would kill herself 'if she had the guts'...Her
conflict appears basically that she does want the baby but feels
that her husband's attitude and circumstances are against
her...Both [husband and wife] feel guilty re having abortion—yet
both wish like hell it had been.

Helen could have deliberately avoided pregnancy, but she slipped
up—possibly because of her competitive jealously. Once pregnant, the
real possibility of having an abortion, even if illegally, gave her too
many choices for any easy decision. She felt abortion to be wrongful,
and had been denied a legitimate one by a medical expert. She feared
for the health of the baby because of her use of drugs and because of the
possibility of hereditary or congenital mental defect. She was in conflict
with her husband, who seems to have been equally ambivalent about
having the child. She already had three children and the family's
economic circumstances were not auspicious for another child.
Helen's response was depressive dithering and admitting herself to a
mental hospital. Nor did the birth of the child resolve her conflict: 'very
depressed and weeping copiously...is self-deprecating, has suicidal
thoughts...strong ideas of guilt'.

Unplanned pregnancies, infertility, miscarriage and stillbirth stood
as possible threats between each woman and the ideal of motherhood.
Each live birth itself was fraught with the possibility of the mother
suffering debilitating depression. Many of the Glenside Hospital casenotes contain the refrain: 'suffered no illness till after the birth of the
child'. (A 1969 British study found that at least half the pregnant
women investigated suffered from depression—'the Blues'—after giving birth, and that almost 11 per cent were more severely depressed to
the point of being diagnosed as suffering from 'psychotic puerperal
depression' (Pitt, 1969; Oakley, 1979:12).)

As well, each mother was faced with the possibility of giving birth to an abnormal baby. Several medical procedures, including ultrasound monitoring and amniocentesis, were developed in the 1970s to check for foetal abnormality, but their availability in Australia has been circumscribed on financial grounds. Even when abnormality can be diagnosed, many women are then placed in the ideological and religious dilemma of having an abortion, even a therapeutic one, when this goes against their well-engrained beliefs and sense of femininity.

Already, the cases of Katie Allen and Helen Vane have shown the maternal worry and blame attendant upon bearing retarded and epileptic children. Giovanna Talbot was in a similar situation. Her notes are never clear on whether her son, John, was retarded or an epileptic. Whatever his disability, he caused considerable unhappiness to Giovanna, and a broad rift between her and her husband. 'She says she has had "a lot of ups and downs and the little chap is to blame".' Mr Talbot wanted his son placed in an institution. Giovanna wanted to look after him (as a good mother was required to), but eventually realised that she was unable to do so. Each spouse blamed the other for the failure of the family:

> [1954] Giovanna says husband says 'she is nuts and so is John'...Says husband is getting his revenge by having her in hospital...Since in Adelaide, 'nothing but talk of mental hospitals' and husband says 'son takes after her and her side of the family'.
> [1959] Mr Talbot says his wife deserted him a year ago because she believed him the cause of her 'breakdowns'. He thinks she still believes that. He has just about 'had it' with trouble with his wife and son who died in 1957...Wife was well as far as he knows until birth of child ten years ago.

The physical failures of motherhood were possible at the stages of conception, pregnancy and birth. However, success, or normality, at these points did not end the physical jeopardy. Next came the imperative to keep the child healthy. Again, failure came to be viewed as fault not fate. If a child became physically or mentally ill, the mother was to blame. Thus, Katie Allen was 'totally pre-occupied' with the variety of her children's abnormalities: epilepsy, retardation, emotional problems, nightmares, religious mania, kleptomania. Her self-recrimination fuelled her depression. 'Nothing seems to turn out right...I'm just a burden to everybody.'

The ideology of motherhood proclaimed that mothers must protect their children from all physical harm. But this was more easily declared than done, since mothers must not overprotect and hence smother their children's growing independence (cf. Chafe, 1972:201–2; Friedan, 1965:167–9). The line between was thin and worrisome. Leonie Bertrams admitted herself to Glenside Hospital in 1969 because she could not successfully negotiate that line.

Present illness dates from birth of last child 5½ years ago. Eight months after birth, found herself getting increasingly slower in coping with household tasks...Constantly preoccupied with thoughts of the necessity for correct personal hygiene...A precipitating factor at that time was an attack of diarrhoea affecting both children and herself. Her baby daughter would have as many as six bowel motions in one day and would need to be stripped and bathed on each occasion. Leonie felt compelled to go over things in the home, when cleaning, time and time again. She felt anxious and apprehensive. Fear that unless things kept clean some dreadful disease due to lack of cleanliness would strike the family and be regarded as her fault...Last six months, increasingly affected and upset by her 'fussiness'—fears that she will ruin the children's lives through insistence on handwashing and neatness and scrupulous care when they go to the toilet.

Throughout the first few decades of the twentieth century, mothers' ignorance, negligence and dirtiness had been consistently blamed for the high infant-mortality rate in Australia, as discussed in chapters 5 and 6. Domestic hygiene and cleanliness could not be insisted upon too much according to the childrearing advice of those early years. Once the mortality rate had declined and stabilised by the 1930s, a high standard was thereafter simply assumed, maintained by maternal fear and guilt, reinforced by the advertising campaigns of the producers of soap and cleaning equipment. Then entered notions of the child's psychological health, which was predominantly affected by its relationship with its mother. Her standards were now thrown into disarray. How much of everything was enough, and how were they to be balanced to nurture perfection in her child? Fear and guilt were compounded.

The obverse of guilt within the gender ideology of maternity was punishment. Those women who deviated too far from the path of feminine motherhood were denied the right to be mothers at all. The unsuitable or unfit mother could have her child physically removed from her care. In extreme cases, she could be sterilised to prevent her from ever again aspiring to the feminine status of mother.

Until the 1960s, the very fact of an illegitimate birth was enough to make a woman an unfit mother. Morally and economically, single motherhood was a contradiction in terms. Both religious and secular welfare bodies took for granted that the only course to take—in the interests of both baby and mother—was the adoption of the child by a fit (married, monogamous, heterosexual and respectable) mother. Such removal of her child was a punishment hard to bear for any woman. A baby was a reward, and the status of motherhood a prize within the gender order.

Deidre Quilper (see chapter 7) bore an illegitimate child to a married man in 1950. She stayed in a Catholic refuge for several months until just after the birth. The nuns thought her 'well liked' and they 'understood that it was her first lapse'. The baby was placed for adoption almost immediately, and Deidre went with her mother to Port Augusta 'where another sister was in difficulties with a sick family'.

> Deidre did not seem very happy, lost a little weight, and was not very easy to get on with. Her family thought it best that she forget about the baby and the subject was hardly mentioned. [Her mother] thinks now that Deidre must have been under considerable strain, having to care for her sister's young children.

After five months, Deidre returned to Adelaide, seeking her baby who had already been adopted. She was put up for the night at the refuge, and the sisters admitted her to hospital the next morning. 'Has ideas of persecution, talks irrationally. Says people stand over her bed.' The Glenside psychiatrists recorded her claim: 'I haven't given the final signature and I want him back, that's why I came back from Port Augusta'. She remained in hospital for six months, then was released to the care of her mother who 'states that she intends to stay and look after Deidre. She now blames herself for not being more sympathetic and understanding towards Deidre.'

Deidre's maternal unfitness was seen and punished by her family, religious welfare workers, and psychiatrists. Once adoption had removed the sign of her failure, these agents of the gender order could support and help her. But their sympathy was not enough since they could or would not restore to Deidre her chance at feminine fulfilment. 'The Child Welfare Department state that the child has been legally adopted and the case is now closed.' While Deidre improved enough to leave hospital, became calmer and more settled than 'at any time since the start of her troubles eighteen months ago', she nonetheless 'impresses as being in a state of apathy'. The notes do not reveal how long afterwards she remained in this state, nor whether she ever managed to expiate her transgression sufficiently to be allowed a new attempt at legitimate motherhood and true femininity.

To bear an illegitimate child was a standard form of unfitness. It could be at least partially rectified by abandoning the baby to the state, or by contracting a hasty marriage. Even so, the stigma took a long time, if it ever did, to disappear from the mother's, and others', memories. On the other hand, the unfitness could be compounded, rendering the woman not simply mistaken and redeemable, but positively vicious and an enemy of the gender order. Such a one was Gwen Kirk, part of whose story was discussed in chapter 7.

In 1961 at the age of 13, Gwen became pregnant to a married man. This brought her to the attention of both judicial and welfare authorities. She was placed under the custody and control of the

Department of Child Welfare until eighteen. After the birth of her child, she went to work as a live-in attendant at a day nursery, while her mother looked after the baby. The fact that her mother was prepared to care for the child is a crucial difference between Gwen's and Deidre's cases. Apart from the possession of a substantial and independent income, such familial support was the only barrier against the necessary abandonment of the baby until 1973. (In that year, the federal government acknowledged the changed gender ideology in relation to illegitimacy, and provided a pension as of right to unmarried mothers, within the general category of women who were supporting dependent children without the aid of a male breadwinner.) Gwen and her mother, however, disagreed over the best childrearing methods, and after two years, Gwen gave the baby up for adoption. Conflict induced by the baby was too great, despite the fact that 'she was pleased to have the baby as it was something for her to look after and someone to love her'.

At the age of 20, Gwen gave birth to another illegitimate child, whom she looked after alone. A year and a half later (1970), she became pregnant again and procured an abortion. (It is not clear whether this was a legal operation or not. The Criminal Law Consolidation Act of South Australia was amended in 1969 to liberalise the grounds of legal abortion.) Two years later again, Gwen had another, this time legal, abortion. After eight years, four pregnancies and five psychiatric admissions, Gwen, now aged 24 and still unmarried, was described by her psychiatrist:

> this unfortunate young woman shows features of gross personality disorder of the hysterical type, characterised by demanding, manipulative, exhibitionistic, histrionic, destructive and seductive behaviour over many years.

Gwen's psychiatrist was thoroughly frustrated by her refusals to adhere to the imperatives of normal femininity and her abuse of her physical female powers. He therefore advocated that she be denied the reward of maternity. 'Social worker informed that Gwen may be an unfit mother...Have suggested tubal ligation—she refuses emphatically.' That the motivation behind these suggestions was moral and ideological repugnance rather than scientific assessment was suggested by an earlier, and remarkably candid, confession by her psychiatrist:

> Whether one regards [this behaviour] primarily as the manifestation of cerebral dysrhythmia, or the firing off of a low frustration tolerance, or plain acting (of the acting out variety) is probably mainly a value judgement and subject to a Doctor's or nurse's emotional preference...It is difficult for us to stomach. But how angry shall we have to get in turn?

Gwen was not sterilised, nor was her child taken away from her. Threat, but not compulsion was used. The fact, however, that the issues were even raised points to the ideological nature of motherhood and to the physical forms of punishment of those who transgressed its norms. Such punishments could also, of course, be desired and inflicted by women themselves after transgression of their own, internalised, norms of femininity. Women accused themselves of being unfit mothers, sent 'their children away because they could not look after them properly, sought hysterectomies or sterilisation because of feeling unworthy to be mothers. Within the ideology of femininity, even the apparently physical dimension of motherhood was social.

The good child

As discussed in chapters 5 and 6, from the early years of the twentieth century, the protection of the child from avoidable harm—whether from inheritable defects, dirt and germs, accidents, poverty or an unsuitable home environment—was established as crucial to true motherhood. The physical welfare of the child was paramount. But as the century progressed, the gender ideology diversified and added the insubstantiality of psychological welfare and discipline to the burden of maternity. Such welfare was given content by an ever expanding variety of beliefs about infant psychology expressed in a plethora of childrearing books published from the 1920s, and in the practices of the increasing numbers of regulatory professionals involving themselves in child bearing and rearing (cf. Newson & Newson, 1974).

This responsibility of mothers for the psychological and emotional health of their offspring, and for their social discipline, was exercised positively as encouragement and ambition, and negatively as punishment for transgression of both family and social norms. Failure in both of these aspects can be, once again, illustrated from the casenotes of Katie Allen.

Katie and her young family migrated from England in the mid-1950s, presumably seeking, along with most other British migrants, a better life in better economic conditions for the children (Appleyard, 1964:213). But nothing worked out right. Katie herself worked hard, as a wife, as a mother, and in the paid workforce. But her ambitions for her husband, her children and herself were incompatible. She got 'fed up with being a housewife', and sought paid work. This doubled her workload, she became exhausted, and she felt guilty every time something went wrong with her children because it meant that she was not a good mother. She exerted 'considerable pressure' on her eldest son to continue his education, wanting him to advance himself, and thereby the family. He, however, sought spiritual rather than material advancement. Another son failed at school and took a dead-end job. A third deliberately thwarted his own career and Katie's ambition for him by shoplifting. Katie's maternal responsibility, reinforcing her purpose in migrating—social mobility and material improvement carried on into the next generation—was a broken dream. Katie's positive mothering was a failure.

Moreover, Katie was often in danger of failure even in the negative aspect of mothering. On at least three occasions, mentioned in her casenotes, she was unable to discipline her children sufficiently to prevent the intervention of external authorities into her family life. She had borne an epileptic son whose unhappiness upset the whole family. She was advised to take him to hospital which she did, and his fits were controlled: medicine saved the family as an ally of the mother. She had nurtured a thief, indicating, according to the gender ideology, some moral deficiency in the family for which she was responsible. The police and the law punished the son and, through denying him a job, stigmatised the family in order to protect society. Katie had fostered a religious fanatic, and was advised to have him certified as insane. She was 'reluctant to act'. Psychiatry hovered on the outskirts of the family, willing to intervene as mother's ally should internal disruption prove too great, ready to intervene punitively as mother's supervisor should she be unable to prevent her children from becoming a menace to society beyond the family.

Bringing up children, the heart of mothering, was a social activity in which women became increasingly beset by a farrago of standards and a confusion of judges. The first level of judgment was, of course, that of the mother of herself. Thus, Martha Crafers was concerned that her worry over her son's behaviour might drive her to violence against him. Such a response would be clearly excessive and would compound her failure as a mother rather than expiating it. So she sought psychiatric help. Martha was fifty when she admitted herself to Glenside Hospital in 1960. Her son, by her first marriage, was seventeen. He had been

> expelled [from school] following an affair with a girl. Now an
> apprentice, in debt with car, seldom able to pay board at home.
> Martha has remonstrated with him over his behaviour; several times
> has lost her temper. Feels unable to control herself when in temper,
> feels may do him considerable harm. 'Has not used the knife yet' but
> feels she might...Temper not associated with alcohol...I do not feel
> she is very depressed at the moment but believe a short stay in
> hospital will enable her to re-think her problems. It will be as well to
> have a talk with her son concerning his and his mother's behaviour.

Clearly, Martha had failed to inculcate in her son appropriate sexual and economic discipline. Moreover, she failed in self-discipline—a cardinal fault in a mother. But she did retain a sense of responsibility towards the social order. Rather than compounding her failure through violence, she subordinated herself to authority, accepting psychiatry's legitimacy to judge and to modify her behaviour to a more appropriate maternity.

An enforced rest, psychotropic drugs, and the intervention of professionals into her family life—re-ordering her standards and sanctions of child discipline—seemed to work. Within three weeks, Martha returned home where 'everything "very good" '. Martha had failed in the social-control aspect of mothering, but she did the best she could to conform to its other standards. She monitored her own behaviour, then volunteered to have modified those practices that she believed to be deviant.

Such monitoring, however, was not solely a personal task. It was very thoroughly socialised. There were many agents of surveillance—relatives, neighbours, friends, police, social workers, doctors—whose reports could lead to compulsory modification of maternal behaviour. For example, Christine Perkins was informed against by her sister. Christine was certified in 1955 at the age of 38. She received messages from 'one above', was at times aggressive and hostile towards her husband 'for no reason at all', and she thought that everyone else was ill and needed electroconvulsive therapy. She had had a number of previous psychiatric admissions. On this occasion, after a series of electroconvulsive treatments, her psychiatrist reported, 'I think she is about as good as she is likely to be and may be able to adjust herself reasonably well although she will probably still have delusions'. The next entry, however, sealed her fate for the next six months:

> Sister called and said Christine is spoiling her children, carries a boy of 9 years old about like a baby, dresses him and takes him to the toilet, doing everything for him as if he were a baby. For sake of children, it would be better if she were transferred [to a long-stay ward].

By whatever method a familied woman came to the attention of the psychiatrists, and whatever her symptoms and diagnosis, her mothering would be placed under scrutiny. Judgment of her mothering would be made according to the moral or.gender standards of the psychiatrists. Failures on such criteria would be translated into medical facts, objective symptoms of mental illness.

Rosalind Hughes was fifty six when certified in 1950. She had been living with her 33-year-old daughter who eventually found her unmanageable and sought to prevent her further deterioration through medical intervention. Rosalind was dirty and slipshod, heard voices which kept her awake all night, and was heavily addicted to a morphine-based patent medicine. Such behaviour, however, was not sufficient for her psychiatrist, who needed to import into his medical

diagnosis an ideological judgment of her femininity. (I am not suggesting here that interviewing Rosalind to uncover evidence of her opinions
and attitudes was an inappropriate medical procedure—it was not.
Rather, I am trying to establish that the psychiatrist's moral judgments
of Rosalind's particular attitudes came to influence his apparently
scientific medical diagnosis of her illness.)

She dismisses major issues as being of little importance, such as her
marriage [she never lived with her husband after the war, for which
she blames her parents], and the fact that her daughter is living with
another man and her children while separated from her husband.

Beyond self-monitoring, and surveillance by family and professionals, a woman's training of her children was hedged around by legislation. Each mother was directly under obligation to the state. She was
responsible for the child's physical well-being. She was also required,
on pain of legal punishment, to enforce her child's minimal conformity
to the economic and gender orders' standards. She must ensure her
child's attendance at school between certain ages. She must prevent its
employment, wandering the streets, smoking, drinking alcohol and
gambling. She must monitor its companions and reading matter.
Maternal duty and responsibility as such were not spelt out. It was the
commission or omission of certain specific acts that invoked state
intervention and maternal punishment. The state had an interest in the
maintenance of a minimal social discipline that could not be simply left
to the power of ideological or moral persuasion.

This aspect of social control thus had two sides: it was the mother's
responsibility to discipline her child into socially appropriate behaviour, to make of it a good child. In the process, she herself was
ensnared by the gender ideology's discipline of maternity. Such discipline she was expected to embrace willingly. If she did not, she could be
coerced into it or, ultimately, punished for her refusal or failure.

The end of mothering

The pattern of a woman's life after her children had grown up was an
ambivalent one within the gender order. During the heyday of the
population ideology, from the turn of the century till the 1930s, motherhood was proclaimed the fulfilment and culmination of a good woman's
life. The status of grandmother was a peripheral or additional one. In
the 1890s in Australia, the average life expectancy of women was 55
years, average age at marriage was about 24, and the average number
of surviving children was seven. Thus, statistically, grandmothers existed in profusion. But it was active mothering that was the task and
identity that generally coincided with almost all of an adult woman's

life. Many women would become grandmothers while still mothering their own younger children, and die before the last-born child married.

The status of grandmother alone, not combined with that of mother, was less common, and only very rough guidelines existed within the gender ideology for the correct pursuit of post-maternal femininity. A grandmother should try to provide a home for her family should they ever need to return to it in an emergency. She should advise her daughters and daughters-in-law on the finer points of mothering. She should befriend her grandchildren in a way not possible for the busy mother of young children. She should bestow upon her family the calmness and wisdom of age. In many ways, grandmothering was but an extension of mothering, and overlapped with it over many years.

Progressively throughout the century, however, grandmothering became more and more distinct from mothering. Women married earlier, completed their child bearing and rearing earlier, and lived longer. Certainly, the dependency of childhood was extended through the invention of teen-age and adolescence, and by the prolongation of schooling. But, by the 1960s, a woman faced about 30 more years after her last child married, for the last 16 of which she would probably be a widow (Bower, 1978:161–2).

At this very time—from the 1950s—when demographic circumstances were producing increasing numbers of grandmothers, the gender ideology virtually abandoned them. In these decades, all the emphasis upon motherhood and wifehood, upon the two-generation nuclear family. This was the era of 'togetherness', of 'do-it-yourself' domesticity. Permissive consumerism declared it the age of youth. Sexual attractiveness was increasingly a major attribute of all phases of femininity. Young families were relatively affluent, and did not require the minimal emergency support offered by grandmother. Regulatory professionals claimed a monopoly on childrearing advice, and deprecated the wisdom of experience. Grandmothers were ignored as women. Only slowly did they begin to receive some little consideration: as problems, as workers, as consumers.

Post-maternal women emerged as the possessors of the 'empty-nest syndrome' in the 1970s. Women who believed in the old population ideology of femininity and had dedicated themselves totally to motherhood found themselves at a loss when the last of the children left home while they were still in middle age. Their years of sacrifice to their families ended abruptly without reward or compensation, and their talents were no longer useful. The consequence for such good women was depression, often so severe as to need long-term treatment: therapy, drugs, hospitalisation. Depression is, par excellence, a middle-aged woman's problem (cf. Bart, 1971; Silverman, 1968).

At a later stage in her life, the post-maternal woman became part of another problem: the aged. Old age did not emerge as a social issue in

Australia until the late 1970s, when demographic trends indicated the rapid aging or 'greying' of the Australian population. The first major problem identified as afflicting the elderly was poverty. At the time of the 1975 Commission of Inquiry into Poverty, they constituted the largest, though not poorest, group of the poor (Poverty in Australia, 1975:234). A new academic discipline of social gerontology developed in the early 1980s to consider these issues, but was unfortunately plagued with the usual gender bias. Despite the fact that women comprise the majority of the elderly, the category is treated as a masculine universal. Old workers, old migrants, old Aborigines, old pensioners are assumed to be men, and women are tacked on as an afterthought (Howe, 1981:7).

Post-maternal women, of course, are not necessarily either depressed or old. Many cease mothering and embark upon grandmotherhood in their middle forties. Increasingly from the 1960s, such women became, or remained, paid workers in the commanding economy, working either full- or part-time. However, those years she had spent mothering would be held against her in this masculine sphere. Her male age-peers, with whom she might have begun work after leaving school, would now all be senior and superior to her within the gendered workplace. More than likely, she would not be welcomed back into her old job. Not only was the commanding workforce divided by gender but also by age. Many of the attractive female jobs were designated for young women only. In the 1980s, the gender ideology does not yet fully accommodate the older, post-maternal woman as a paid worker.

Further, the ideology of permissive consumerism, which supplanted the old population ideology by the 1960s, does not yet fully accommodate such women. The expected time of spending and buying are those years when the family is growing up. The target unit of consumption is the intact nuclear family household. By the time the children have left home, most of the consumer durables have been bought. For a while, the woman probably has more disposable income if both she and her husband continue to work. The older couple is just coming to be exploited as a market by the producers of luxuries: holidays and leisure or fitness activities, more sophisticated goods for home entertainment that children would monopolise or wreck. Eventually, however, the woman's income drops as she retires, as her husband retires and perhaps dies. She is no longer a lucrative consumer. She is no longer a worker. She is no longer an active mother.

For these post-maternal years, the gender ideology has nonetheless developed a certain direction for the good woman. It has established a process of gradual abandonment of the active pursuit of femininity. When the first child marries, she becomes a mother-in-law. With the birth of her daughter's or daughter-in-law's first child she may become the younger woman's adviser and support. As the child grows, she settles into being a grandmother. Late in life, if she becomes frail or senile, she reverts to a condition of uselessness, a virtually de-gendered dependent.

At the marriage of her first child, a mother reaches her penultimate triumph, unequivocal proof of at least some success as a good woman. She has reared a new adult who is obedient to the ideology of the gender order. But at this very moment decline sets in. This is especially the case if it is a son who marries. Male approval is critical for the good woman. She receives her validation from men. With her son's marriage, she loses intimacy with, control over, and responsibility for a man who, in one way or another, has meant a great deal to her for twenty or so years. She must now share his masculine validation of her femininity with another woman.

Such sharing becomes, in some cases, a competition. Whether true in each case or not, some mothers feel the son's wife to be unworthy of him (of her creation). Some wives feel their mother-in-laws to be interfering and domineering. In the years after the second world war, this situation came under extreme misogynist scrutiny in America, just at that time when the gender order was in the throes of transition. For these critics, the problem was labelled the 'mother-in-law syndrome' and 'momism'. A 'pathological emptiness in women's lives' led to their failure 'in the elemental maternal function of weaning [their] offspring emotionally as well as physically' (Chafe, 1972:201–2). How widely accepted this ideological imagery was in Australia is not known. But some wives' fear of their mothers-in-law was certainly apparent.

Katie Allen, according to her casenotes, felt herself to be a victim of the mother-in-law syndrome: judged wanting as a suitable wife, treated shabbily, unfairly criticised. She described her husband's mother as 'a very dominant woman...no one could live harmoniously with her'. Her mother-in-law successfully drove a wedge between Katie and her husband: 'things not the same between husband and myself since they left'. Her husband claimed that 'he went out of his way to be offhand with parents when they were here'. But Katie believed that 'husband was loyal to them and not to her'.

In a similar vein, another Glenside patient, Vera King, was apparently in great fear of her mother-in-law who stood, physically and metaphorically, between Vera and her hope of marital happiness:

> 'She said I was not fit to be her son's wife, and was so unpleasant that I would not go to their home even with my hubby.' When she died they were married...It appears that when they were married, the fear of Mrs King remained...(What did she seem like to your imagination Vera?) 'A big hard woman, but she was really only quite small.' (What did she seem like to you?) 'Like an ogre...' [1945]

The mother-in-law of the syndrome refused to hand on the mantle of mother long after her children were adult. Sometimes, of course, it was the children who refused to allow her to retire gracefully. Sons might compare wives with mothers, and opt to return to the latter. However the pattern was motivated, the older woman was looked at askance within the gender ideology.

In 1964, Ada Norris, whose case was discussed in chapter 8, was fifty nine and had seven children, six boys and one girl, the youngest of whom was twenty eight. She was depressed and had admitted herself to hospital for the fifth time in two years. A social worker submitted a report on her home life, obtained from an informal interview with an unsuspecting neighbourhood gossip:

> The eldest and youngest boys were not married and lived at home. Two other boys were parted from their wives and expected Ada to be able to look after them and their children.

According to the neighbour, Ada was mothering three generations: her invalid husband, her sons, both married and unmarried, and her grandchildren. There is no evidence in the casenotes, but it would be possible to suppose that the estranged wives of Ada's sons may have feared Ada as an interfering mother-in-law. The very fact that she was willing to take back and care for her sons and their children rather than insisting that they make their own ways with their new families suggests this possibility. Certainly, it was a thought that occurred to the social worker:

> I asked the neighbour did she think Mrs Norris may have interfered with the sons and their wives. The neighbour's opinion is that Mrs Norris certainly would not have. She feels Mrs Norris will never be able to cope while they all expect her to do so much for them. She feels that it is time that they started to help Mrs Norris for a change.

The wife's mother-in-law was a stranger to her, linked to and sharing in her husband's superior power, a continuing source of judgment of the wife's femininity. In the best of cases, there would be some benificent conspiracy in the interests of the man they both loved; in the worst, there would be resentment, hostility, and fierce competition. The mother-in-law's power and the wife's fear were usually greatest before the wife had children of her own. The birth of the first child in the correct circumstances—within legal marriage—was the fundamental symbol of the achievement of full adult status for both women and men throughout twentieth-century Australia. Other rites of passage existed, but tended to be more ambiguous. The usual pattern, still remarkably uniform in the 1970s, was for young women to leave school, start work, then leave home at the time of marriage (Young, 1980:47). Depending upon a number of factors, such as class, occupation, economic climate and housing availability, the young woman might still remain at home after marriage, with her new husband, or live with his parents, while the new couple accumulated the capital to buy a house or furnish a rented one. Until the second world war, it was usually expected that a woman would leave work upon marriage. It was desired by many women because of their limited job options and low pay. It was insisted upon by many employers who relied for profitability on a fairly rapid turnover of junior female staff. It was sanctioned by many men who saw non-working wives as symbols of respectability and working ones as competitors for their own jobs. It was encouraged by state legislation placing disabilities upon married women workers in the interests of gender discipline for economic and domestic harmony. During the war, these considerations were patriotically (and profitably) suspended, and thereafter, the increasing tendency was for women to work until sometime during the first pregnancy.

Within the variability of these circumstances of work and living arrangements, it was the certainty of the event of the first legitimate child that remained the definite sign of the assumption of the responsibilities of adulthood. Thereafter, everyone's status took on a new dimension: the mother-in-law became a grandmother; the son/husband became a father; the wife, a mother. The wife now stood, potentially, in a new bargaining-position because she had enhanced her femininity through maternity, and because she possessed, physically, a hostage or a pawn in the generational power game.

Her erstwhile competitor was diminished. Unless the original mother–mother-in-law–grandmother retained control of disposable property, thereby retaining some parental authority over adult children, at this moment she was pushed a large step away from an active definition of femininity. By such changes, for example, Iris Wentworth ended up on the outer in the struggle with her son's wife. As a mother, Iris had failed to inculcate correct sexual discipline in her son, who 'had to get married' in 1968. She probably viewed with extreme disfavour the young woman whose own lax discipline had allowed revelation of this failure. Nonetheless, the consequence was a speeded-up process of devolution of her maternal status to her daughter-in-law once the child was actually born within wedlock.

> Daughter-in-law complains that Iris has been ringing her up continually and doesn't let them lead their own life. 'She is always talking about sex.' Iris feels that her daughter-in-law is in need of treatment herself, and she won't let her take any interest in her grandchild. [1969]

With the birth of the wife's first child, the relationship between her and either or both her own mother and her mother-in-law could change substantially. Before the birth, the attention of both generations of women was upon the adult male. After the birth, it was more particularly upon the infant (who, in the childrearing literature throughout the century, was inevitably male). There is considerable historical and anthropological literature indicating that this relationship has been a particularly significant one in western societies over many centuries. Through maternity, a woman entered a special world of women, of female relatives and friends, in which experiences and skills were shared, and reassurance and security given. Within this world, the new mother pursued the highest goal of femininity, that of good motherhood, and central to this mission was the model and physical assistance of her own mother (cf. Bernard, 1981; Smith-Rosenberg, 1975; Bott, 1957).

Most commentators have indicated a change in this system of maternal networks in the past few decades, with pregnant women and new mothers having fewer kin around them, and relying more on friends and experts. This is not to say, however, that the importance of the mother–daughter relationship at the time of the daughter's child bearing and rearing has been completely eclipsed. As an obvious example, the importance of grandmothers as babysitters and childminders is still well recognised (by mothers themselves) as the best substitute when mothers leave home occasionally or regularly. (By 1980, over a quarter of the children of women in the paid workforce were being cared for by relatives—mainly grandmothers (Women's Bureau, 1981:38–9; Harper & Richards, 1979:120–1).)

Another fairly common example was that of the wife's mother continuing to provide a protective familial haven, the one place where an adult woman with children could possibly go when there was nowhere else. For example, Yve Markeby provided a permanent haven for her daughter:

> This woman has been twice widowed and her last husband died sixteen months ago...She has a married daughter and her three children living with her. At present this daughter is divorcing her husband, but this does not worry her. 'He has never been any good to her.'

Comparison with two cases discussed above is relevant to Yve's situation. Firstly, her position was the opposite of Ada Norris', whose sons, not daughter, returned to their mother's home with their children—a fairly uncommon occurrence. In general, upon separation or divorce, the children of the marriage remained in the custody of their mother, although since the late 1970s, under the operations of the Family Law Court, there has been an increase in paternal custody. Secondly, as was the case with Rosalind Hughes, Yve's mothering evoked a moral response from her psychiatrist. The gender ideology held by such men was obviously in favour of women maintaining the integrity of the two-generational nuclear family as their feminine duty.

Much of the historical and sociological discussion of mother–daughter relationships has emphasised them as benign, educative and supportive kinship rituals. But this is only one side. As with all the relationships so far discussed, the mother–daughter bond is embedded within the gender ideology of femininity. There is thus the inevitability, in individual experience, of failure to attain the impossible ideal.

Two extreme situations of failure are exposed in the casenotes of two young women who were admitted to Glenside Hospital in the 1960s. Gwen Kirk's story has been recounted above: she bore an illegitimate child at the age of 13, and her mother cared for the child for about two years, after which it was put up for adoption. The relationship between Gwen and her mother was clearly fraught with antipathy, but tempered by necessity and duty:

> On many occasions before [Gwen's pregnancy] her mother had said that when the father had died she would kick her out of the house. After the baby was born the mother took care of it while Gwen went to work in the City. At weekends the girl would go home and visit the baby but found that the mother was looking after the baby in a way contrary to what Gwen thought right...Six months ago Gwen gave up the baby for adoption...There is evidence of...overt aggression towards her mother...Gwen jealous of mother re baby...Mother shows no interest in Gwen at all.

In Gwen's eyes, her mother had failed twice: firstly in her relationship with Gwen herself, and secondly in her improper mothering of her grandchild. Gwen dealt with these failures by sending the baby away from the family altogether and, later, when legally and economically able to, by removing herself from it. Meanwhile, her mother's justification for looking after the child as its social mother was that Gwen, as its biological mother, was unfit because of extreme youth.

A rather more wretched relationship, indicating the same sorts of maternal failure, apparently existed between Eve Innes and her mother. Eve was admitted in 1961, aged 20.

> Eve's florid symptoms date from an astonishing sequence of violence a few years ago. Her husband suicided after seven weeks of marriage, leaving her pregnant. Before that, he beat her. Then her twin sister's husband robbed Eve's belongings, later he killed the twin sister's five week old baby, which was nearly the age of Eve's own daughter...Her stepfather, she says, beats her mother, and to a less extent herself...Three months ago Eve left home to try and get cheaper board elsewhere because she was paying £4 a week from her £5/10/0 p.w. pension. The baby fretted, however, and Eve returned to her mother despite the heavy board...Eve says mother drinks all the time and expects Eve to do all the work...mother hits her...Can't get a job because of child—mother doesn't care.

[Second admission, 1961] The surrounding world worries Eve.
Wanted to hit people. Has hit her child...Mother claims Eve is cruel
to her child (2 years old).

[1962] During last weekend trial-leave Eve threatened to kill her
daughter and mother and then herself.

[1963] One must be very concerned that Eve's small daughter is
not exposed to further violent assault.

[1965] [Interview with mother: admits husband beats her and son
beats him.]

[1965] Recurrence of depression. In particular she feels resentful
and disappointed in her daughter (5½y.) who has been telling her to
return to this hospital and that she doesn't want to have any further
dealings with her. 'They are turning the child against me.'...The
mother is emphatic in not wanting to have Eve.

[1966] [Letter from mother:] 'I am writing to let you know Dr that
Eve *can not come home to sleep any more* it is not fair for my little Grand
Daughter to have to give up her own bed from Friday to Sunday. I've
got *no* thanks whatever from Eve by allowing her to come home.'

[1966] Hostel arrangements made: Cost $12.00 p.w., pension
$19.50 p.w. (widows), leaves $7.50 p.w. of which mother wants $6.00
for upkeep of child. Eve says she will only pay $4.00.

[1967] Visits mother twice each week to see her daughter.

[1968] Relationship with man X. Eve's mother is writing Eve
nasty letters saying X is married etc., and doubtless she will try to
break up the relationship with X or write to the pensions
department.

[1969] Doing well, living with X.

Even more than in Gwen's case, here was a mother who refused to
allow her daughter adult feminine, maternal status. To be a widow at
seventeen was somehow careless. The process of marrying, leaving
home, bearing a child was skewed. Both mother and daughter had
failed in their pursuit of ideal motherhood. Soon the young child was
also drawn into the power play between the two women, learning at the
same time the patterns of failure. Here were three generations of
women, caught in a cycle of violence and vindictiveness, unable to
conform to appropriate gender patterns, failing to transmit and to learn
the discipline of true maternity.

The gender ideology proclaimed mothering to be the central activity
of the good woman. Grandmotherhood was a more passive status, a
retirement after success in launching the next generation into its own
pursuit of the ideals of the gender order. But for specific circumstances,
specific qualifications were introduced. In both Gwen's and Eve's
cases, these qualifications were too subtle. When these young women
bore children, everyone became caught in status ambiguities. Gwen
and Eve were considered (by both their own mothers and by state
authorities) to be too young to be mothers, so they remained daughters.
Their mothers then remained mothers, taking on the new infants as

their own, rather than changing their status to grandmothers. As the daughters grew older, however, they tried to take up the superior status their biological motherhood should have given them, and came into conflict with their mothers' unwillingness to relinquish their mothering for the lesser status of grandmother.

Such ambiguity is rarely so openly expressed, but it nonetheless lies close to the heart of the ideal of motherhood. The desire to become a mother has been that component of the gender ideology most universally accepted by women and most encouraged by all the gender order's institutions and agencies. And at the end of mothering, there is nothing else to do. The feminine ideal dissipates, never having been truly achieved.

By her mid-sixties, she who had been mother would be but a survivor of a bygone generation. She would be economically dependent upon the government rather than her husband, eligible for either the old-age pension or the widows' pension. She would possibly live in poverty. Her only feminine function remaining within a gender order that had virtually abandoned her would be as an occasional babysitter. Some women, of course, continued active lives into their old age, in community activity, or in personal pursuits. Such activity was often honoured (especially with OBE's), but it was usually viewed as curiously degendered activity. Until the 1970s, the only women acknowledged in the public—masculine—sphere of politics and the administration of power had been a few older women. Such women had relinquished their feminine (reproductive) sexuality; they had completed their feminine (maternal) duty. They could now be granted a sort of neutral status which allowed them entry to some parts of the masculine world. Most women, however, stayed in the feminine world, gradually losing status and purpose as their feminine attributes faded and their feminine tasks declined. Within the Australian gender order the notion of an old woman is a derogatory one.

What remained for an elderly widow within that order was for her to relinquish finally and irrevocably all claim to feminine and maternal status (except in name and complaint), and to become, instead of its dispenser, the recipient of maternal care—if available. Such availability was determined, in the first place, by hereditary succession. That is, women needed to have daughters whom they had taught to pursue true femininity and who were willing to accept the maternal mantle of three-generational family responsibility. (A study in 1954 revealed that one in four elderly widows were beneficiaries of this system and lived in their daughters' households (Bower, 1978:163).)

It might be noted here the importance of women bearing daughters. The gender ideology has traditionally inculcated the desire for sons to carry on the family name and to inherit the family business or follow in father's occupation. But caring for the aged is and always has been in

Australia 'women's work'. Sons look after money, not mothers. Thus, a woman who had borne only sons would be in trouble when old unless the sons had made enough money to buy her institutional care, or they had married women who could be prevailed upon, as daughters-in-law, to undertake the task.

In general, this was the case with all familial caring—only women, of whatever generation, did it. It was part of the gender discipline, exercised within and around the family, centring upon the mother. It was strongly reinforced, throughout the century, by the various regulatory professionals and their institutions, and by the state and its parsimonious welfare provision, both before and after the second world war and the rise of the so-called welfare state.

The three-generational family tended to be rather difficult for a mother to run, requiring a fine sense of balance to adjust relations among family members, and between the family and professional or institutional supervisors. Such juggling is revealed in several of the cases. Thus, Lettie Banks was an 84-year-old widow who had 'lived alone, functioning very well with minimal support of daughter'. Two weeks before she was admitted in 1970, she had become disturbed and moved in with her daughter and her family. But Lettie kept the household awake at night with her complaints and screams, so her daughter had her certified. Her age, the acuteness of her disturbance, and the fact that her daughter had her own family to care for led to this certification. Lettie was not being a good mother or grandmother, so she was turned into a patient. She was a burden but she was not simply abandoned. Her two children and their families visited at least twice in the month she was in hospital, before her death.

A similar situation occurred in the case of Rita Grant, a 67-year-old widow who lived alone, but who often visited her daughter and her family. There, she quite directly threatened the harmony of the next generation.

> Her daughter is becoming afraid of her and the grandchildren are
> very upset by her shouting at them. She once raised a carving knife to
> her daughter in a threatening attitude, but did not use it. She is
> making libellous statements in public about various relatives.
> Becomes very depressed and emotional.

Rita was obviously no good, even as a babysitter, while in this state, so she was removed. Her daughter, however, retained her filial–maternal concern and was 'willing to take her mother as soon as she is well enough'. This also was the case with Rosalind Hughes' daughter, who had Rosalind certified because she could not care for and keep clean either herself or her room and was looking and acting strangely. The daughter, however, remained 'anxious to look after mother and be responsible for her'. In both instances, the daughters did take care of their mothers after discharge.

In other casenotes, there was a certain taken-for-grantedness about this female caring on the part of the recording psychiatrist. Fifty-one-year-old Sarah Irving, diagnosed as chronic schizophrenic, was commented upon by her outpatients doctor in 1965: 'mental state as previously. To have 84 year old mother living with her and son and grandson whilst new baby born. Undergoing hypnosis'. Or there was Iris Wentworth, whose family history read in part: 'Mother very childish for her last 3½ years; cared for by her daughters, mainly Iris. Everyone loved her.'

Such love for old women who had served and been subservient to men and their children all their adult lives was the promised reward of the gender ideology for the dedicated pursuit of femininity. But the gender order and its ideology cannot guarantee love, or affection, which cannot be produced on command. Ultimately, the pursuit of femininity must be its own reward.

10

Conclusion

*I*n the period covered by this book, the meaning of femininity passed through three phases. The years between the 1910s and the 1950s were a time of considerable stability in gender relations. These years were bounded at both ends by times of transition, at the turn of the century and in the 1960s and 1970s. In both of these transition periods, significant changes in both economy and ideology coincided with the emergence of new groups of social managers. From these associations, new directions were forged for femininity, new meanings were given to the ideal of the good woman.

At the turn of the century, the commanding masculine economy was firmly established as a modern mixed capitalism, balancing agriculture, manufacturing and services, with the majority of men employed in towns and cities. The domestic-service economy had reached its height and was in decline, and the rest of the feminine economy was divided. Some single women worked in female pockets of the commanding economy; other women were hidden in the local economy, with the home as their workplace. The commonsense view of the world to which everyone was increasingly adhering was underpinned by a preoccupation with the size and quality of the population. This preoccupation pushed the medical profession to the fore as that body of experts who could best ensure the strength and well-being of the population. The meaning of woman became centred in the home, as married mother of the race.

Meanwhile, the demographic transition was in full swing, with women having fewer children. Few individual families could sustain the rigid segregation of breadwinning husband and dependent wife, and women were compelled to make ends meet through both paid and unpaid work in the home. The medical profession ordained strict standards to ensure the physical health of children, but in the process

198

denigrated individual women's maternal abilities, demoting them to junior partners with medicine as the true protector of the population. Over the next 40 years, these contradictions of the gender order were played out in the lives of individual women. There was pride in making the best of a difficult job. There was shame and guilt in the face of failure. Through two wars and a depression, the meaning of femininity remained fairly constant. Real and striking changes in women's lives were seen as mere aberrations, temporary alterations that would soon return to normal.

But in the 1960s the contradictions and changes in the ideal of the good woman emerged again as social, not just individual, problems. The capitalist marketplace had extended into every corner of life. The home could no longer be seen as a separate and private place but was more visible as part of the social world. The local, domestic economy was exposed as its patterns of work time and work space were organised according to the imperatives of corporate profit. The ideology of permissive consumerism broke down the apparently unified ideal of the good woman as dependent mother. The new good woman was more complex, with new needs and desires and responsibilities, whose fulfilment could come only through the purchase of an infinitely diversifying range of goods and services. The rapid expansion of education in the postwar period had created, by the 1960s, a large group of new professionals. Their task was the management of economy and ideology so, inevitably, they were drawn into the management of women. They supervised and regulated the new complexity of femininity. They did not resolve its contradictions; rather they added to them.

In both periods of transition, many groups and individuals competed to fill the empty shell of femininity with prescriptions suited to their own ends. What a good woman's work should be, how she should exercise her sexuality, how she should conduct her mothering: these questions formed the main lines of debate and struggle. The answers were a myriad of detail and interpretation and disagreement. Even during the stability of the 1910s to 1950s, these details were the subject of daily contention in the power relations between individual women and men.

Every change in the patterns of the gender order brought new opportunities for women, and closed off others. Across the century, the feminine dance is curiously constant: one step forward, one step sideways, one step back. Certainly, the second transition in the 1960s and 1970s seemed to open up opportunities, to replace the narrow definition of the good woman with a more comprehensive one. But for many individual women, more apparent freedom meant more fear and guilt, more failure. This paradox came about because each woman was not in control of her choices: they all had strings attached. She could no longer abstain but was directed to make specific choices, all of which carried responsibilities, and her exercise of those responsibilities was stringently policed. Control was increasingly appropriated by experts.

In this book, I have mapped out the patterns of Australian society that affected the lives of women over the past century, that have determined the meaning of being a woman. Such a map can only be a guide, a two-dimensional simplification of the world in which real people live and travel. It indicates only those features of the landscape that impress themselves upon the cartographer. What has most impressed me as a feminist, looking at the world of Australian women, has been the restrictions and denials imposed upon us.

My map of the landscape of Australian femininity shows it as a maze. Women enter this maze as infants, and are compelled to seek the true path throughout life. We are faced constantly by dead ends, by refusals of entry, by compulsions to turn this way or that. New and enticing paths are constantly opening up, but they are as obstructed by barriers as the old.

Individually and collectively we push through some of these barriers, only to find new ones hastily erected on the other side. The true path through this maze involves an intense narrowing of our choices, of our desires and behaviour. When our choices are so narrow, there is in fact no real choice. Rather, we are compelled to pursue this minimal femininity through fear of failure, fear of punishment.

This is not to say that such restriction is all there is to Australian women's lives. Because, for example, heterosexuality is compulsory it does not mean that those women who accept it are merely passive victims of oppression, nor that those who reject it are merely hounded and persecuted rebels. For all women there is happiness and laughter and joy. But such good times occur despite, not because of our entrapment in the maze. Only when the path of feminine sexuality is widened to accommodate the choice of, for example, lesbianism and celibacy as validly as that of heterosexuality will the precondition for genuine sexual happiness exist. (This precondition implies, of course, true equality among and between women and men.) Similarly with the other dimensions of femininity: work and mothering. Within the constraints of the capitalist gender division of labour, and the medical and professional control of family life, women can find satisfaction and pleasure. But the precondition of genuine happiness lies in equality and choice.

I am not arguing here for the total abolition of the maze. I cannot imagine an ungendered world. The existence of some distinctions between people on the basis of gender seems to me to be inevitable. But such distinction need not be the polar opposition of femininity and masculinity that we confront today. Femininity and masculinity need not be so limiting and controlled. Our bodies, our identities and our sense of group definition need not conform to such uniform and narrow ideals. Our choices need not be so circumscribed and policed. These possibilities seem to me to be the driving inspiration of feminism: the attempt to restructure the gender order, to oppose compulsory definitions of femininity and widen the real choices open to women, to create ourselves as autonomous individuals.

Across the century, women have sought to wrest control of their lives from the authorities who oppressed them, from individuals, institutions and ideals. Resistance to some of the imperatives of the gender order has sometimes been successful. At other times, attempts to ease its restrictions and to create alternatives have been savagely repressed. The strength of the gender order's standard of femininity lies in its individual imposition. Its contradictory and illusory character means that its pursuit by each woman is always attended by some failure and guilt. For there is no end to the maze, no successful way out. The inevitability of failure debilitates women. As well, because individuals take the standard so much for granted, they allow violators to be picked off. Those women who not only fail to live up to but deliberately disregard the tenets of femininity become legitimate objects of punishment and examples to other women of the dangers of non-conformity.

On the other hand, the strength of feminist attempts to restructure femininity and widen its meaning lies in collective effort on our own behalf. The realisation of the historical construction of our individual sense of failure can open up new possibilities that we are not afraid to try. The creation of 'safe places' like refuges, health centres and consciousness-raising groups can provide protection for women seeking alternatives to particularly destructive situations. The establishment of feminist groups wherever women are creates the possibility of gaining some control over the direction of gender relations in that place: in workplaces, in trade unions, in childcare groups, in tennis clubs, in parliament, in schools, in neighbourhoods and families.

If freedom is granted by those in authority, they can always take it away again. The opportunities and possibilities that they open up are always hedged around by new restrictions and compulsions. Only that freedom won in struggle and continuously defended is real. The crucial goal of feminism is thus autonomy and self-determination for all women. The expansion of women's opportunities and the breaking down of restrictions on choice are not enough. The way of emancipation, of liberation, of freedom always poses the question of power and control. Feminism stands for women's control of our own lives.

Appendix:

Glenside Hospital casenotes

*B*etween 1945 and 1970, the reports of the Director-General of South Australian Medical Services reveal that there was a total of approximately 11 500 people admitted to Glenside Hospital (formerly Parkside Mental Hospital), with an annual total ranging from about 290 in 1945 to 790 in 1960 to 230 in 1970. The fluctuations in annual admissions (shown in part in the table on p. 203), have no clear-cut relation to the level of madness in South Australian society, but rather relate to administrative and ideological changes within the psychiatric profession: to changes in admission policy at Glenside Hospital, and at the other major South Australian public mental hospital, Hillcrest; to changes in the relations between the hospitals and their receiving houses and wards; to changes in the geographical 'catchment areas' of each of these institutions; and to a major change in the mid-1960s from a conception of 'institutional' treatment of the mad to one of 'community' responsibility.

As well as fluctuations in numbers admitted annually, there was also considerable change in the types of patient received. For example, over the years, alcoholic and mentally retarded patients were alternately admitted to the hospital despite professional discouragement and hidden away in back wards, were encouraged to seek treatment and placed in special wards, then were segregated out, discouraged from hospital admission and sent to specialised institutions elsewhere. Within such variations it is possible, nonetheless, to make a very rough division of the patient intake into Glenside Hospital over the 25 years.

By the early decades of the twentieth century, psychiatrists had conclusively proved that certain types of madness were caused by physical, hereditary or organic accident, malfunction or disease. On the other hand, there remained a large number of categories of madness that, even by the 1970s, could not be shown to have any organic cause. These latter categories were defined solely in term of peculiarities of behaviour, and can be termed 'behavioural' or 'functional' disorders to distinguish them from 'organic' disorders. Within the classification system accepted by Glenside Hospital in the 1960s (Section V of the *International Classification of Diseases* (1967)) organic madness (including such disorders as general paralysis, Korsakov's psychosis, senile dementia) were covered by categories 290–94 and 309–15; while functional madness (including such disorders as schizophrenia, depression, paranoia) were covered by categories 295–308.

For the purposes of this book, being concerned with the social behaviour that defined 'good' women, I was interested in functional madness only, so I set about dividing the hospital population along organic and functional lines. This was possible by using the Hospital Admissions Register of Patients, a register that the institution was obliged to keep by law. Each person admitted or re-admitted to the hospital had an entry recorded chronologically in the register, and was given a number which became the identifying number of her or his casenotes. As well, each entry included the category, 'form of mental disorder'. Beginning with the register of 1945, and taking that of every fifth year to 1970, I separated out those admissions whose diagnoses fell within the functional categories, then took a random sample of ten female functional admissions for each year, making 60 in all. The numbers involved are shown in the Table:

Table 6   Total admissions and functional admissions to Glenside Hospital 1945–1970

Year[a]	total admissions[a]	total functional admissions[b]	female functional admissions[b]
1945 (45–6)	261 (291)	98	52
1950 (50–1)	417 (378)	178	87
1955 (55–6)	403 (329)	165	85
1960 (60–1)	703 (786)	417	227
1965 (65–6)	603 (556)	357	152
1970 (70–1)	331 (229)	182	92

Notes: [a]Years and numbers in brackets are the equivalent statistics from the Annual Reports of the Director-General of Medical Services. The distinction between the statistics from the Hospital Admissions Register and the Annual Reports is explained, firstly, from the fact that the published statistics covered the periods July to June, while the register recorded from January to December; secondly, the published figures were partly corrected for discrepancies in the register arising from administrative procedures, e.g., recording of transfers of patients from one section of the hospital to another, transfers between different hospitals and receiving houses, and readmissions after trial leave Functional Admissions are only roughly calculated

Source: [b]Admissions Registers, Glenside Hospital (Parkside Mental Hospital), and *South Australian Parliamentary Papers*, No. 21, 1946–71.

The 60 female functional patients thus selected were then traced through their casenotes. These casenotes varied considerably in the quantity and quality of information they contained—from year to year, and from patient to patient. The usually limited nature of the records from 1945 to 1960, and their relative expansion in the next ten years, was explained by the hospital staff (in 1974) in terms of, firstly, the increased numbers of staff over the years which allowed more time for the keeping of records, and secondly, the fact that casenotes used to be kept in a central, and hence isolated, room in the Administration Building and were written up only once a week, whereas later they were kept in the wards with the relevant patient, and were therefore much more accessible after each visit or examination.

The casenotes of these 60 women belong to Glenside Hospital, not to the women who were their subjects and who were never given access to them. I was granted permission to use the notes by the South Australian Director of Mental Health Services, the Superintendent of Glenside Hospital, and the Glenside Hospital Research Committee, all of whom placed upon me the responsibility to preserve the privacy and confidentiality of the particular patients whose notes I had access to. I have taken great care to discharge this responsibility, and to respect the rights of the women involved and their families and friends. The casenotes were selected by random process, coded, and the women given invented names which bore no resemblance to their real ones. All identifying details have been changed.

The use of the casenotes, and hence the lives of real women, was important to my analysis in that they provided the individual unity, social complexity, and precision of detail necessary to follow through the relations of the gender order: the meaning of being a woman; the relations between individual women, individual men, and specific institutions; the discrepancies between the ideal of the good woman and the lives of real women. Their use is in their individual detail. As an overview, however, the following list establishes the broad sociological and historical outlines of their 60 lives:

Birth dates: 1884 to 1953;
First admission dates: 1932 to 1970;
Age at first admission: 15 to 84;
Place of residence: 7 in the City of Adelaide, 14 in the country, 3 in hostels or
    camps, the rest in the Adelaide suburbs;
Nationality: 12 were migrants, of 7 nationalities (Greek, Italian, English,
    Polish, Maltese, Yugoslav, American), and 6 of them were said to have a
    'language problem' (2 Italians, 3 Poles, 1 Greek);
Marital status: 16 were single, 4 divorced or permanently separated, 5
    widowed, 2 in de facto relationships, and 33 married;
Occupation: according to the Admissions Register, only 11 worked in the
    public economy (1 nun, 1 ballet dancer, 4 domestics, 2 office workers, 2
    process workers, 1 unemployed); on following through the case notes, a
    further 14 women, initially classified as 'home duties,' were shown to have
    worked in the public economy at some stage (4 unknown, 4 domestics, 3
    skilled or unskilled manual workers, 2 teachers, 1 office worker);
Hospital career: 51 were certified at some stage, with information given
    variously by husbands, parents, children, relatives, in-laws, neighbours,
    landladies, nurses, nuns, police; 4 died and 1 committed suicide; number
    of admissions per person ranged from 1 to 17; overall time spent in
    hospital per person ranged from 10 days to 31½ years.

Of the 60 cases collected, I have discussed only 31 in this book. (A further 23 are discussed in my doctoral thesis (Matthews, 1978), and a final six were omitted because they contained no social histories of the patients.) There is no particular difference between the cases discussed and the remainder of the sample: nationality, admission dates, marital status and diagnosis are fairly evenly spread. The 31 cases contained enough within themselves for my argument since I was using them qualitatively, not quantitatively. The other cases were either not so explicitly useful, or merely duplicated the types of experience I had already discussed.

The following is a brief tabulation of the 31 cases used according to the formula: name; birth date and place; marital status (s. = single; m. = married; w. = widowed; def. = de facto); number of children (ch); first admission to Glenside Hospital (Adm.); first attack (in brackets); diagnosis (diag.).

Allen, Katie   b.1926 U.K.   m. 5 ch.   Adm. 1959 (1958)
    diag. Depressive reaction
Arndt, Karen   b. 1909   m. 2 ch.   Adm. (1945 (1940)
    diag. Schizophrenia hebephrenia
Banks, Lettie   b. 1886   w. 2 ch.   Adm. 1970
    diag. Severe endogenous depression
Bertrams, Leonie   b. 1926   m. 2 ch.   Adm. 1960
    diag. Obsessive–compulsive neurosis with secondary depression
Carter, May   b. 1888   m.   Adm. 1955 (1947)
    diag. Chronic paraphrenia with florid features
Crafers, Martha   b. 1910   m. 1 ch.   Adm. 1960 (1934)
    diag. Depressive reaction
Dolci, Nicola   b. 1911 ?U.S.A. m. ?2 ch.   Adm. 1945 (1944)
                               ?Italy
    diag. Acute mania; schizophrenia hebephrenia
Grant, Rita   b. 1893   w. 1 ch.   Adm. 1960 (1930)
    diag. Schizophrenic reaction, paranoid type
Gniada, Carmella   b. 1935 Italy   m. 3 ch.   Adm. 1970 (1968)
    diag. ?Atypical depression ?Paranoid schizophrenia ?Puerperal psychosis
Hughes, Rosalind   b. 1894   m. 2 ch.   Adm. 1950 (1947)
    diag. Obsessional neurosis with anxiety tension; overall mild personality
    deterioration
Innes, Eve   b. 1941   w. 1 ch.   Adm. 1961 (1951)
    diag. ?Inadequate personality ?psychopath
Irving, Sarah   b. 1914   m. 2 ch.   Adm. 1957 (1951)
    diag. Schizophrenia
Johns, Fay   b. 1947   s.   Adm. 1965
    diag. Inadequate personality; adolescent immaturity reaction
King, Vera   b. 1900   m. 2 ch.   Adm. 1944
    diag. Melancholia; schizophrenia hebephrenia
Kirk, Gwen   b. 1948   s. 1 ch.   Adm. 1965 (?)
    diag. Immature personality disorder of adolescence
Lawson, Heather   b. 1948   s.   Adm. 1965
    diag. Inadequate personality
Markeby, Yve   b. 1904   w. 2 ch.   Adm. 1960 (1932)
    diag. Acute depressive illness in cyclothymic personality
Masters, Claire   b. 1916   def. 12 ch.   Adm. 1955
    diag. Depression
Nehler, Annabelle   b. 1916   s.   Adm 1957
    diag. Schizophrenia
Norris, Ada   b. 1904   m. 7 ch.   Adm. 1962
    diag. Depressive reaction
Norton, Joyce   b. 1953   s.   Adm. 1968

diag. Unspecified personality disorder
Parnell, Catherine   b. 1906   s.   Adm. 1937
diag. Agitated melancholia, paraphrenia
Perkins, Christine   b. 1917   m. 3 ch.   Adm. 1955 (1949)
diag. Paranoid schizophrenia
Quennall, Doris   b. 1906   m. 3 ch.   Adm. 1950
diag. Paranoid schizophrenia
Quilper, Deidre   b. 1920   s. 1 ch.   Adm. 1950
diag. Reactive depression
Radetzky, Eugenia   b. 1923 Poland m. 1 ch.   Adm. 1950 (1947)
diag. Depressive psychosis; affective disorder seen in Continentals in the
U.K.
Talbot, Giovanna   b. 1924 Malta m. 1 ch.   Adm. 1955 (1950)
diag. Schizophrenia
Vane, Helen   b. 1924   m. 3 ch.   Adm. 1963
diag. Reactive depression
Weiman, Irma   b. 1925 Poland m. 2 ch.   Adm. 1960
diag. Schizophrenia; no mental abnormality
Wentworth, Iris   b. 1908   m. 2 ch.   Adm. 1968
diag. Depression
York, Jean   b. 1925   m. 1 ch. Adm. 1961
diag. Schizophrenia

Bibliography

Abbott, Sidney & Love, Barbara (1973) *Sappho was a right-on woman. A liberated view of lesbianism* New York: Stein & Day

ABS [Australian Bureau of Statistics] (1978) *Social Indicators* 2, Canberra

—— (1980a) *Social Indicators* 3, Canberra

—— (1980b) *Marriages Australia 1980* Canberra

—— (1981) *Year Book Australia* Canberra

Adler, D.L. (1965) 'Matriduxy in the Australian family' in A.F. Davies & S. Encel (eds) *Australian society. A sociological reader* Melbourne: Cheshire

Aitken, Jan (1978) 'The prostitute as worker' [First] *Women and Labour Conference Papers* II Sydney pp. 9–12

Albury, Rebecca, and others (1983) 'Forum. Dynamic labour market or work on the wane?' *Social Welfare Research Centre Newsletter* 9, pp. 19–24

Alford, Katrina (1981) 'Academic and media views of married women's employment' in Norma Grieve & Patricia Grimshaw (eds) *Australian women. Feminist perspectives* Melbourne: Oxford University Press

Allen, Judith (1982) 'Octavius Beale reconsidered. Infanticide, babyfarming and abortion in N.S.W. 1880–1939' in Sydney Labour History Group *What rough beast? The state and social order in Australian history* Sydney: George Allen & Unwin and The Australian Society for Labour History

Allport, Carolyn.(1983) 'Women and suburban housing: post-war planning in Sydney 1943–1961' in P. Williams (ed.) *Social process and the city* Urban Studies Yearbook I Sydney: George Allen & Unwin

ANZCP [Australian and New Zealand College of Psychiatrists] (1972) 'Homosexuality' Position Statement No. 3 Victoria

—— (1973) 'Homosexuality' Clinical Memorandum No. 6 Victoria

Appleyard, R.T. (1964) *British emigration to Australia* Canberra: ANU

Auchmuty, Rosemary (1979) 'The truth about sex' in Peter Spearritt & David Walker (eds) *Australian popular culture* Sydney: George Allen & Unwin

Australian Government Commission of Inquiry into Poverty (1975) *Poverty in Australia* First Main Report, Canberra: AGPS

Australian News and Information Bureau (1942) *The job Australia is doing* New

York
Bacchi, Carol (1980a) 'Evolution, eugenics and women. The impact of scientific theories on attitudes towards women 1870–1920' in Elizabeth Windschuttle (ed.) *Women, class and history. Feminist perspectives on Australia 1788–1978* Melbourne: Fontana/Collins
—— (1980b) 'The nature–nurture debate in Australia 1900–1914' *Historical Studies* 19, 75, pp. 199–212
Barbalet, Margaret (1983) *Far from a low gutter girl. The forgotten world of state wards: South Australia 1887–1940* Melbourne: Oxford University Press
Barrett, Michèle (1980) *Women's oppression today. Problems in Marxist Feminist analysis* London: Verso
Bart, Pauline B. (1971) 'Depression in middle-aged women' in Vivian Gornick & Barbara K. Moran (eds) *Woman in sexist society. Studies in power and powerlessness* New York: Basic Books
Basic Wage Commission [Report of the Royal Commission on the Basic Wage] (1920–21) *Commonwealth Parliamentary Papers 1920–21* vol. 4
Benét, Mary Kathleen (1972) *Secretary: an enquiry into the female ghetto* London: Sidgwick & Jackson
Benston, Margaret (1969) 'The political economy of Women's Liberation' *Monthly Review* 21, pp. 13–27
Berk, Sarah F. (ed) (1980) *Women and household labour* California: Sage
Bernard, Jessie (1972) *The future of marriage* New York: Bantam
—— (1981) *The female world* New York: Free Press
Blackburn, Jean & Jackson, Ted (1963) *Australian wives today* Melbourne: Victorian Fabian Society
Bollen, J.D. (1972) *Protestantism and social reform in New South Wales 1890–1910* Melbourne: Melbourne University Press
Bott, Elizabeth (1957) *Family and social network* London: Tavistock
Bower, Herbert (1978) 'Aged families and their problems' in Jerzy Krupinski & Allen Stoller (eds) *The Australian family. Social, demographic and psychological aspects* 2nd edn, Sydney: Pergamon
Boyd, Robin (1978) *Australia's home. Why Australians built the way they did* 2nd edn, England: Penguin
Brake, Mike (1982) 'Sexuality as praxis—a consideration of the contribution of sexual theory to the process of sexual being' in Mike Brake (ed.) *Human sexual relations. A reader in human sexuality* England: Penguin
Braverman, Harry (1974) *Labor and monopoly capital. The degradation of work in the twentieth century* New York: Monthly Review Press
Brennan, Teresa (1982) personal communication
Broverman, I.K., Broverman, D.M., Clarkson, F.E., Rosenkrantz, P.S. & Vogel, S.R. (1970) 'Sex role stereotypes and clinical judgments of mental health' *Journal of Consulting and Clinical Psychology* 34, 1, pp. 1–7
Bryson, Lois (1975) 'Husband and wife interaction in the Australian family. A critical review of the literature' in Jan Mercer (ed.) *The other half* Victoria: Penguin
Building Act Inquiry Committee (1940) First Progress Report No. 30; Second Progress Report No. 32; Third and Final Report No. 34 *South Australian Parliamentary Papers*
Butlin, N.G. (1972) *Investment in Australian economic development 1861–1900* Can-

berra: Department of Economic History, Research School of Social Sciences, ANU

Caldwell, John (1980) 'Long-term perspectives on the Australian family' in Dorothy Davis, Geoff Caldwell, Margaret Bennett & David Boorer (eds) *Living together: family patterns and lifestyles. A book of readings* Canberra: Centre for Continuing Education, ANU

Calwell, A.A. (1945) Ministerial statement *Commonwealth Parliamentary Papers No. 3 1945–1946* vol. 4

Campion, Edmund (1982) *Rockchoppers. Growing up Catholic in Australia* Victoria: Penguin

CBCS [Commonwealth Bureau of Census and Statistics] (1939) *Demography 1938* Canberra: Government Printer

Chafe, William (1972) *The American woman. Her changing social, economic, and political roles 1920–1970* New York: Oxford University Press

Chodorow, Nancy (1978) *The reproduction of mothering. Psychoanalysis and the sociology of gender* California: University of California Press

Christo, C. (1974) The South Australian Boy-Immigration Scheme 1913–1929, Adelaide: B.A. Hons thesis, History Department, Adelaide University

Clark, C.M.H. (ed.) (1965) *Select documents in Australian history 1788–1850* Sydney: Angus & Robertson

Clark, David (1974) *Social therapy in psychiatry* England: Penguin

Cochrane, Peter (1982) Company time. Management ideology and the labour process 1940–1960, Sydney: unpublished paper presented at History '82 Conference

Coleman, Peter (1974) *Obscenity, blasphemy, sedition. 100 years of censorship in Australia* Sydney: Angus & Robertson

Connell, R.W. & Irving, T.H. (1980) *Class structure in Australian history. Documents, narrative and argument* Melbourne: Longman Cheshire

Connell, W.F., Stroobant, R.E., Sinclair, K.E., Connell, R.W. & Rogers, K.W. (1975) *12 to 20: studies of city youth* Sydney: Hicks Smith

Cowie, C. & Lees, S. (1981) 'Slags or drags' *Feminist Review* 9, pp. 17–31

Crowley, F.K. (1954) 'The British contribution to the Australian population 1860–1919' *University Studies* 2, 2, pp. 55–88

—— (1973) *Modern Australia in documents 1901–1939; 1939–1970* 2 vols, Melbourne: Wren Publishing

CURA [Centre for Urban Research and Action] (1976) *'But I wouldn't want my wife to work here...' A study of migrant women in Melbourne industry* Research Report for International Women's Year, Victoria: CURA

Davey, Constance M. (1956) *Children and their law-makers. A social–historical survey of the growth and development from 1836 to 1950 of South Australian laws relating to children* Adelaide: Griffin Press

Daniels, Kay & Murnane, Mary (1980) *Uphill all the way. A documentary history of women in Australia* Queensland: University of Queensland Press

Davidoff, Leonore (1973) *The best circles. Society, etiquette and the season* London: Croom Helm

—— (1974) 'Mastered for life. Servant and wife in Victorian and Edwardian England' *Journal of Social History* 7, 4, pp. 406–28

—— (1979) 'The separation of home and work? Landladies and lodgers in nineteenth and twentieth-century England' in Sandra Burman (ed.) *Fit work for women* London: Croom Helm

Davison, Graeme (1979) *The rise and fall of marvellous Melbourne* Melbourne: Melbourne University Press

Day, Lincoln H. (1970) 'Divorce' in A.F. Davies & S. Encel (eds) *Australian society. A sociological introduction* 2nd edn, Melbourne: Cheshire

Deacon, Desley (1982a) Political arithmetic. The nineteenth century census and the construction of the dependent woman, Canberra: unpublished papper, Department of Sociology, ANU

—— (1982b) 'The employment of women in the Commonwealth Public Service: the creation and reproduction of a dual labour market' *Australian Journal of Public Administration* 41, 3, pp. 232–50

Department of Immigration (1967) *Woman's angle on Australia* Immigration Information Pamphlet, Canberra

—— (1973) *Australian immigration. Consolidated statistics* Canberra: AGPS

Department of Labour and National Service (1967) *Women in the work force. Facts and Figures* Melbourne

Dingle, A.E. (1980) '"A truly magnificent thirst": an historical survey of Australian drinking habits' *Historical Studies* 19, 75, pp. 227–49

Dinnerstein, Dorothy (1976) *The mermaid and the minotaur. Sexual arrangements and human malaise* New York: Harper & Row

Doherty, Maree (1980) 'An historical background to the predominance of women in clerical employment' *Second Women and Labour Conference Papers* I, Melbourne, pp. 41–51

Donzelot, Jacques (1979) *The policing of families* Transl. from the French by Robert Hurley, New York: Pantheon

Edwards, Meredith (1981) *Financial arrangements within families* A research report for the National Women's Advisory Council, Canberra

Ehrenreich, Barbara & English, Deidre (1979) *For her own good. 150 years of the experts' advice to women* London: Pluto

Encel, Sol, Mackenzie, Norman & Tebbutt, Margaret (1974) *Women and society. An Australian study* Melbourne: Cheshire

Evans, Raymond (1975) '"Soiled doves": prostitution and society in colonial Queensland' *Hecate* 1, 2, pp. 6–24

Ewen, Stuart (1976) *Captains of consciousness. Advertising and the social roots of the consumer culture* New York: McGraw-Hill

Fanon, Frantz (1968) *Black skin, white masks* Transl. from the French by Charles Lam Markman, London: MacGibbon & Kee

Finlay, H.A. (1978) 'The family and the law' in J. Krupinski & A. Stoller (eds) *The family in Australia. Social, demographic and psychological aspects* 2nd edn, Sydney: Pergamon

Firth, S. (1971) 'Social values in the N.S.W. Primary School 1880–1914. An analysis of school texts' in E.L. French (ed.) *Melbourne Studies in Education 1970* Melbourne: Melbourne University Press

Fisher, S.H. (1981) 'An accumulation of misery?' *Labour History* 40, pp. 16–28

Foreman, Lynne (1975) *Children or families? An evaluation of the legislative basis for child-protective statutory welfare services in the Australian States and Territories* Canberra: Australian Government Social Welfare Commission

Forster, C. (ed.) (1970) *Australian economic development in the twentieth century* London: George Allen & Unwin

Forsyth, W.D. (1942) *The myth of open spaces. Australian, British and world trends of population* Melbourne and London: Melbourne University Press in association with Oxford University Press

Foucault, Michel (1967) *Madness and civilization. A history of insanity in the Age of Reason* Transl. from the French by Richard Howard, London: Tavistock
—— (1979) *The history of sexuality Vol. 1 An Introduction* Transl. from the French by Robert Hurley, London: Allen Lane

Fox, Greer Litton (1978) '"Nice girl": social control of women through a value construct' *Signs* 2, 4, pp. 805–17

Fransella, Fay & Frost, Kay (1977) *On being a woman. A review of research on how women see themselves* London: Tavistock

Friedan, Betty (1965) *The feminine mystique* England: Penguin

Fry, E.C. (1956) 'Outwork in the 'eighties. An examination of outwork in the infant industries of the eastern Australian colonies, c. 1880–90' *University Studies in History and Economics* 2, 4, pp. 77–93

Gadlin, Howard (1976) 'Private lives and public order: a critical view of the history of intimate relations in the U.S.' *Massachusetts Review* 17, 2, pp. 204–30

Game, Ann & Pringle, Rosemary (1979) 'The making of the Australian family' *Intervention* 12, pp. 63–83
—— (1983) *Gender at work* Sydney: George Allen & Unwin

Gandevia, Bryan (1978) *Tears often shed. Child health and welfare in Australia from 1788* Sydney: Charter Books and Boards of Directors, Prince Henry and Prince of Wales Hospitals

Gatens, Moira (1983) 'A critique of the sex/gender distinction' in Judith Allen & Paul Patton (eds) *Beyond Marxism? Interventions after Marx* Sydney: Intervention Publications

Gavron, Hannah (1966) *The captive wife. Conflicts of housebound mothers* England: Penguin

Gelb, Lester A. (1973) 'Masculinity–femininity. A study in imposed inequality' in Jean Baker Miller (ed.) *Psychoanalysis and women* England: Penguin

Gershuny, J.I. & Pahl, R.E. (1979–80) 'Work outside employment: some preliminary speculations' *New Universities Quarterly* 34, 1, pp. 120–35

Golder, Hilary & Allen, Judith (1980) 'Prostitution in New South Wales 1870–1932: restructuring an industry' *Refractory Girl* 18–19, pp. 17–24

Gordon, Linda (1977) *Woman's body, woman's right. A social history of birth control in America* England: Penguin
—— & Hunter, Allen (1978) *Sex, family and the new right* Massachusetts: New England Free Press

Gordon, Michael (1968) 'Infant care revisited' *Journal of Marriage and the Family* 30, pp 578–83

Grimshaw, Patricia & Willett, Graham (1981) 'Women's history and family history: an exploration of colonial family structure' in Norma Grieve & Patricia Grimshaw (eds) *Australian Women. Feminist perspectives* Melbourne: Oxford University Press

Haire, Norman (1943) *Sex problems of today* Sydney: Angus & Robertson

Hall, Stuart (1980) 'Reformism and the legislation of consent' in National Deviancy Conference (ed.) *Permissiveness and control. The fate of the sixties legislation* London: Macmillan

Hamilton, Paula (1982) "'Tipperarifying the moral atmosphere." Irish Catholic immigration and the state 1840–1860' in Sydney Labour History Group *What rough beast? The state and social order in Australian history* Sydney: George Allen & Unwin and The Australian Society for the Study of Labour History

Hargreaves, Kaye (1982) *Women at work* Victoria: Penguin

Harper, Jan & Richards, Lyn (1979) *Mothers and working mothers* Victoria: Penguin

Harrison, K. (1980) 'Child custody and parental sexuality: just another factor?' *Refractory Girl* 20–21, pp. 7–14

Hasluck, P. (1970) *The government and the people 1942–1945* Australia in the war of 1939–1945 Series 4: Civil Vol. 2, Canberra: Australian War Memorial

Harvester Case (1907) ex parte H.V. McKay *2 Commonwealth Arbitration Reports* pp. 1–25

Heagney, Muriel (1933) *Are women taking men's jobs? A survey of women's work in Victoria with special regard to equal status, equal pay and equality of opportunity* Melbourne: Hilton & Veitch

Herzog, Marianne (1980) *From hand to mouth. Women and piecework* Transl. from the German by Stanley Mitchell, introduction by Sally Alexander, England: Penguin

Hetzel, Basil S. (1974) *Health and Australian society* Victoria: Penguin

Hicks, Neville (1978) *'This sin and scandal.' Australia's population debate 1891–1911* Canberra: ANU Press

Higgins, Winton (1978) 'State welfare and class warfare' in Graeme Duncan (ed.) *Critical essays in Australian politics* Melbourne: Edward Arnold

Hirst, J.B. (1983) *Convict society and its enemies* Sydney: George Allen & Unwin

HMSO (1957) Report of the Committee on Homosexual Offences and Prostitution (Wolfenden Report) Cmnd. 257, London: HMSO

Horne, Donald (1964) *The lucky country. Australia in the sixties* Victoria: Penguin

Housewives, Association of Australia (South Australian Division) (1930) 'Editorial Notes.Necessity for the Housewives, Association' *The Housewife* 1, 7

Howe, Anna L. (1981) *Towards an older Australia. Readings in social gerontology* Queensland: University of Queensland Press

Human Relationships (1977) See Royal Commission on Human Relationships (1977)

Hunt, Su-Jane & Bolton, Geoffrey (1978) 'Cleansing the dunghill. Water supply and sanitation in Perth 1878–1912' *Studies in Western Australian History* 2, pp. 1–17

Hyslop, Anthea (1980) 'Agents and objects. Women and social reform in Melbourne 1900 to 1914' in Margaret Bevege, Margaret James & Carmel Shute (eds) *Worth her salt. Women at work in Australia* Sydney: Hale & Iremonger

Immigration Advisory Council (1969) *Immigration and the balance of the sexes in Australia* Report to the Minister of State for Immigration, Canberra

International Classification of Diseases (1967) See World Health Organization (1967)

James, T.E. (1951) *Prostitution and the law* London: Heinemann

Jones, F.L. (1979) Status attainment and earnings amongst the other half in Australia. The cost of being a woman, Canberra: unpublished paper presented at the 1979 Meeting of the Sociological Association of Australia and

New Zealand
—— (1983) Is it true what they said about women? The census 1801–1911 and women in the economy, Canberra: unpublished paper, Department of Sociology, Research School of Social Sciences, ANU

Joske, Percy Ernest (1952) *The laws of marriage and divorce in Australia and New Zealand* 3rd edn, Sydney: Butterworth

Keating, Michael (1967) The growth and composition of the Australian work force 1910–11 to 1960–61, Canberra: PhD thesis, ANU

Kelly, Elizabeth (1978) 'Sociological aspects of family life. The fictitious family' in J. Krupinski & A. Stoller (eds) *The family in Australia* 2nd edn, Sydney: Pergamon

Kewley, T.H. (1973) *Social security in Australia 1900–72* 2nd edn, Sydney: Sydney University Press

Kingston, Beverley (1975) *My wife, my daughter and poor Mary Ann. Women and work in Australia* Melbourne: Nelson

Krupinski, J. (1967) 'Sociological aspects of mental ill-health in migrants' *Social Science and Medicine* 1, pp. 267–81

—— (1978) 'Demographic data on marriage and the family' in J. Krupinski & A. Stoller (eds) *The family in Australia. Social, demographic and psychological aspects* 2nd edn, Sydney: Pergamon

Lake, Marilyn (1981) '"Building themselves up with aspros": pioneer women re-assessed' *Hecate* 7, 2, pp. 7–19

Larmour, Constance (1975) 'Women's wages and the WEB' in Ann Curthoys, Susan Eade & Peter Spearritt (eds) *Women at work* Canberra: Australian Society for the Study of Labour History

Larson, Magali Sarfatti (1977) *The rise of professionalism. A sociological analysis* Berkeley: University of California Press

Laster, Kathy (1982) The forgotten crime: infanticide. The Infant Life Protection Act 1890, Sydney: unpublished paper presented at History '82 Conference

Lawler, Ronald, Wuerl, Donald W. & Lawler, Thomas C. (eds) (1976) *The teaching of Christ. A Catholic catechism for adults* Indiana: Our Sunday Visitor

'Lesbian custody—a personal account' (1980) *Refractory Girl* 20–21, pp. 2–6

Lewis, Jane (1980) *The politics of motherhood. Child and maternal welfare in England 1900–1939* London: Croom Helm

Lewis, Milton (1976) Populate or perish: aspects of infant and maternal health in Sydney 1870–1939, Canberra: PhD thesis, ANU

—— (1980) 'Milk, mothers and infant welfare' in Jill Roe (ed.) *Twentieth century Sydney. Studies in urban and social history* Sydney: Hale & Iremonger in association with The Sydney History Group

Litherland, John Charles (1940) *The law relating to child welfare affiliations and adoptions (Child Welfare Act 1939)* Sydney: Law Book Co.

Lomax, Elizabeth M.R. (1978) *Science and patterns of child care* San Francisco: W.H. Freeman & Co.

Lopata, Helena (1971) *Occupation: housewife* London: Oxford University Press

Lynch, P. (1970) *The woman's role in immigration* Australian Department of Immigration Reference Paper, Canberra

Lynzaat, Ann Marie (1979) 'Respectability and the outworker' in Judy Mackinolty & Heather Radi (eds) *In pursuit of justice. Australian women and the law 1788–1979* Sydney: Hale & Iremonger

McBride, Theresa M. (1976) *The domestic revolution. The modernisation of household service in England and France 1820–1920* New York: Holmes & Meier

McCoy, Alfred W. (1980) *Drug traffic. Narcotics and organised crime in Australia* Sydney: Harper & Row

MacCulloch, Jennifer (1980) '"This store is our world." Female shop assistants in Sydney to 1930' in Jill Roe (ed.) *Twentieth century Sydney. Studies in urban and social history* Sydney: Hale & Iremonger in association with The Sydney History Group

McDonald, Peter F. (1974) *Marriage in Australia. Age at first marriage and proportions marrying 1860–1971* Australian Family Formation Project Monograph No. 2, Canberra: Department of Demography, ANU

McGrath, E.C. (1943) 'The future of women in industry' *Australian Quarterly* 15, 2, pp. 39–45

McIntosh, Mary (1978) 'Who needs prostitutes? The ideology of male sexual needs' in Carol Smart & Barry Smart (eds) *Women, sexuality and control* London: Routledge & Kegan Paul

McKinlay, John B. (1972) 'The sick role—illness and pregnancy' *Social Science and Medicine* 6, pp. 561–72

McRobbie, Angela (1978) 'Working class girls and the culture of femininity' in Women's Study Group, Centre for Contemporary Cultural Studies (ed.) *Women take issue: aspects of women's subordination* London: Hutchinson

Mainardi, Pat (1970) 'The politics of housework' in Leslie B. Tanner (ed.) *Voices from Women's Liberation* New York: Signet

Markey, Ray (1980) 'Women and labour 1880–1900' in Elizabeth Windschuttle (ed.) *Women, class and history* Melbourne: Fontana

Martin, Jean (1965) *Refugee settlers: a study of Displaced Persons in Australia* Canberra: ANU Press

—— & Richmond, Catherine M.G. (1968) *Working women in Australia* HRH The Duke of Edinburgh's Third Commonwealth Study Conference, Australia, Background Paper 11

Marx, Karl (1968) 'The eighteenth Brumaire of Louis Bonaparte' in Karl Marx & Frederick Engels *Selected Works* Moscow: Progress Publishers

Matthews, Jill (1978) Good and mad women. A study of the gender order in South Australia 1920–1970, Adelaide: PhD thesis, University of Adelaide

—— (1982) 'Deconstructing the masculine universe: the case of women's work' *Third Women and Labour Conference Papers* II South Australia pp. 474–82

—— (1983) 'Education for femininity. Domestic Arts education in South Australia' *Labour History* 45, pp. 30–53

Mayo, Helen (1960) 'Some aspects of the history of infant welfare in South Australia' *Medical Journal of Australia* II, pp. 970–72

Mechling, Jay (1975) 'Advice to historians on advice to mothers' *Journal of Social History* 9, 1, pp. 44–63

Mendelsohn, Ronald (1979) *The condition of the people. Social welfare in Australia 1900–1975* Sydney: George Allen & Unwin

Mildura Fruitpickers' Case (1912) The Rural Workers Union and the South Australian United Labourers' Union v. The Mildura Branch of the Australian Dried Fruits Association and others 6 *Commonwealth Arbitration Reports* pp. 61–88

Minc, Salec (1972) 'Medical and health problems of immigrants' in Hew

Roberts (ed.) *Australia's immigration policy* Nedlands: University of Western Australia Press

Mitchell, Juliet (1974) *Psychoanalysis and feminism* London: Allen Lane

Murnane, Mary & Daniels, Kay (1979) 'Prostitutes as "purveyors of disease": venereal disease legislation in Tasmania 1868–1945' *Hecate* 5, 1, pp. 5–21

Murray, Robert (1970) *The split. Australian Labor in the fifties* Melbourne: Cheshire

Myrdal, Alva & Klein, Viola (1968) *Women's two roles. Home and work* 2nd edn, London: Routledge & Kegan Paul

National Population Inquiry (1975) *Population and Australia. A demographic analysis and projection* First Report 2 vols + index, Canberra: AGPS

Newson, John & Newson, Elizabeth (1974) 'Cultural aspects of child-rearing in the English-speaking world' in Martin P.M. Richards (ed.) *The integration of a child into a social world* London: Cambridge University Press

New South Wales Law Reform Commission (1981) *De factor relationships* Issues paper, Sydney: NSW Law Reform Commission

New York Radicalesbians (1974) 'Woman-identified-woman' in Women's Press Collective *Lesbians speak out* California: Women's Press Collective

Oakley, Ann (1974a) *The sociology of housework* London: Martin Robinson

—— (1974b) *Housewife* England: Penguin

—— (1979) *From here to maternity. Becoming a mother* England: Penguin

O'Brien, Eris (1950) *The foundation of Australia (1786–1800). A study in European criminal practice and penal colonization in the eighteenth century* 2nd edn, Sydney: Angus & Robertson

O'Donnell, Carol & Craney, Jan (1982) 'The social construction of child abuse' in Carol O'Donnell & Jan Craney (eds) *Family violence in Australia* Australian Studies Series, Melbourne: Longman Cheshire

OECD Study, Women's Bureau Department of Labour (1974) *The role of women in the economy* Background Information, Australia, Canberra: AGPS

O'Farrell, Patrick (1977) *The Catholic church and community in Australia. A history* Melbourne: Nelson

Office of the Status of Women (1983) *Women's contribution to economic recovery* National Economic Summit Conference, Information on the Economy, Second Addendum, Canberra

Orbach, Susie (1978) *Fat is a feminist issue...The anti-diet guide to permanent weight loss* New York & London: Paddington Press

Owen, Mary & Shaw, Sylvie (1979) *Working women. Discussion papers from the Working Women's Centre Melbourne* Melbourne: Sisters

Padgug, Robert A. (1979) 'Sexual matters: on conceptualizing sexuality in history' *Radical History Review* 20, pp. 3–23

Palmer, George (1967) *A guide to Australian economic statistics* Melbourne: Macmillan

Parsons, Talcott (1952) *The social system* London: Tavistock

Perrott, Monica (1983) *A tolerable good success. Economic opportunities for women in New South Wales 1788–1930* Macquarie Colonial Papers, Sydney: Hale & Iremonger

Phillips, Walter (1980) '"Six o'clock swill": the introduction of early closing of hotel bars in Australia' *Historical Studies* 19, 75, pp. 250–66

Pitt, B. (1968) '"Atypical" depression following childbirth' *British Journal of*

Psychiatry 114, pp. 1325–35

Poverty in Australia (1975) See Australian Government Commission of Inquiry into Poverty (1975)

Power, Margaret (1975) 'Women's work is never done—by men. A socioeconomic model of sex-typing in occupations' *Journal of Industrial Relations* 17, 3, pp. 225–39

Pringle, Rosemary (1981) 'Women and consumer capitalism' Sydney: unpublished paper, School of Behavioural Sciences, Macquarie University

Quiggin, P. (in progress) The female role in the decline in fertility in Australia 1860-1900, Canberra: MA thesis, Department of Demography, ANU

Rawson, Don (1982) 'The ACTU—growth yes, power no' in Kathryn Cole (ed.) *Power, conflict and control in Australian trade unions* Victoria: Penguin

Red Fems (1980) 'The implications of technological change for women workers in the public sector' in Margaret Bevege, Margaret James & Carmel Shute (eds) *Worth her salt. Women at work in Australia* Sydney: Hale & Iremonger

Rich, Adrienne (1977) *Of woman born. Motherhood as experience and institution* London: Virago

—— (1980) 'Compulsory heterosexuality and lesbian existence' *Signs* 5, 4, pp. 631–60

Richards, Lyn (1978) *Having families. Marriage, parenthood and social pressure in Australia* Victoria: Penguin

Richardson, Alan (1974) *British migrants and Australia. A psychosocial inquiry* Canberra: ANU Press

Rickard, John (1976) *Class and politics. New South Wales, Victoria and the early Commonwealth 1890–1910* Canberra: ANU Press

Roberts, Helen (1981) 'Women and their doctors: power and powerlessness in the research process' in Helen Roberts (ed.) *Doing feminist research* London: Routledge & Kegan Paul

Roe, Jill (ed) (1976) *Social policy in Australia 1901–1975* Sydney: Cassell

Ronalds, Chris (1979) *Anti-discrimination legislation in Australia* Sydney: Butterworth

Rosenkrantz, P., Vogel, S., Bee, H., Broverman, I., Broverman, D.M. (1968) 'Sex role stereotypes and self-concepts in college students" *Journal of Consulting and Clinical Psychology* 32, 3, pp. 287–95

Rowse, Tim (1978) *Australian liberalism and national character* Melbourne: Kibble

Royal Commission on Human Relationships (1977) *Final Report* 5 vols, Canberra: AGPS

Ruzıcka, Lado T. & Caldwell, John (1977) *The end of demographic transition in Australia* Australian Family Formation Project Monograph No. 5, Canberra: Department of Demography, ANU

Ryan, Edna (1984) personal communication

—— & Conlon, Anne (1978) *Gentle invaders. Australian women at work 1788–1974* Melbourne: Nelson

—— & Prendergast, Helen (1982) '"Unions are for women too!"' in Kathryn Cole (ed.) *Power, conflict and control in Australian trade unions* Victoria Penguin

Ryan, Penny & Rowse, Tim (1975) 'Women, arbitration and the family' in Ann Curthoys, Susan Eade & Peter Spearritt (eds) *Women at work* Canberra: Australian Society for the Study of Labour History

Safilios-Rothschild, Constantina (1970) 'The study of family power structure.

A review 1960–1969' *Journal of Marriage and the Family* 32, 4, pp. 539–52

Sawer, Marian (ed.) (1982) *Australia and the new right* Sydney: George Allen & Unwin

Schaechter, Frieda (1962) 'A study of psychoses in female migrants' *Medical Journal of Australia* II, pp. 458–61

Scheff, Thomas J. (1966) *Being mentally ill: a sociological theory* London: Weidenfeld & Nicolson

Searle, G.R. (1971) *The quest for national efficiency. A study in British politics and social thought 1899–1914* California: University of California Press

Shaw, A.G.L. (1974) '1788–1810' in Frank Crowley (ed) *A new history of Australia* Melbourne: Heinemann

Shields, John (1982) 'A dangerous age. Bourgeois philanthropy, the state and the young unemployed in NSW in the 1930s' in Sydney Labour History Group *What rough beast? The state and social order in Australian history* Sydney: George Allen & Unwin and The Australian Society for Labour History

Sihombing, Judith (1979) 'When romance fades. Cohabitation property rights' in Judy Mackinolty & Heather Radi (eds) *In pursuit of justice. Australian women and the law* Sydney: Hale & Iremonger

Silverman, Charlotte (1968) *The epidemiology of depression* Baltimore: Johns Hopkins

Sinclair, W.A. (1976) *The process of economic development in Australia* Melbourne: Cheshire

—— (1982) 'Women and economic change in Melbourne 1871–1921' *Historical Studies* 20, 79, pp. 278–91

Skolnick, Arlene (1975) 'The family revisited: themes in recent social science research' *Journal of Interdisciplinary History* 4, pp. 703–19

Smart, Carol (1976) *Women, crime and criminology. A feminist critique* London: Routledge & Kegan Paul

Smith, L.R. (1980) *The Aboriginal population of Australia* Canberra: ANU Press

Smith, Martin (1975) 'Sodomy and transportation. Some attitudes concerning sodomy in Britain and Australia (1765–1850): and a short bibliography of sources' *GLP: A Journal of Sexual Politics* 8, pp. 48–61

Smith-Rosenberg, Caroll (1975) 'The female world of love and ritual. Relations between women in nineteenth-century America' *Signs* 1, 1, pp. 1–28

Spearritt, Peter (1975) 'Women in Sydney factories c. 1920–50' in Ann Curthoys, Susan Eade & Peter Spearritt (eds) *Women at work* Canberra: Australian Society for the Study of Labour History

Stephen, Ann (1981) 'Agents of consumerism. The organisation of the Australian advertising industry 1918–1939' in Judith Allen and others (eds) *Media Interventions* Sydney: Intervention Publications

Stephenson, Rosalie (1970) *Women in Australian society* Melbourne: Heinemann Educational

Storr, Catherine (1974) 'Freud and the concept of parental guilt' in Arlene Skolnick & Jerome H. Skolnick (eds) *Intimacy, family and society* Boston: Little, Brown

Summers, Anne (1975) *Damned whores and God's police. The colonization of women in Australia* Victoria: Penguin

Thame, Claudia (1974) Health and the state. The development of collective responsibility for health care in Australia in the first half of the twentieth century, Canberra: PhD thesis, ANU

Tilley, Louise A. & Scott, Joan W. (1978) *Women, work and family* New York: Holt, Reinhart & Winston

Vanek, Joann (1979) 'Time spent in housework' in Nancy F. Cott & Elizabeth H. Pleck (eds) *A heritage of her own. Toward a new social history of American women* New York: Simon & Schuster

Wade, John H. (1981) *De facto marriages in Australia* Sydney: CCH Australia

Warrior, Betsy & Leghorn, Lisa (1974) *Houseworker's Handbook* Massachusetts: Women's Centre

Webbly, Irene A. (1982) 'Women Who Want to be Women' in Marion Sawer (ed.) *Australia and the new right* Sydney: George Allen & Unwin

Weeks, Jeffrey (1981) *Sex, politics and society. The regulation of sexuality since 1800* London & New York: Longman

Weinbaum, Batya & Bridges, Amy (1976) 'The other side of the paycheck: monopoly capital and the structure of consumption' *Monthly Review* 28, pp. 88–103

Whalley, P. (1972) Laws relating to contraceptives in Australia, Canberra: unpublished paper, Department of Demography, ANU

White, Richard (1981) *Inventing Australia. Images and identity 1688–1980* The Australian Experience, Sydney: George Allen & Unwin

Williams, Graham (1983) 'Housing Commission may help singles' *Sydney Morning Herald* 6 December

Williams, R.D. (1968) 'White-collar unions' in P.W.D. Matthews & G.W. Ford (eds) *Australian Trade Unions. Their development, structure and horizons* Melbourne: Sun Books

Wimshurst, Kerry (1981) 'Child labour and school attendance in South Australia 1890–1915' *Historical Studies* 19, 76, pp. 388–411

Windschuttle, Elizabeth (1974) 'Wages for mothers?' *Refractory Girl* No. 5, pp. 42–7

Wolfenden Report (1957) See HMSO (1957)

Wolfers, Howard (1980) 'The big stores between the wars' in Jill Roe (ed.) *Twentieth century Sydney. Studies in urban and social history* Sydney: Hale & Iremonger in association with The Sydney History Group

Women's Bureau (1981) *Facts on women at work in Australia 1980* Canberra: Department of Employment and Youth Affairs

Wood, G.L. (1928) 'Immigration in relation to primary and secondary industries' in P.D. Phillips & G.L. Wood *The peopling of Australia* Melbourne: Macmillan & Melbourne University Press

World Health Organization (1967) *Manual of the international statistical classification of diseases, injuries, and causes of death* 8th Revision, Geneva: World Health Organization

Young, C.M. (1980) 'Leaving home and lifestyle. A survey analysis of young adults' in Dorothy Davis, G. Caldwell, M. Bennett & D. Boorer (eds) *Living together: family patterns and life styles. A book of readings and reports* Canberra: Centre for Continuing Education, ANU

Young, I. (1975) 'Forgotten workers' *Women: a journal of liberation* 4, 2, pp. 39–40

Yudkin, Marcia (1978) 'Transsexualism and women: a critical perspective' *Feminist Studies* 4, 3, pp. 97–106

Index

219